Academic
Reading
Builder

3

Bin Walters
- MA in TESOL: Macquarie University, Australia
- Grade 6-12 Teacher's Certification: Loyola University, USA

Will Link
- MA in Literature, Florida State University, USA
- Co-author of *How to Master Skills for the TOEFL® iBT Listening Intermediate*

Academic Reading Builder 3

Publisher Kyudo Chung
Editorial Director Dongho Lee
Editors Hwagohn Kim, Jun Hwang
Proofreader Tasha Y. Otenti
Translator Kyungran Lee
Designer Soojung Koo

First published in May 2009
By Darakwon, Inc.
Darakwon Bldg., 211, Munbal-ro, Paju-si, Gyeonggi-do 10881
Republic of Korea
Tel: 82-2-736-2031 (Ext. 250)
Fax: 82-2-732-2037

Copyright © 2009 Darakwon, Inc.

All rights reserved. No part of this publication may be reproduced, stored in a retrieval system, or transmitted in any form or by any means, electronic, mechanical, photocopying or otherwise, without the prior consent of the copyright owner. Refund after purchase is possible only according to the company regulations. Contact the above telephone number for any inquiries. Consumer damages caused by loss, damage, etc. can be compensated according to the consumer dispute resolution standards announced by the Korea Fair Trade Commission. An incorrectly collated book will be exchanged.

ISBN 978-89-5995-988-4
      978-89-5995-985-3 (set)

www.darakwon.co.kr

Components Main Book / Answer Book
13 12 11 10 9 8 7   23 24 25 26 27

Academic Reading Builder

Bin Walters • Will Link

3

Contents

Anthropology
- Overview — 10
- Basic Knowledge Building — 11
- Unit 01　The Hohokam — 15
- Unit 02　Clovis Culture — 19
- Vocabulary Expansion — 23

Business
- Overview — 26
- Basic Knowledge Building — 27
- Unit 03　Types of Advertising Appeals — 31
- Unit 04　Product Pricing Policies — 35
- Vocabulary Expansion — 39

Genetics
- Overview — 42
- Basic Knowledge Building — 43
- Unit 05　Gregor Johann Mendel — 47
- Unit 06　Stem Cell Research — 51
- Vocabulary Expansion — 55

Political Science
- Overview — 58
- Basic Knowledge Building — 59
- Unit 07　Tyranny in Ancient Greece — 63
- Unit 08　The Patricians and the Plebeians of Republican Rome — 67
- Vocabulary Expansion — 71

Geography
- Overview — 74
- Basic Knowledge Building — 75
- Unit 09　Greenland — 79
- Unit 10　The Mississippi River and Its Dams — 83
- Vocabulary Expansion — 87

Contents

Mass Communication
Overview	90
Basic Knowledge Building	91
Unit 11 Joseph Pulitzer	95
Unit 12 The History of Magazines	99
Vocabulary Expansion	103

Psychology
Overview	106
Basic Knowledge Building	107
Unit 13 Howard Gardner and Multiple Intelligences	111
Unit 14 Behaviorism, Cognitivism, and Constructivism	115
Vocabulary Expansion	119

Economics
Overview	122
Basic Knowledge Building	123
Unit 15 John Ruskin	127
Unit 16 The Theory of Marginal Utility	131
Vocabulary Expansion	135

Law
Overview	138
Basic Knowledge Building	139
Unit 17 Major Legal Systems	143
Unit 18 The Code of Hammurabi	147
Vocabulary Expansion	151

Ecology
Overview	154
Basic Knowledge Building	155
Unit 19 Keystone Species	159
Unit 20 Mutualism *vs.* Commensalism	163
Vocabulary Expansion	167

Answer Book

Introduction

The **Academic Reading Builder** series is designed to provide intermediate to upper-intermediate EFL students with a sound, extensive knowledge base for academic success. The series consists of three books, each of which contains 20 units in 10 subject areas in a wide range of academic fields, such as arts, humanities, social sciences, life sciences, and natural sciences. Each book will help students become familiar with various academic topics through extensive reading.

In the book, every subject area in focus is first introduced with an accessible explanation about it and simple aptitude-finding questions. Then the subject area is explored through 12 short passages of about 100 words and two main passages of about 400 words. The short passages are followed by a simple true/false question and the main passages by reading comprehension questions, note-taking and summarizing activities, and challenging vocabulary expansion activities. All the readings deal with basic concepts, important historical events, or noteworthy figures in the given subject area.

Each book in the series contains an MP3 with recordings of all reading passages. They are recorded in American and British accents to help students get accustomed to two major English accents. Also, at the end of the book is an answer book that includes a full answer key, word lists, and Korean translations.

The **Academic Reading Builder** series is an optimum extensive reading course for those who are preparing for the TOEFL® iBT test or the College Scholastic Ability Test.

The **Academic Reading Builder** series has the following features:

- Extensive reading in a wide range of academic fields, including topics from the TOEFL® iBT
- An accessible introduction to major subject areas followed by interesting aptitude-finding questions
- Reading comprehension questions that build skimming, scanning, and inference skills
- Clear exercises to enhance information-organizing and summarizing skills
- Vocabulary exercises designed to facilitate the learning and expansion of academic vocabulary
- Full answer key and Korean translations
- MP3 with recordings of all reading passages

How to Use This Book

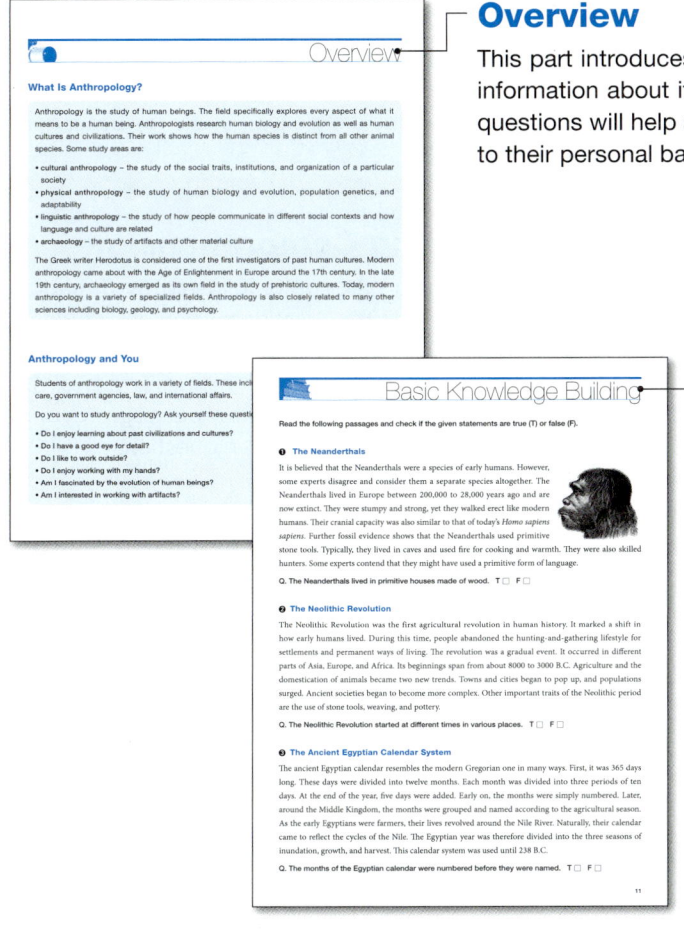

Overview
This part introduces students to a specific subject area with basic information about it and several aptitude-finding questions. These questions will help students think about the subject area in relation to their personal backgrounds.

Basic Knowledge Building
This part provides students with 12 short passages dealing with basic concepts, historical events, or important figures in a specific subject area. Each passage is about 100 to 120 words in length and is accompanied by a true/false question.

Thinking about the Topic
This is one of the two pre-reading activities. Students are asked to look at two images and answer the given questions. There are no set answers to these questions. It is best to elicit as many answers from students as possible in order to activate their background knowledge about the topic.

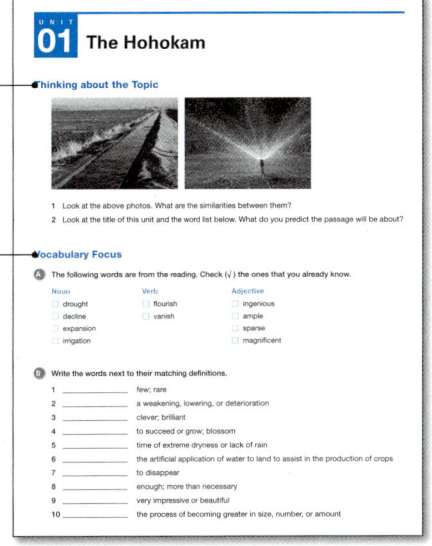

Vocabulary Focus
This is the other pre-reading activity. It presents 10 vocabulary words necessary for students effectively to understand the main passage. Students are asked to check the words they already know and to write the words beside their matching definitions.

How to Use This Book

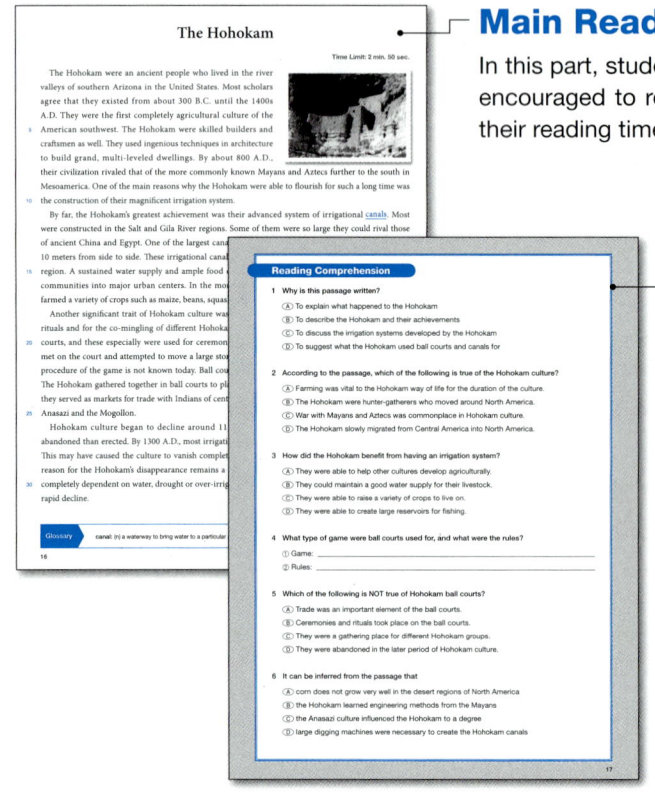

Main Reading

In this part, students read a passage of about 400 words. They are encouraged to read the passage within a given time and to mark their reading time. Difficult words are glossed under the passage.

Reading Comprehension

Each main passage is followed by 6 reading comprehension questions. They ask students about the main idea or main purpose, factual or negative factual information, and the information implied in the passage. One of these questions is an open question.

Organizing & Summarizing

In this part, students are asked to complete the given table or chart to organize information from the main reading. Then they are also asked to summarize the passage based on the organized information. For both tasks, students need to distinguish the major information from the minor information in the passage.

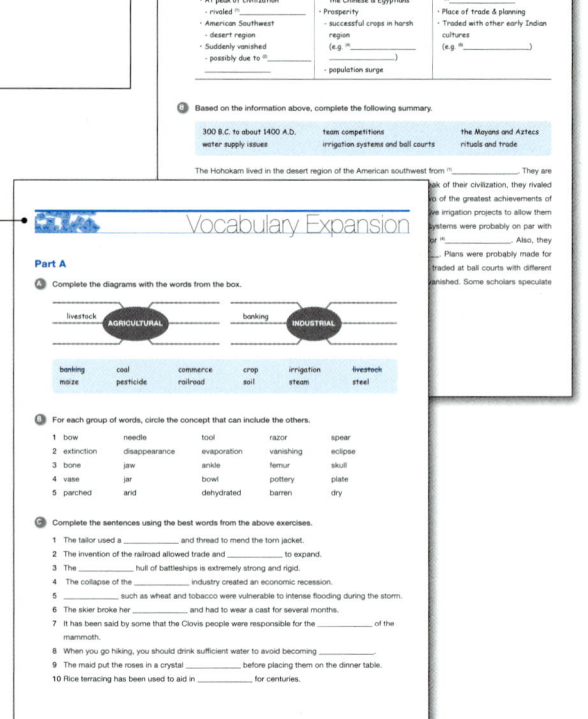

Vocabulary Expansion

This part consists of somewhat challenging activities that build on the words students encountered earlier in the background knowledge building passages and the main passages. Students are encouraged to classify or categorize the given words in light of their sense relations and to use them in appropriate sentences.

Anthropology

Overview
Basic Knowledge Building
Unit 01 The Hohokam
Unit 02 Clovis Culture
Vocabulary Expansion

Overview

What Is Anthropology?

Anthropology is the study of human beings. The field specifically explores every aspect of what it means to be a human being. Anthropologists research human biology and evolution as well as human cultures and civilizations. Their work shows how the human species is distinct from all other animal species. Some study areas are:

- **cultural anthropology** – the study of the social traits, institutions, and organization of a particular society
- **physical anthropology** – the study of human biology and evolution, population genetics, and adaptability
- **linguistic anthropology** – the study of how people communicate in different social contexts and how language and culture are related
- **archaeology** – the study of artifacts and other material culture

The Greek writer Herodotus is considered one of the first investigators of past human cultures. Modern anthropology came about with the Age of Enlightenment in Europe around the 17th century. In the late 19th century, archaeology emerged as its own field in the study of prehistoric cultures. Today, modern anthropology is a variety of specialized fields. Anthropology is also closely related to many other sciences including biology, geology, and psychology.

Anthropology and You

Students of anthropology work in a variety of fields. These include teaching, research, museums, health care, government agencies, law, and international affairs.

Do you want to study anthropology? Ask yourself these questions:

- Do I enjoy learning about past civilizations and cultures?
- Do I have a good eye for detail?
- Do I like to work outside?
- Do I enjoy working with my hands?
- Am I fascinated by the evolution of human beings?
- Am I interested in working with artifacts?

Basic Knowledge Building

Read the following passages and check if the given statements are true (T) or false (F).

❶ The Neanderthals

It is believed that the Neanderthals were a species of early humans. However, some experts disagree and consider them a separate species altogether. The Neanderthals lived in Europe between 200,000 to 28,000 years ago and are now extinct. They were stumpy and strong, yet they walked erect like modern humans. Their cranial capacity was also similar to that of today's *Homo sapiens sapiens*. Further fossil evidence shows that the Neanderthals used primitive stone tools. Typically, they lived in caves and used fire for cooking and warmth. They were also skilled hunters. Some experts contend that they might have used a primitive form of language.

Q. The Neanderthals lived in primitive houses made of wood.   T ☐   F ☐

❷ The Neolithic Revolution

The Neolithic Revolution was the first agricultural revolution in human history. It marked a shift in how early humans lived. During this time, people abandoned the hunting-and-gathering lifestyle for settlements and permanent ways of living. The revolution was a gradual event. It occurred in different parts of Asia, Europe, and Africa. Its beginnings span from about 8000 to 3000 B.C. Agriculture and the domestication of animals became two new trends. Towns and cities began to pop up, and populations surged. Ancient societies began to become more complex. Other important traits of the Neolithic period are the use of stone tools, weaving, and pottery.

Q. The Neolithic Revolution started at different times in various places.   T ☐   F ☐

❸ The Ancient Egyptian Calendar System

The ancient Egyptian calendar resembles the modern Gregorian one in many ways. First, it was 365 days long. These days were divided into twelve months. Each month was divided into three periods of ten days. At the end of the year, five days were added. Early on, the months were simply numbered. Later, around the Middle Kingdom, the months were grouped and named according to the agricultural season. As the early Egyptians were farmers, their lives revolved around the Nile River. Naturally, their calendar came to reflect the cycles of the Nile. The Egyptian year was therefore divided into the three seasons of inundation, growth, and harvest. This calendar system was used until 238 B.C.

Q. The months of the Egyptian calendar were numbered before they were named.   T ☐   F ☐

❹ Sumerian Civilization

The Sumerians are believed to have established one of the earliest civilizations in human history. They lived in southern Mesopotamia, the area of the world that is now Southern Iraq and Southwestern Iran. Experts believe the civilization began between 5000 and 4000 B.C. The city-state was the foundation of their well-organized society. Sometimes the city-states were united; other times they functioned separately. The Sumerians relied mainly on farming for survival. Thus, they created the earliest forms of canals and irrigation systems. They also thrived at metalworking. Another important invention of the Sumerians was cuneiform. It was an early form of writing. Symbols were pressed into clay tablets to record and transfer information. The Sumerians were absorbed by the Babylonians around the 18th century B.C.

Q. The early Sumerians were most likely hunter-gatherers. T ☐ F ☐

❺ Clovis Culture

Archaeologists believe the Clovis people lived about 13,500 years ago in North America. They were probably the first humans to settle the continent. Their culture became known after Clovis artifacts were discovered in New Mexico in the 1930s. Common artifacts found at Clovis sites are Clovis points. These are sharp flint stone heads used for spears. Clovis points suggest that the Clovis people hunted big game, such as bison and mammoths. Thus, some experts believe the Clovis people were responsible for the extinction of the mammoth. It is estimated that Clovis culture flourished for 500 years or so. Afterwards, the Clovis people were most likely replaced by other regional peoples.

Q. The Clovis people hunted the mammoth and bison to the point of extinction. T ☐ F ☐

❻ Stonehenge

Stonehenge is a grouping of ancient stones in southern England. These prehistoric megaliths were probably constructed in phases over a long span of time. Archaeologists estimate that the first phase began about 3000 B.C. and finished around 1600 B.C. The stones are arranged in concentric circles. Stonehenge is one of modern man's great mysteries. No one knows who built Stonehenge. Furthermore, the exact reason for its construction remains a matter of debate. However, one common theory is that it was a place of worship. Modern excavations clearly show that at one time it was a place of burial. Another belief is that it was used as an ancient solar and lunar observatory.

Q. Experts are convinced of Stonehenge's original purpose and function in society. T ☐ F ☐

❼ The Olmec

The Olmec were an ancient Mexican people. They lived in the southern region of Mesoamerica. Archaeologists believe they existed between 1300 and 400 B.C. Present-day sites reveal that they lived along rivers and on vast plains. There is evidence that the Olmec were adept fishermen. They were also skilled sculptors. Two of their favorite mediums were jade and  basalt. Massive sculpted ceremonial heads still survive today. Some of them weigh tens of tons. The Olmec also built large ceremonial mounds and pyramids at their settlements. They established a broad culture base for future Mesoamerican civilizations.

Q. Rituals probably played an important role for the Olmec.   T ☐   F ☐

❽ Anasazi Culture

The Anasazi are the early ancestors of modern Pueblo Indians. They lived in the Four Corners area of the United States, the dry region where the states of Colorado, Utah, New Mexico, and Arizona meet. The word Anasazi means the "ancient ones" in Navajo. Anasazi culture is believed to have begun 2,000 years ago. Some experts even date it much earlier than that. The earliest Anasazi lived in pit houses made of mud and brick. As their culture developed, they began to carve elaborate dwellings from the walls of cliffs and canyons. Initially, the Anasazi were hunter-gatherers. However, they began to farm corn, squash, and beans in later periods. They also produced fine baskets, pottery, ornaments, and tools. Their survival in so arid a region as a desert is remarkable. It shows that they were a determined, inventive early American people.

Q. Over the years, the Anasazi built only one type of dwelling.   T ☐   F ☐

❾ The Scythians

The Scythians were a disorganized network of nomadic people. They inhabited regions of southern Russia. Although their origins are not clear, they probably existed from the 7th century B.C. to the 1st century B.C. It is believed that their society was centered on horses. They were skilled horsemen who used their four-footed steeds to conquer and intimidate their enemies. It is said that Scythian women also were warriors and fought on horses like men. Some experts even believe the Scythians were the first people to ride on horseback. Horses gave them great range to explore and encounter other cultures and peoples such as the Greeks. Much of what we know today about the Scythians is attributed to the Greek historian Herodotus.

Q. Scythian warriors may have included both genders.   T ☐   F ☐

⑩ Fremont Culture

The Fremont people lived in the areas of Utah, Colorado, and Idaho in the present-day U.S. Their culture was at its height from 700 to 1250 A.D. They shared many similarities with the Anasazi. For example, they were originally hunter-gathers, lived in pit houses, and relied on corn as their staple food. They wisely developed granaries to store food for the harsh winter months. They also developed artwork. Common art forms were pottery and pictographs. Fremont pictographs usually depict human forms on rocks or cave walls. The Fremont culture vanished between 1250 and 1500 A.D. Climate may have been a cause. It is possible that other tribes might have displaced the Fremont people, as well.

Q. Fish were not the main food source for the Fremont people.   T ☐   F ☐

⑪ Inca Civilization

The Incas were an ancient people of South America. They thrived from the 12th to 16th century A.D. Their great empire swept the mountain regions from Ecuador to northern Chile. Their empire was a network of independent tribes. Each tribe had a strict hierarchy with a tribal head at the top. Thus, their empire was more of a confederation of tribes with a single people in control. The Incas were gifted farmers and engineers. They built roads and ingenious terraces for mountain agriculture. They also built tunnels and bridges in the Andes. Safe above the forest floor at an elevation of 8,000 feet, the remains of the ancient Incan city Machu Picchu still exist in Peru. Unfortunately, the Inca civilization was wiped out by the conquest of the Spanish led by Francisco Pizzarro in 1531.

Q. Engineering was one of the strong points of the Inca civilization.   T ☐   F ☐

⑫ Cultural Diffusion

Cultural diffusion is the term used to describe the transfer or sharing of cultural traits between people. They may be shared between individuals or cultures. However, cultural diffusion is not limited to only ideas. Anything novel, such as art or music, can qualify. Often, cultural diffusion can be direct or indirect. Direct diffusion occurs when two cultures lie close to one another. Direct contact such as trade will lead to a blend of both cultures. Indirect diffusion happens when a middle person or country introduces new traits to two other cultures. Today, the Internet is the main facilitator of indirect cultural diffusion.

Q. Cultural diffusion happens in just one way.   T ☐   F ☐

UNIT 01 The Hohokam

Thinking about the Topic

1 Look at the above photos. What are the similarities between them?
2 Look at the title of this unit and the word list below. What do you predict the passage will be about?

Vocabulary Focus

A The following words are from the reading. Check (√) the ones that you already know.

Noun	Verb	Adjective
☐ drought	☐ flourish	☐ ingenious
☐ decline	☐ vanish	☐ ample
☐ expansion		☐ sparse
☐ irrigation		☐ magnificent

B Write the words next to their matching definitions.

1 _____ few; rare
2 _____ a weakening, lowering, or deterioration
3 _____ clever; brilliant
4 _____ to succeed or grow; blossom
5 _____ time of extreme dryness or lack of rain
6 _____ the artificial application of water to land to assist in the production of crops
7 _____ to disappear
8 _____ enough; more than necessary
9 _____ very impressive or beautiful
10 _____ the process of becoming greater in size, number, or amount

The Hohokam

The Hohokam were an ancient people who lived in the river valleys of southern Arizona in the United States. Most scholars agree that they existed from about 300 B.C. until the 1400s A.D. They were the first completely agricultural culture of the American southwest. The Hohokam were skilled builders and craftsmen as well. They used ingenious techniques in architecture to build grand, multi-leveled dwellings. By about 800 A.D., their civilization rivaled that of the more commonly known Mayans and Aztecs further to the south in Mesoamerica. One of the main reasons why the Hohokam were able to flourish for such a long time was the construction of their magnificent irrigation system.

By far, the Hohokam's greatest achievement was their advanced system of irrigational canals. Most were constructed in the Salt and Gila River regions. Some of them were so large they could rival those of ancient China and Egypt. One of the largest canals measured over 24 kilometers in length and over 10 meters from side to side. These irrigational canals allowed the Hohokam to thrive in the dry desert region. A sustained water supply and ample food enabled the Hohokam to develop sparse, regional communities into major urban centers. In the more advanced stages of their culture, the Hohokam farmed a variety of crops such as maize, beans, squash, cotton, and tobacco.

Another significant trait of Hohokam culture was the ball court. It served as an important place for rituals and for the co-mingling of different Hohokam communities. Some communities had large ball courts, and these especially were used for ceremonial games. Two teams from different communities met on the court and attempted to move a large stone or rubber ball to a goal. Unfortunately, the exact procedure of the game is not known today. Ball courts also served as places of trade and organization. The Hohokam gathered together in ball courts to plan agricultural projects and future expansion. Also, they served as markets for trade with Indians of central Mexico as well as neighboring tribes such as the Anasazi and the Mogollon.

Hohokam culture began to decline around 1150 A.D. Over the years, more sites began to be abandoned than erected. By 1300 A.D., most irrigation systems had reached their environmental limits. This may have caused the culture to vanish completely in just another hundred years, but the ultimate reason for the Hohokam's disappearance remains a question. However, when a civilization's survival is completely dependent on water, drought or over-irrigation become a plausible cause for the civilization's rapid decline.

Glossary

canal: (n) a waterway to bring water to a particular area or for boats to carry goods and passengers

Reading Comprehension

1. Why is this passage written?

    Ⓐ To explain what happened to the Hohokam
    Ⓑ To describe the Hohokam and their achievements
    Ⓒ To discuss the irrigation systems developed by the Hohokam
    Ⓓ To suggest what the Hohokam used ball courts and canals for

2. According to the passage, which of the following is true of the Hohokam culture?

    Ⓐ Farming was vital to the Hohokam way of life for the duration of the culture.
    Ⓑ The Hohokam were hunter-gatherers who moved around North America.
    Ⓒ War with Mayans and Aztecs was commonplace in Hohokam culture.
    Ⓓ The Hohokam slowly migrated from Central America into North America.

3. How did the Hohokam benefit from having an irrigation system?

    Ⓐ They were able to help other cultures develop agriculturally.
    Ⓑ They could maintain a good water supply for their livestock.
    Ⓒ They were able to raise a variety of crops to live on.
    Ⓓ They were able to create large reservoirs for fishing.

4. What type of game were ball courts used for, and what were the rules?
    ① Game: _____
    ② Rules: _____

5. Which of the following is NOT true of Hohokam ball courts?

    Ⓐ Trade was an important element of the ball courts.
    Ⓑ Ceremonies and rituals took place on the ball courts.
    Ⓒ They were a gathering place for different Hohokam groups.
    Ⓓ They were abandoned in the later period of Hohokam culture.

6. It can be inferred from the passage that

    Ⓐ corn does not grow very well in the desert regions of North America
    Ⓑ the Hohokam learned engineering methods from the Mayans
    Ⓒ the Anasazi culture influenced the Hohokam to a degree
    Ⓓ large digging machines were necessary to create the Hohokam canals

Organizing & Summarizing

A Complete the following table to arrange the information about the Hohokam.

The Hohokam

Background	Irrigation Systems	Ball Courts

• 300 B.C. to 1400s A.D.
  - renowned for engineering & building
  - agricultural society
• At peak of civilization
  - rivaled (1)_____
• American Southwest
  - desert region
• Suddenly vanished
  - possibly due to (2)_____
	• Built in the Salt & Gila River regions
	• (3)_____
	  - equaled or surpassed those of the Chinese & Egyptians
	• Prosperity
	  - successful crops in harsh region
	  (e.g. (4)_____)
	  - population surge
		• For ritual purposes
		• Where different communities congregated
		• Team competitions in (5)_____
		• Place of trade & planning
		• Traded with other early Indian cultures
		  (e.g. (6)_____)

B Based on the information above, complete the following summary.

300 B.C. to about 1400 A.D.	team competitions	the Mayans and Aztecs
water supply issues	irrigation systems and ball courts	rituals and trade

The Hohokam lived in the desert region of the American southwest from (1)_____. They are renowned for their early skill at building and engineering. At the peak of their civilization, they rivaled other high cultures of the time like that of (2)_____. Two of the greatest achievements of the Hohokam were their (3)_____. They built long massive irrigation projects to allow them to survive and prosper in the harsh desert climate. Their irrigation systems were probably on par with those of the Chinese and Egyptians. The ball courts were used for (4)_____. Also, they allowed different villages time to congregate for (5)_____. Plans were probably made for future joint agricultural projects and expansion. The Hohokam also traded at ball courts with different Indian peoples like the Anasazi. However, the Hohokam suddenly vanished. Some scholars speculate that this was due to (6)_____.

UNIT 02 Clovis Culture

Thinking about the Topic

1. Look at the above images. What are the differences between the ways of their hunting?
2. Look at the title of this unit and the word list below. What do you predict the passage will be about?

Vocabulary Focus

A The following words are from the reading. Check (√) the ones that you already know.

Noun	Verb	Adjective
☐ hypothesis	☐ collapse	☐ monstrous
☐ pursuit	☐ migrate	☐ marshy
☐ terrain	☐ seal	☐ well-preserved
☐ utensil		

B Write the words next to their matching definitions.

1. _____ very large; massive; huge
2. _____ close or stop
3. _____ an area of land
4. _____ fresh; well-kept
5. _____ a tool or object, esp. for eating food
6. _____ to travel to another place
7. _____ wet and muddy
8. _____ a theory or assumption
9. _____ the act of searching or hunting
10. _____ to fall into ruin

Clovis Culture

The Clovis people were a prehistoric Paleoindian group that first appeared in North America around 13,500 years ago at the end of the last ice age. Their culture first became known to archaeologists in 1932 when some artifacts were discovered near Clovis, New Mexico. This is why they are now called the Clovis. Today, it is understood that they lived in settlements throughout Central as well as North America. Initially, the Clovis were thought to be the earliest human inhabitants of North America. But recent discoveries have revealed peoples older than the Clovis.

How the Clovis people arrived in North America and where they came from is still highly debated. One theory proposes that they originated in the Alaskan region and migrated south in pursuit of prey. Another hypothesis argues that the ancestors of the Clovis came from South America. Scholars point to pre-Clovis sites in Brazil and Chile which share similar traits with the Clovis culture. A more recent idea is that the Clovis came from Europe to North America by boat, keeping close to the edges of ice sheets that spanned from Greenland to New York. However, none of these theories has been fully accepted by archaeologists.

A variety of well-preserved artifacts provide a glimpse into the Clovis way of life. Evidence unearthed at various sites includes fluted stone points now dubbed Clovis points. They were probably attached to a type of spear and used for hunting big game. The length of most Clovis points found at the sites ranges from one to five inches. Larger points were necessary to hunt big game such as  the monstrous mastodon and mammoth. These giant animals were preferred because meat from a single animal could provide sufficient food for a large tribe for about a month. Besides the meat, the Clovis also used the bones, tusks, and hides to build shelters and fashion, cooking utensils, tools, and other weapons. It is likely that the Clovis used ambush-hunting techniques as their prey congregated at marshy watering locations. The soft terrain would have hindered the movement of the animals.

Most estimates concur that the Clovis culture lasted for about five hundred years. It seems that the people suddenly vanished, much like the mammoth, without a trace. Numerous theories attempt to explain their sudden disappearance. One is directly related to the mammoth. It claims that the Clovis might have over-hunted the mammoth and other big game, thereby erasing their main food source and sealing their own fate. However, a more likely scenario is a post-glacial climate change which led to an overall collapse in the environment.

Glossary: seal someone's fate: (phr) to show or decide that something bad will definitely happen to someone

Reading Comprehension

1. Why is this passage written?

   Ⓐ To discuss the origins and way of life of the Clovis people
   Ⓑ To determine how the Clovis people hunted big game
   Ⓒ To show the migration patterns of the Clovis people
   Ⓓ To illustrate the downfall of the Clovis people

2. Which of the following is true about the origins of the Clovis?

   Ⓐ Greenland is most likely the point of their origin.
   Ⓑ Recent evidence shows that they came from Central America.
   Ⓒ Experts have contrasting views as to where they came from.
   Ⓓ It is not possible that they used land bridges to reach North America.

3. Which of the following is true about Clovis points?

   Ⓐ They were used for both hunting and cooking.
   Ⓑ They were usually longer than the hunter's arm.
   Ⓒ They were attached to arrows and shot from a bow.
   Ⓓ They are one of the best-preserved Clovis artifacts.

4. What type of big game did the Clovis people hunt, and what did they use the game for?
   ① Big game: _____
   ② Use: _____

5. Which of the following is NOT true about Clovis culture?

   Ⓐ It was eventually absorbed by other Indian groups.
   Ⓑ It suddenly vanished about 13,000 years ago.
   Ⓒ It was based on hunting rather than farming.
   Ⓓ It was established in both North and Central America.

6. Which of the following can be inferred from the passage?

   Ⓐ The Clovis people lived in Canada and moved south toward a warmer climate.
   Ⓑ Artifacts which predate Clovis culture have been unearthed.
   Ⓒ Clovis hunters used horses to hunt large beasts like the mastodon.
   Ⓓ Agriculture was important for the Clovis people early on.

Organizing & Summarizing

A Complete the following table to arrange the information about the Clovis culture.

Clovis Culture

The People	Origins	Way of Life

• Prehistoric Paleoindians
  - emerged in North America
  (1)_____
  - also lived in Central America
• Curious disappearance
  - culture lasted for about 500 years
  - theory 1: (2)_____ killed off vital big game
  - theory 2: (3)_____ harmed environment
	• Unclear
	  - theory 1: they migrated south (4)_____
	  - theory 2: they crossed over (5)_____ by following ice sheets.
		• Clovis points
		  - best-preserved artifact
		  - (6)_____ for hunting
		• Big game hunters
		  - (7)_____
		  - mastodon & mammoth
		  → meat of one animal could feed whole village for 1 month
		  → (8)_____ used to make tools
		  → hides for clothing & dwellings

B Based on the information above, complete the following summary.

from Europe to Greenland	due to over-hunting	Clovis points
the bones and ivory	about 13,500 years ago	mastodons and mammoths

The Clovis people were ancient Paleoindians in North America who lived (1)_____. They also settled in Central America. However, their origins are unclear. Some experts think they might have migrated south from the Alaskan region. Others believe they crossed over in boats by following ice sheets (2)_____ and finally to the continent. The Clovis way of life centered on big game hunting. The meat from just one animal could feed an entire tribe for about a month. The hide provided shelter, and (3)_____ were used for tools. They used stone-tip spears and ambush-hunting techniques to kill (4)_____. These spear tips called (5)_____ are the best-preserved artifacts from the culture. After about 500 years of existence, the Clovis suddenly disappeared. The definite reason is not known. However, some experts believe it was (6)_____. Others think a drastic climate change that produced a dire effect on the environment was the cause.

Vocabulary Expansion

Part A

A Complete the diagrams with the words from the box.

- livestock — **AGRICULTURAL**
- banking — **INDUSTRIAL**

| banking | coal | commerce | crop | irrigation | livestock |
| maize | pesticide | railroad | soil | steam | steel |

B For each group of words, circle the concept that can include the others.

1	bow	needle	tool	razor	spear
2	extinction	disappearance	evaporation	vanishing	eclipse
3	bone	jaw	ankle	femur	skull
4	vase	jar	bowl	pottery	plate
5	parched	arid	dehydrated	barren	dry

C Complete the sentences using the best words from the above exercises.

1 The tailor used a _____ and thread to mend the torn jacket.
2 The invention of the railroad allowed trade and _____ to expand.
3 The _____ hull of battleships is extremely strong and rigid.
4 The collapse of the _____ industry created an economic recession.
5 _____ such as wheat and tobacco were vulnerable to intense flooding during the storm.
6 The skier broke her _____ and had to wear a cast for several months.
7 It has been said by some that the Clovis people were responsible for the _____ of the mammoth.
8 When you go hiking, you should drink sufficient water to avoid becoming _____.
9 The maid put the roses in a crystal _____ before placing them on the dinner table.
10 Rice terracing has been used to aid in _____ for centuries.

Part B

A Complete the diagrams with the words from the box.

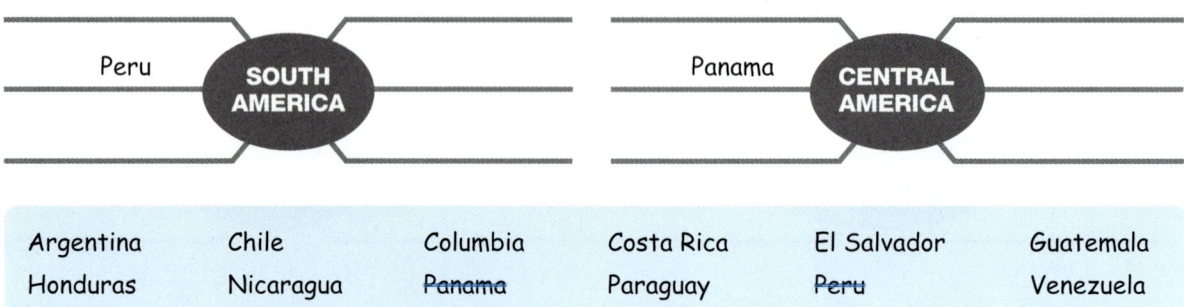

| Argentina | Chile | Columbia | Costa Rica | El Salvador | Guatemala |
| Honduras | Nicaragua | ~~Panama~~ | Paraguay | ~~Peru~~ | Venezuela |

B For each group of words, cross out the word that does not belong.

1 complex   detailed   elaborate   intricate   concentric
2 trait   feature   quality   appearance   property
3 confront   encounter   surrender   experience   face
4 constant   temporary   permanent   everlasting   perpetual
5 clumsy   adept   expert   skilled   adroit

C Complete the sentences using the best words from the above exercises.

1 _____ occupies most of the western coast of South America.
2 She has _____ satisfaction and success in her new job.
3 You need an _____ eye to check if your diamond ring is genuine.
4 _____ housing or shelters were the homes of ancient nomadic cultures.
5 _____ is an important region for shipping because of its canal system.
6 The troops _____ once they realized there was no hope of winning.
7 Nobody knows why the Stonehenge stones are arranged in _____ circles.
8 Rick is so _____ that he is always tripping over his shoe laces or bumping into people.
9 Many consumers consider _____ to be most important when making a purchase.
10 Thousands of people took part in the parade, many of them wearing _____ costumes.

Business

Overview
Basic Knowledge Building
Unit 03 Types of Advertising Appeals
Unit 04 Product Pricing Policies
Vocabulary Expansion

Overview

What Is Business?

Business is the study of producing and selling goods or services to earn profits. It basically includes the study of marketing and management strategies. Some of the other study areas of business are:

- **accounting and finance** – the study of how money is managed
- **advertising** – the study of consumer needs and public promotions of products and services
- **industrial organization** – the study of strategic behavior of businesses and their interaction with markets
- **entrepreneurship** – the study of investing and managing a business and the risks involved
- **investment** – the study of asset purchases for later profit

The first types of "business" were based on barter systems—i.e. simply trading one thing for another. During ancient Greece and Rome, hard currencies made business a more complex system. By the Middle Ages, societies were breaking away from subsistence economies. Later, free enterprise and capitalism boomed during the Industrial Revolution. Since then, new technologies have made businesses central not just to local economies but to the global economy as well.

Business and You

People who study business work in a broad range of settings. These include accounting, investment, finance, real estate, management, universities, politics, non-profit organizations, and consulting.

Do you want to study business? Ask yourself these questions:

- Am I intrigued by profit strategies?
- Am I good with numbers and calculations?
- Do I like to work both in an office and outdoors?
- Do I have good social and communication skills?
- Do I have a knack for recognizing patterns and trends?
- Do I stick to my short-term and long-term goals?

Basic Knowledge Building

Read the following passages and check if the given statements are true (T) or false (F).

❶ Samuel Slater

Samuel Slater is the father of the American textile industry. He was born in England in 1768. There he learned the art of textile manufacturing. Later, he illegally immigrated to the U.S. taking his knowledge of textiles and textile technology with him. Before long, he designed the first cotton mill in Rhode Island in 1793. This is considered the beginning of the American Industrial Revolution. Once in business for himself, he established numerous other mills and became wealthy. Eventually, the livelihood of entire towns in New England revolved around many of his mills. Slater died in 1835.

Q. Samuel Slater moved freely to America to begin a textile company.　T ☐　F ☐

❷ American Transcontinental Railroad

The first transcontinental railroad in the U.S. was completed in 1869 to link the east with the west. It was crucial to spawning population and development in the American west. Rapid economic growth was witnessed along its main line. Populations surged while commerce between states increased. The transcontinental railroad provided a vital link between the natural resources of the west and the urban markets of the east. Minerals were mined in the west and transported easily to industrial plants in the east. The railroad allowed the U.S. to advance quickly as a nation in almost every aspect.

Q. The transcontinental railroad helped develop the American west from its inception.　T ☐　F ☐

❸ The Zipper

The zipper was invented in 1890 by Whitcomb Judson, an American inventor and salesman. The earlier zipper was more of a slide fastener. Judson patented it in 1893. Investors took notice and supported his invention, so Judson continued to revise and improve it. The zipper was first introduced to soldiers in World War I. It helped them fasten their jackets and vests quickly. However, it was not until the 1920s that it was introduced to the public. The zipper's design was continually tweaked over the years. Sales climbed. Today, zippers are used for everything from pencil cases to blue jeans.

Q. Early zippers probably looked little like modern ones.　T ☐　F ☐

❹ Kress Five-and-Dimes

S.H. Kress & Co. was founded by Samuel Kress in 1896. The company built a chain of five-and-dime stores across the U.S. The stores were popular for inexpensive goods. However, Kress five-and-dime buildings also exhibited beautiful aesthetics. The buildings were attractively designed and decorated. They were often located in the central business districts of cities. The blend of aesthetics and shopping attracted customers. One of Kress's chief competitors was Woolworth's, another successful five-and-dime chain. Today, malls have assumed the popularity of five-and-dime stores. Yet, many Kress buildings still grace downtown areas and house new businesses or offices.

Q. Most Kress buildings were made with little ornamentation.　T ☐　F ☐

❺ Early Labor Movement in America

The first labor movements in the U.S. started during the late 19th and early 20th centuries. One of the first unions was the Knights of Labor. It was organized in 1869 and fought for the welfare of all workers in the U.S. However, it lacked cohesion because the great diversity of its members caused internal conflict. Before long, it lost popularity. Another early union was the American Federation of Labor, which was founded in 1886. It was made up of hourly workers from various trade unions. It strove for better working conditions and higher wages. However, management usually favored dealing with workers on an individual basis. Strikes and demonstrations often occurred. Often, the government had to use troops to maintain public order.

Q. The Knights of Labor mainly represented the interests of hourly workers.　T ☐　F ☐

❻ Scientific Management

Scientific management or "Taylorism" was developed by steel foreman Frederick Taylor in the late 19th century. Taylor devised this system to maximize the productivity of workers. He divided factory work into the simplest jobs and sequenced them in a way to achieve maximum efficiency. He then let skilled managers oversee semi-skilled or unskilled workers. This method saved time and increased output. As Taylorism spread, work areas became highly regimented. Workers felt more pressure. Yet, the scientific management system proved to be successful. Workers were provided incentive pay for higher output. The influence of Taylorism may still be felt today in many management systems around the world.

Q. Workers were more strictly controlled under Taylorism.　T ☐　F ☐

❼ Management by Walking Around

Management by Walking Around (MBWA) is a concept originally developed in the 1940s by the founders of Hewlett-Packard. It emphasizes a hands-on approach by managers. They should be visible and accessible to their workers. They should also be approachable for questions as well as feedback. Also, MBWA supports managers in actually knowing how to perform each of their workers' roles. Face-to-face talks override memos, faxes, emails, or even meetings. In the end, this one-on-one style often leads to more meaningful contributions from the workers themselves. MBWA attempts to dissolve the often intimidating lines between management and staff.

Q. MBWA allows managers to seek more input from their employees.   T ☐   F ☐

❽ Buzz Marketing

Buzz marketing is a marketing technique used to boost sales or product awareness. It is based on pre-existing social conditions. That is, it relies on customers to spread positive feedback about a given product. In this sense, it is much like word of mouth. However, with today's technology such as the Internet and Podcasts, it can also spread positive feedback like a virus. In this case, it is called viral marketing. For example, marketers target certain populations or groups, hoping to "infect" them with an enticing ad. Once a few target customers are infected, the ad can spread within their circle. Buzz or viral marketing techniques continue to be used by a variety of industries from movies to music today.

Q. Buzz marketing is distinguished from viral marketing.   T ☐   F ☐

❾ Market Segmentation

Market segmentation is a business strategy. A large market is split up into smaller groups. The consumers in each smaller group have a common demographic. For example, they are in a similar age group or have the same gender. Education and income levels are other traits marketers consider. Market segmentation is a tool used by businesses to better understand the consumer's needs. A benefit of this technique is new product ideas. Another is increased market share in both segmented populations and broader demographics. Companies may even poll consumers. This helps them address their specific needs. It can also help increase customer loyalty in the long run.

Q. In market segmentation, companies target a certain demographic.   T ☐   F ☐

❿ Franchising

A franchise is a type of business. A mother company or franchiser grants a license to an individual or franchisee to sell its product. The franchisee often receives special training for the given business and brand. Also, the franchisee receives name recognition in the market. Advertising is another benefit to the franchisee. The franchiser usually funds ads or commercials. Franchising has become a popular business model in the U.S. Companies like Coca-Cola and Burger King are highly successful examples. Today, many franchises are recognized globally. They extend well beyond fast food and beverage companies to the clothing industry and beyond.

Q. A new franchise must pay for its own advertising. T ☐ F ☐

⓫ Forms of Business Ownership

There are four common types of business ownership: cooperative, corporation, partnership, and sole proprietorship. The cooperative is comprised of a group of individuals. They come together to form a business. This is because they can be more successful together than on their own. It is most common today in the agricultural sector. A corporation is a legal entity created by shareholders. They can profit from the corporation. Yet, they are not responsible for losses. A management board is elected to oversee business matters. A partnership is a contract between two or more people. They are the co-owners of a business. Finally, sole proprietorship is when one person owns and controls a business for profit. This is the most basic form of business.

Q. In a corporation, shareholders take responsibility for losses. T ☐ F ☐

⓬ Electronic Publishing

Electronic publishing is the digital publication of words. Articles, e-books, and even entire libraries can be published this way. DVDs and CDs, along with the Internet, are common means of electronic publishing. One advantage of electronic publishing is that it allows materials to reach an audience quicker than paper. Still, some electronic publishing eventually makes its way into paper form. Another advantage is that it is more environmentally friendly. Less paper means less pulp and entire forests can be saved. Finally, electronic publishing can store enormous amounts of information in very little space. Therefore, a vendor can provide even more titles than a bookstore or library. This can be invaluable for out-of-print or obscure documents.

Q. DVDs are considered a form of electronic publishing. T ☐ F ☐

UNIT 03 Types of Advertising Appeals

Thinking about the Topic

1 Look at the above images. What similarities or differences exist between these two advertisements? Who is their target audience?

2 Look at the title of this unit and the word list below. What do you predict the passage will be about?

Vocabulary Focus

A The following words are from the reading. Check (√) the ones that you already know.

Noun	Verb	Adjective
☐ annoyance	☐ associate	☐ covert
☐ coincidence	☐ dictate	☐ subtle
☐ intrusion	☐ encompass	☐ unwarranted
☐ standby		

B Write the words next to their matching definitions.

1 _____ secret; undetected

2 _____ source of irritation or bother

3 _____ to influence; to command

4 _____ someone or something that is always ready or available if needed

5 _____ to connect; to link

6 _____ an accidental happening

7 _____ not easy to sense; not obvious; indirect

8 _____ to surround; to include; to contain

9 _____ a forced entrance; interruption

10 _____ unnecessary; needless

Types of Advertising Appeals

Time Limit: 2 min. 40 sec.

Advertising is a major component of the business world. When it is successful, companies can look forward to record production and profits. However, lackluster advertising can spell doom for a product or company. In the past fifteen years, the Internet has opened up whole new possibilities in brand marketing and recognition. But this does not mean the old standbys of advertising are no longer relevant. Media is one type of advertising appeal which remains vital to many larger companies. It makes up the bulk of all advertisements. Other types of advertising appeals include covert and outdoor advertising approaches.

Media advertising encompasses a large, diverse realm in the marketing world. Broadcast advertising involves television and radio. Print advertising is commonly adopted by newspapers and magazines. With broadcast media, commercial spots are paid for by companies on certain television or radio networks. The popularity of the network and program as well as airtime length dictates the cost of the commercial. Similarly, a business may purchase ad space in a magazine. Again, the size of the ad and the circulation of the print media determine the cost of the advertisement. Because television programs and print media attract audiences from certain demographics, companies can market their product to a specific client base quickly.

Covert and outdoor advertising appeals also continue to influence consumer spending. First, covert advertising is most commonly seen in movies. It is a more subtle form of advertising. For example, in a certain scene of a movie, a famous actor may drink a can of Coca-Cola. This is by no means a coincidence. Coca-Cola has paid to have their product visible in the scene. Thus, potential customers will hopefully associate the drink with the actor and purchase more of it. Second, outdoor advertising is another successful technique. Billboards are a common example. However, businesses also advertise their name or products in other places easily visible to the public, like on the sides of buses or taxis, on park benches, in subways, and in sports stadiums.

The Internet is another more recent form of advertising appeal. Spam mail and website pop-ups are common methods. However, while some are from successful, reliable companies, most represent unproven companies or services and are viewed as annoyances by many Internet users. Even special web tools have been created to block their unwarranted intrusions. Avoiding unwelcome advertising is difficult with traditional forms of advertising such as print and broadcast media. Advertisers therefore dedicate the majority of their revenue to the upkeep of the most popular forms of entertainment and information.

Your Time: _____ min. _____ sec.

Glossary	lackluster: (adj) dull or boring
	billboard: (n) a large, flat board for advertisements, usually on the sides of roads

Reading Comprehension

1. Why is this passage written?

   Ⓐ To show how advertising increases sales
   Ⓑ To explain how advertising relates to demographics
   Ⓒ To compare major types of advertising and their effects
   Ⓓ To illustrate common methods used for advertising

2. Which of the following is true about media advertising?

   Ⓐ It has always been the most limited form of advertising appeal.
   Ⓑ The popularity of the medium influences the cost of the advertisement.
   Ⓒ Television advertising is more effective in attracting a broader range of clients.
   Ⓓ It is generally less expensive than advertising in newspapers and on the Internet.

3. According to the passage, covert advertising

   Ⓐ is usually found in movies or television shows
   Ⓑ relies on common, unknown actors to popularize products
   Ⓒ is not a planned form of advertising and occurs by chance
   Ⓓ is a new phenomenon which started a couple of years ago

4. What type of advertising appeal do billboards exemplify?

   _____

5. Which of the following is NOT true about Internet advertising?

   Ⓐ Consumers are able to restrict somewhat the ads they see.
   Ⓑ Advertising appeals on the Internet are sometimes ignored by web surfers.
   Ⓒ Spam email and website pop-ups are used frequently in Internet advertising.
   Ⓓ The Internet has overtaken television as the most successful outlet for ads.

6. What can be inferred from the passage?

   Ⓐ Internet ads are more trustworthy than their media counterparts.
   Ⓑ The most successful commercials are found in magazines.
   Ⓒ Print advertising predates broadcast media advertising.
   Ⓓ The overall cost of television ads has dropped in recent years.

Organizing & Summarizing

A Complete the following table to arrange the information about types of advertising appeals.

Types of Advertising Appeals

Types	Characteristics	Examples
Media	• Companies purchase ad space & time - cost dependent on (1)_____ • Most common advertising appeal • Can target (2)_____	• Broadcast: television & radio • Print: newspapers & magazines

Covert	• Products placed in movie scenes deliberately
	  - (3)_____
	  - gives (4)"_____" to the good or service
	• So subtle often unnoticed
		• An actor drinking a particular beverage in a movie scene

Outdoor	• Large advertisements in public areas - constant visibility	• Large ads placed (6)_____
Internet	• Reach consumers via the WWW • Tools available to block unwanted ads • (5)_____	• Spam mail or pop-ups

B Based on the information above, complete the following summary.

circulation size	their brand with superstars	social demographic
ad space or time	often unavoidable	indirect marketing

There are several types of advertising appeals. Media is the largest form of advertising appeal. Typical mediums for media ads include television, newspapers, and magazines. Companies purchase (1)_____ in the form of print ads or commercials. Advertising costs are determined by the popularity of the program and (2)_____. Media allows companies to target a specific (3)_____. Covert advertising appeals are a form of (4)_____ often found in movies. Companies have their products included in movie scenes. In this way, audiences associate (5)_____. Outdoor advertising is usually found on billboards, on taxis, or in other public spaces. Most recently, advertising appeals have found their way to the Internet. Pop-ups and spam mail are usual methods. Tools have even been designed to reject these types of advertising appeals. This is one advantage consumers have compared to television or radio commercials, which are (6)_____.

UNIT 04 Product Pricing Policies

Thinking about the Topic

1 Look at the above photos. What factors might influence the price of a product or service?
2 Look at the title of this unit and the word list below. What do you predict the passage will be about?

Vocabulary Focus

A The following words are from the reading. Check (√) the ones that you already know.

Noun	Verb	Adjective
☐ assumption	☐ entice	☐ bargain
☐ clientele	☐ react	☐ illegal
☐ monopoly	☐ subside	
☐ pitfall	☐ switch	

B Write the words next to their matching definitions.

1 _____ against the law
2 _____ danger; hazard
3 _____ to attract
4 _____ the control of an entire market by only one business
5 _____ cheap; inexpensive
6 _____ to respond; to reply
7 _____ to decrease; to decline
8 _____ something expected
9 _____ to change; to shift
10 _____ a group of customers

Product Pricing Policies

Time Limit: 2 min. 45 sec.

Pricing is a crucial element of marketing, and the final price of a good or service is often determined only after careful consideration. Competitors and profit objective are commonly taken into consideration. However, types of pricing strategies are also important in successful marketing. The two most
5 common strategies used today are skimming and penetration pricing.

Price skimming is the act of initially setting a high price for a product with the intention of lowering it over time later. Companies base the price on the highest amount consumers will pay in relation to demand. In other words, companies first target a group of customers willing to pay a premium for a particular good or service. Once that demand has been met and subsides, the price is adjusted for
10 the next layer of customers. Skimming continues until each group is satisfied. Price skimming can be successful when certain circumstances are present. First, sufficient numbers of high-paying customers must exist. Second, the high price must be equated with high quality. One of the greatest risks of price skimming is competition. Often, price skimming takes time, which allows competitors to imitate the product or produce an alternative at a lower price. This competition will significantly affect the profit
15 structure of the product.

In contrast, penetration pricing is the opposite of skimming. This strategy sees a company price a product or service at an initially low price. The intention is to entice new customers. Penetration pricing is based on the assumption that consumers will switch brands based on competitive pricing. At first, profit is sacrificed for the building of new clientele. This allows the company to gain a superior hold
20 on the market before competitors can react. Penetration pricing can be highly efficient because cost controls must be established from the onset. However, this strategy has its pitfalls as well. One of the most dangerous is image. Consumers may associate the company with bargain prices. This image makes it difficult to later raise prices to more competitive market levels.

In certain market environments, both penetration and skimming pricing can prove successful. Yet, in
25 both cases, the law must be carefully observed as well. With skimming, companies must be careful that they do not enter into price discrimination. It is illegal in some countries. Likewise, extreme penetration pricing can become predatory pricing, which is also illegal in many countries. Predatory pricing can create a monopoly for the practicing company as it makes it impossible for other competitors to enter the market.

Your Time: _____ min. _____ sec.

Glossary

price discrimination: (phr) the practice of a company selling the same product at different prices
predatory pricing: (phr) the practice of a company selling a product at a very low price in order to drive or keep competitors out of the market

Reading Comprehension

1. What is the main purpose of the passage?

    Ⓐ To explain why alternative methods of pricing are necessary
    Ⓑ To show how price skimming and penetration pricing can violate the law
    Ⓒ To illustrate ways companies manipulate what consumers pay
    Ⓓ To argue that penetration pricing is more effective than price skimming

2. What element must be present for price skimming to be successful?

    Ⓐ The market has to be saturated with similar products.
    Ⓑ There must be enough consumers willing to pay a premium.
    Ⓒ Profit should not be a long-term goal of the company.
    Ⓓ The quality of the product should be sacrificed for cheap prices.

3. Which of the following is true about penetration pricing?

    Ⓐ It always enhances the image of the company.
    Ⓑ It targets established clients who will pay higher prices.
    Ⓒ Prices can easily be raised in the long-term market scheme.
    Ⓓ It intends to build a new clientele base through low pricing.

4. What is penetration pricing called in extreme cases, and what negative result may happen?
    ① Term: _____
    ② Result: _____

5. Which of the following is NOT true about pricing policies?

    Ⓐ They can be very complex in nature.
    Ⓑ They often affect the competition as well as consumers.
    Ⓒ They create a greater market share in the short term.
    Ⓓ They are rarely altered once established by a company.

6. It is likely that a company practicing predatory pricing

    Ⓐ will face legal troubles if caught by authorities
    Ⓑ intends to cater to customers willing to pay more for quality
    Ⓒ is never a well-established one with a good reputation
    Ⓓ only uses the technique to avoid bankruptcy

Organizing & Summarizing

A Complete the following table to arrange the information about product pricing policies.

Product Pricing Policies

Policy	Details	Potential Problems
Price Skimming	• Price starts high & drops over time • Targets customer group willing to (1)_____ • High price = high quality • (2)_____	• Time-consuming - competition can undermine • Potential (4)_____ - can be illegal
Penetration Pricing	• Low initial price • Used to attract (3)_____ • Profits negligible at first	• Image issues - company may be eternally equated with (5)_____ • Hard to raise price & retain customers • Potential for (6)_____ - can create a monopoly - can be illegal

B Based on the information above, complete the following summary.

maximize profits	a monopoly	on the bargain end
on the high end	time-consuming	low prices

Two main product pricing policies companies use are called price skimming and penetration pricing. In price skimming, prices are set (1)_____ and are aimed at existing customers willing to pay the price. The high price typically suggests a high-quality good or service. Then over time, the price will be reduced in stages to attract every level of consumer. Ideally, companies can (2)_____ via skimming. However, there are some drawbacks. One is that it is (3)_____. This allows competition to enter the market and undermine the strategy. Another is price discrimination, which is often considered against the law. Penetration pricing uses the reverse psychology of skimming. Prices start (4)_____ to lure new customers in. Profits are not considered important at first. Again, over time, prices will be increased. However, a problem can occur with the image of the company. Consumers may always equate the company with (5)_____ and low-quality goods or services. Furthermore, a penetration pricing policy might become predatory, which can lead to (6)_____. This is another illegal practice.

Vocabulary Expansion

Part A

A Complete the diagrams with the words from the box.

```
_____ mall _____          _____ jacket _____
         SHOPPING                        CLOTHING
_____        _____          _____        _____
```

blouse	clerk	consumer	customer	good	jacket
mall	shirt	skirt	trousers	vendor	vest

B For each group of words, circle the concept that can include the others.

1. cooperative   company   partnership   corporation   sole proprietorship
2. radio   magazine   television   media   newspaper
3. location   indoor   rear   outdoor   exterior
4. track   platform   train   turnstile   subway
5. cotton   linen   textile   denim   wool

C Complete the sentences using the best words from the above exercises.

1. A _____ is a legal entity created by shareholders.
2. It is often best to take the _____ in crowded cities to avoid traffic.
3. The _____ of e-books can provide more titles than a bookstore or library.
4. After going through the _____, the woman ran to catch her train.
5. The _____ was a groundbreaking invention of the early 20th century.
6. A man's suit consists of a jacket, _____, and sometimes a waistcoat.
7. The _____ of the building is run down, but its interior is very elegant and graceful.
8. _____ activities like hunting and fishing are very popular in the United States.
9. _____ goods are products purchased by the average customer to be consumed right away.
10. Samuel Slater was the father of the American _____ industry; he designed the first U.S. cotton mill.

39

Part B

A Complete the diagrams with the words from the box.

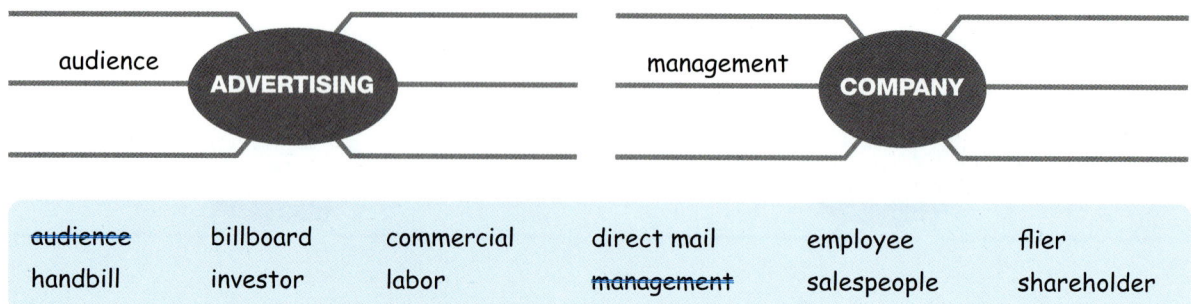

| ~~audience~~ | billboard | commercial | direct mail | employee | flier |
| handbill | investor | labor | ~~management~~ | salespeople | shareholder |

B For each group of words, cross out the word that does not belong.

1 browse   glance   skim   decipher   glimpse
2 target   aim   goal   objective   demographic
3 bountiful   vivid   abundant   plenty   ample
4 obvious   ambiguous   vague   indistinct obscure
5 illegal   unlawful   fair   criminal   illicit

C Complete the sentences using the best words from the above exercises.

1 To overcome the economic crisis, _____ and management agreed to cooperate.
2 The national soccer team beat their rivals by an astonishing four _____.
3 Many children have a very _____ imagination and can tell creative stories.
4 The contract was _____ and open to more than one interpretation.
5 The _____ was charged with a felony and sentenced to five years in prison.
6 A _____ is a particular group of people in society—for example, those in a certain age group.
7 The experts were able to _____ the secret code and complete the task.
8 When Whitcomb Judson patented the zipper, many _____ offered to support his invention.
9 The teacher _____ at the student for a moment and then continued the lecture.
10 The archer _____ his bow and arrow at the deer, but it heard him and ran away.

Genetics

Overview
Basic Knowledge Building
Unit 05 Gregor Johann Mendel
Unit 06 Stem Cell Research
Vocabulary Expansion

Overview

What Is Genetics?

Genetics is the science of inheritance and variation in organisms. Geneticists try to understand the effect that DNA has on different species. They also examine how the environment affects the expression of different genes. Genetics is widely known today for its attempt to influence the development of organisms by altering their genetic makeup. Some study fields of genetics are:

- **molecular genetics** – the study of the structure and function of genes at the molecular level
- **developmental genetics** – the study of how genes influence development
- **evolutionary genetics** – the study of evolution in terms of genetic changes and genotype frequencies within populations
- **population genetics** – the study of the genetic composition and distribution of biological populations
- **behavioral genetics** – the study of the influence of varying genetics on animal behavior
- **clinical genetics** – the study of genetic disorders and diseases

Gregor Johann Mendel was the first scientist to accurately describe the manner in which biological traits are passed down. His work with pea plants in the mid-1800s laid the foundation of classical genetics. However, his theory received little attention until after his death in the late 1800s. At the start of the 20th century, the field quickly grew once DNA was identified as the material of genes. Scientists then learned how to manipulate DNA. Genetics has since grown to influence many other fields of biology.

Genetics and You

People who study genetics work in a wide number of places. These include schools, museums, research institutes, government agencies, pharmaceutical companies, and hospitals.

Do you want to study genetics? Ask yourself these questions:

- Do I like working in labs and enjoy experimenting?
- Do I like gaining knowledge about living organisms?
- Am I interested in figuring out how things work?
- Am I good at seeing relationships between things?
- Am I organized and detail-oriented?

Basic Knowledge Building

Read the following passages and check if the given statements are true (T) or false (F).

❶ Cell Division

Cell division plays two important roles in organisms. The first type, mitosis, is necessary for the overall growth of an organism. As cell division occurs, the number of cells within an organism increases. Without this process, the organism would not be able to grow nor would it be able to replace lost or dead cells. Meiosis, on the other hand, is the division process used to create sex cells. The egg and sperm cells used in reproduction are produced through meiosis. While the two processes are similar, meiosis produces cells with half the number of chromosomes than a regular cell. The full number of chromosomes is restored once an egg and sperm cell fuse together to create a new organism.

Q. After a cell undergoes meiosis, the number of chromosomes decreases by half.   T ☐   F ☐

❷ Chromosomes

Inside the nucleus of a cell is DNA (deoxyribonucleic acid). During cell division, however, the DNA must condense in order to be properly copied, divided, and separated into new cells. First, the DNA coils around ball-shaped proteins called histones. Then the DNA-histone combination is packaged into chromatin, which in turn is wound into a chromosome. There are 46 chromosomes in a human cell. Half are donated from the mother, and the other half from the father. Of these chromosomes, two are sex chromosomes. If an embryo inherits two X chromosomes, it will become a female. If it inherits an X and a Y chromosome, it will become a male.

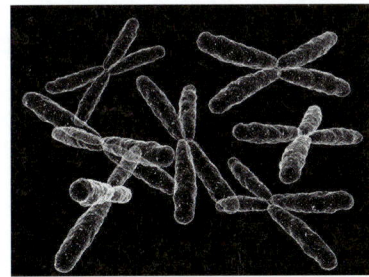

Q. There are a total of 48 chromosomes in a human cell.   T ☐   F ☐

❸ The Structure of DNA

Once DNA was identified as the material which carries genetic information, scientists raced to figure out its structure. James Watson and Francis Crick were the first to identify the unique double helix structure of the DNA molecule. In essence, DNA appears as a twisted ladder. The sides are composed of phosphates and sugars, and the rungs are made of nitrogenous bases. The key to the structure lies in the fact that the bases line up in pairs. When the DNA is unzipped, two new identical strands can be made from each half. This is what enables DNA to make copies of itself and be passed down to each new generation.

Q. The double helix structure is what enables DNA to make copies of itself.   T ☐   F ☐

❹ RNA

RNA (ribonucleic acid) is very similar to DNA; however, it functions very differently in the cell. The two main types of RNA are mRNA (messenger RNA) and tRNA (transfer RNA). Both are used to make proteins in the cell. The mRNA copies a section of DNA in the nucleus. Before leaving the nucleus, extra portions of the DNA are cut out. The mRNA then makes its way to a ribosome where protein synthesis occurs. The ribosome mediates the attachment of tRNA to the mRNA. The tRNA carries amino acids or the building blocks of proteins. The tRNA attaches to the mRNA in a specified order, and amino acids are then connected to one another accordingly. In this manner, DNA controls the production of proteins without ever leaving the nucleus.

Q. RNA is produced and stored in the nucleus where proteins are made.   T ☐   F ☐

❺ The Human Embryo

A woman's egg is fertilized in one of the fallopian tubes. As the zygote makes its way down to the uterus, it divides numerous times. Once it reaches the womb, it implants in the uterine lining and further develops. At this point, it is called an embryo. The human embryo stage lasts for about two months. The brain and spinal cord are among the first organs to develop. By the end of the first month, the heart develops and starts to beat. In addition, small buds appear where the arms and legs will develop. The remaining organs 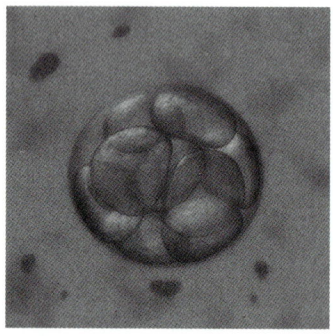 also begin to develop, and the embryo will soon be able to move. By the eighth week, all the major organs have been formed, and the embryo is now considered a fetus.

Q. The embryo stage lasts for approximately eight weeks.   T ☐   F ☐

❻ The Human Genome Project

The Human Genome Project was an international effort to decode all the DNA in a human. While every person has different DNA, many genes are identical person to person. The project began in 1990 when gene studies were just beginning. It was very expensive and time-consuming and took 13 years to complete. Scientists believed that a better understanding of the human genome, or the entire DNA content of a human being, could pave the way for advances in medicine and biotechnology. Already, there have been tangible benefits from the project. Scientists have been able to identify a number of genes responsible for diseases such as breast cancer. As a result, a person can choose to be tested to see if she, as in the case of breast cancer, carries the gene for that disease.

Q. The Human Genome Project has yet to be completed.   T ☐   F ☐

❼ Gene Therapy

A number of diseases are due to faulty genes. The goal of gene therapy is to insert the correct genes into the cells of a patient in order to remedy the disorder. Some initial treatments have been successful. However, gene therapy does have some drawbacks. For one, the treatments must be given repeatedly. In addition, there is a chance the body's immune system will respond negatively and reject the treatment, causing the patient to die. Despite these obstacles, scientists believe that gene therapy offers the potential for medical treatments to be tailored for individual patients. More recent efforts have been successful in restoring sight to patients with retinal disease.

Q. Gene therapy offers the possibility of cures to a number of diseases.   T ☐   F ☐

❽ GMOs

GMOs refer to genetically modified organisms. They are plants or animals that have had new genes inserted into them. The term transgenic is often used to refer to them. The first GMOs were bacteria that had genes inserted into them to produce pharmaceuticals. More commonly, however, plants are genetically engineered to withstand harsh conditions or produce greater yields. Since the safety of eating foods made with GMOs has yet to be proven, there are a number of countries that have banned their use. Critics of the ban argue that transgenic plants are nearly the same as regular plants, and their abilities to grow in various conditions could help end global hunger. Scientists have even created some transgenic animals, using the GMO technology. However, their primary reason has been research-based and not for commercial applications.

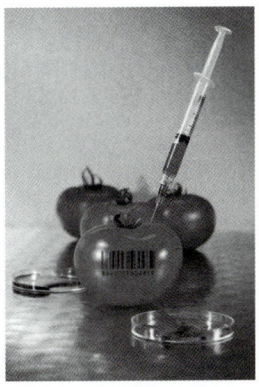

Q. Some people believe GMOs can offer a way to save the world from starvation.   T ☐   F ☐

❾ Recombinant DNA

Recombinant DNA, or rDNA, is DNA that has been modified by the addition of a new gene. The method is fairly simple. Enzymes are used to cut open a circular ring of DNA. Then a new gene is glued into place, and the ring is inserted into a host organism, usually bacteria. The host bacteria will treat the DNA ring as its own DNA. Current uses for rDNA include the production of hormones. A good example is insulin, a very expensive hormone used to treat diabetes. Using rDNA, scientists insert the insulin gene into bacteria. They carefully grow the bacteria to help them produce large amounts of the hormone. Scientists can then simply scoop up the insulin produced and sell it to diabetics at a fraction of the previous cost.

Q. Researchers have yet to find practical applications for recombinant DNA technology.   T ☐   F ☐

⑩ Mutations

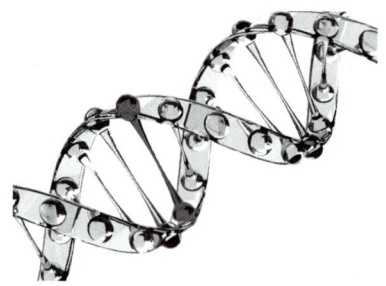

Mutations are changes in the DNA code. They can occur in a number of ways. Most commonly, DNA is miscopied, thus leading to the change. However, some chemicals, radiation, or even viruses can also cause gene mutations. As a general rule, mutations are harmful since they result in the production of an abnormal protein. On occasion, however, mutations can confer an advantage to the host. When they do, they enable the host to be more successful. This increases the spread of mutated genes throughout the population. In this manner, mutations serve as a way for new traits to be introduced into a population. Mutations are the source of all evolutionary progress.

Q. Mutations are usually negative but have some beneficial aspects as well.   T ☐   F ☐

⑪ DNA Fingerprinting

With the exception of identical twins, every person's DNA is unique. Each person has a different sequence of the nitrogenous bases: adenine, guanine, cytosine, and thymine. Thus, every person can be precisely identified by the exact sequence of their bases. DNA fingerprinting is the process of comparing two samples of DNA to see if the DNA sequences match. The process requires restriction enzymes to be added to the DNA 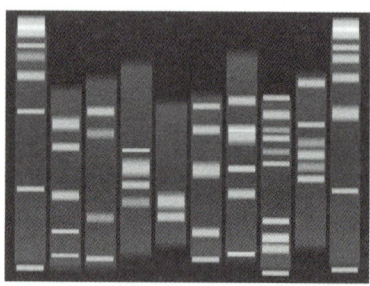 to cut it up into fragments of different lengths. Scientists then put the DNA fragments into a gel and pass an electric current through it. The shorter the fragment, the farther it will move along the gel. If the two DNA samples are the same, then the lines of each gel should be identical.

Q. DNA fingerprinting is used to determine if two DNA samples are the same.   T ☐   F ☐

⑫ Eugenics

After Darwin's publication of his theory of evolution, people began to wonder if it would be possible to improve the human race by preventing certain people from having children. During the early 1900s, there were a number of laws passed which forced people who were considered unfit or inferior to undergo operations that would make them sterile. The basic idea was that by preventing them from having children, the average intelligence of the overall population would increase. However, Hitler's use of eugenics as an excuse for the ethnic genocide of the Jews under his Nazi regime caused it to fall out of favor. Now, genetic screening is used by doctors to detect fetuses with debilitating disabilities. As parents may choose not to keep a severely disabled fetus, genetic screening is a highly controversial technology.

Q. Eugenics has become more widespread with the advent of genetic testing.   T ☐   F ☐

UNIT 05 Gregor Johann Mendel

Thinking about the Topic

1 Look at the above photos. How do the children resemble their parents?
2 Look at the title of this unit and the word list below. What do you predict the passage will be about?

Vocabulary Focus

A The following words are from the reading. Check (√) the ones that you already know.

Noun	Verb	Adjective	Adverb
☐ inheritance	☐ contradict	☐ disastrous	☐ independently
☐ offspring	☐ deduce	☐ intact	
☐ trait	☐ estimate		
	☐ resemble		

B Write the words next to their matching definitions.

1 _____ to calculate approximately
2 _____ particular characteristics or qualities passed down from parent to offspring
3 _____ to disagree; to dispute; to challenge
4 _____ separately; individually
5 _____ to be similar to; to look like; to mirror
6 _____ a characteristic
7 _____ having all parts; whole; undamaged
8 _____ children; descendents
9 _____ to reach a conclusion by reasoning
10 _____ causing extremely bad consequences and effects; very unsuccessful

47

Gregor Johann Mendel

It has been long known that traits are handed down from parents to offspring. People knew that their children looked like them. Farmers saw animals resemble their parents. The exact reasons and mechanisms, however, were shrouded in mystery until the mid-19th century. An Austrian monk, Gregor Johann Mendel discovered that it was mathematically possible to predict which traits parents would give to their offspring. This discovery not only revolutionized agriculture but also shed new light on the mechanism of evolution.

Mendel is perhaps best known for his work with peas. They were cheap, took up little space, and reproduced quickly. He took care of these plants for many years and carefully recorded the offspring of each generation. It is estimated that he grew over 5,000 pea plants per year. By looking at their characteristics such as flower color and pea color, Mendel figured out that traits were passed down intact from parent peas to their offspring. He deduced that some traits could be masked in one generation only to reappear in the next. He also found that the various traits could be inherited independently of each other. His work contradicted the widespread belief of blending. At that time, most scientists believed that offspring were a blend of the parents' characteristics. Mendel's work clearly showed that while traits are passed down from the parents, the trait itself is unchanged.

In 1866, Mendel published his findings in a small local journal and sent copies of his work to a number of scientists. Most of them ignored his research. Only one scientist, Karl von Nägeli showed interest. But his advice to Mendel to study the hawkweed plant proved to be disastrous. Hawkweed reproduces in a very unusual asexual pattern. Thus, when Mendel tried to replicate his findings with the new plant, he was unable to confirm his previous results. He then lost confidence in his theories and abandoned his research.

Mendel's goal for his research was to aid local farmers in producing better crops. He had hoped to create a way to help them grow more useful crops. He did not think that he had stumbled upon a theory of inheritance that could be used to explain nearly every species. He passed away without ever knowing the impact his work would later have. Mendel's work lay undiscovered for nearly a generation. It was not until the 20th century that his work was rediscovered, and Mendel finally received the credit he deserved.

| Glossary | shed new light on: (phr) to make something easier to understand |
| | stumble upon: (phr) to find something unexpectedly |

Reading Comprehension

1. What is the passage mainly about?

   Ⓐ The difficulties Mendel faced in growing peas

   Ⓑ The failure of scientists to recognize Mendel's work

   Ⓒ The origins of a groundbreaking scientific theory

   Ⓓ The importance of verifying findings prior to publication

2. What does the passage say about the ideas of inheritance prior to Mendel?

   Ⓐ They were only discussed and explored among farmers.

   Ⓑ They lacked an explanation for how inheritance occurred.

   Ⓒ They were thought to contradict conventional scientific ideas.

   Ⓓ They were not widely believed since inheritance was not seen.

3. Which of the following is true about blending?

   Ⓐ It was challenged by the results of Mendel's experiments.

   Ⓑ It was not widely accepted at the time of Mendel's work.

   Ⓒ It grew out of Mendel's early work with pea plants.

   Ⓓ It successfully predicted Mendel's observations.

4. According to the passage, what problem did hawkweed cause Mendel?

   _____

5. Which of the following is NOT mentioned as an advantage to working with peas?

   Ⓐ They were inexpensive.

   Ⓑ They created offspring quickly.

   Ⓒ They come in various colors.

   Ⓓ They did not require much room.

6. What can be inferred about the paper that Mendel first published?

   Ⓐ It was enthusiastically received by local farmers.

   Ⓑ It was confirmed by further research by Mendel.

   Ⓒ It was criticized for lacking enough supporting evidence.

   Ⓓ It was considered insignificant by most scientists of the time.

Organizing & Summarizing

A Complete the following table to arrange the information about Gregor Johann Mendel.

Gregor Johann Mendel

Before Mendel	Research on Peas	Research on Hawkweed	Impact
• Commonly believed: traits were passed down → but didn't know how • (1)_____ - offspring were a blend of parents' characteristics	• To help local farmers produce better crops • Low cost, little space & (2)_____ • Findings about traits - passed down intact - (3)_____ • Published the first paper on inheritance (4)_____ - ignored by most scientists	• Suggested by Karl von Nägeli • Problematic - has (5)_____ - failed to replicate his findings • Led Mendel to stop exploring his theories	• Revolutionized agriculture • Discovered fundamental (6)_____ - able to explain nearly every species

B Based on the information above, complete the following summary.

independently of each other	blended together	receive much recognition
inheritance	modern genetics	pea plants

People have long known about (1)_____ and that parents pass on some of their traits to their children. It was not until Gregor Johann Mendel began working with (2)_____, however, that the basic mechanism of inheritance was understood. By studying the characteristics of pea plants and how their traits were passed down from generation to generation, Mendel was able to devise a way to predict what future generations would be like. In addition, his work proved that traits are not (3)_____. They remain intact and can be passed down (4)_____. Although he published his remarkable findings, he did not (5)_____ from the scientific community. The advice that he received actually served to dissuade him from additional research. He died not knowing the impact that his work would have. Decades later, his work was rediscovered and he was credited with being the father of (6)_____.

UNIT 06 Stem Cell Research

Thinking about the Topic

1 Look at the above photos. What are the similarities and differences between identical and fraternal twins?

2 Look at the title of this unit and the word list below. What do you predict the passage will be about?

Vocabulary Focus

A The following words are from the reading. Check (√) the ones that you already know.

Noun	Verb	Adjective
☐ ban	☐ halt	☐ ethical
☐ embryo	☐ hinder	☐ illegal
☐ stalemate	☐ constitute	
☐ advocate	☐ culture	

B Write the words next to their matching definitions.

1 _____ a supporter; a proponent
2 _____ prohibition; restriction
3 _____ prohibited by law; unlawful
4 _____ to grow something in or on a controlled medium
5 _____ an organism in an early stage of development
6 _____ to stop; to cease
7 _____ to compose or make up
8 _____ a deadlock; an impasse
9 _____ related to moral or correct behavior
10 _____ to slow the progress of something

Stem Cell Research

Reading Time: 2 min. 55 sec.

Stem cells are capable of becoming any type of cell in the human body. They can be harvested from the inner cell mass of an early-stage embryo or isolated from adult tissues. Of these two types, embryonic stem cells are believed to have greater potential in treating disease. There are already a number of embryonic cell lines established. Current work on these lines has already shown their potential for many medical benefits. However, stem cell research is controversial. Its advocates and opponents are stuck in an ongoing debate.

The primary objection to stem cell research is that it requires the use of human embryos. Opponents of stem cell research feel that life begins at conception. Thus, they consider abortion as a means of collecting stem cells from human embryos unethical. They oppose it on moral and religious grounds. Advocates, however, argue that an embryo is not life until it develops human form or is born. They believe the potential discovery of cures to life-threatening diseases outweighs any objection to the research. The sharp disagreement over what constitutes life has put stem cell research on the rocks.

In fact, many nations have decided to severely restrict but not halt further embryonic stem cell research. It is considered illegal in those countries to create an embryo for the purpose of experimentation. As a result, only donated embryos can be used now. As these embryos would be destroyed anyways, the ban addresses some of the concerns that critics have. Researchers, on the other hand, consider this a stopgap measure that fails to fully address the issue.

Cloning is the other major issue of stem cell research. Cloning would be required if scientists were to develop new organs to replace failing ones in sick patients. A valuable technology, it allows new organs to exactly match patients' old organs and minimize the risk of rejection from the body's immune system. Cloning, however, raises the same concerns. The embryo would be destroyed after the tissues to be implanted in the recipient had been cultured. In addition, if this technique were to become a reality, it would also introduce the possibility of cloned humans.

As of now, there is a ban on both the cloning of human embryos and the creation of embryos for stem cell research in many countries. Their governments are currently debating the ethics of such research. Yet, not every country is restricting embryonic stem cell research. As a result, many top researchers are considering moving to institutions where their work will not be hindered. They argue that ethical problems are not as important as life-saving treatments which could be created. Thus, the countries that chose not to participate in human embryonic stem cell research may find themselves lagging behind other nations. This concern has increased the pressure to resolve the debate as quickly as possible in those countries.

Your Time: _____ min. _____ sec.

Glossary	on the rocks: (phr) in a very difficult situation
	stopgap measure: (phr) a temporary solution; a makeshift

Reading Comprehension

1. What is the primary purpose of the passage?

    Ⓐ To highlight weaknesses in an argument

    Ⓑ To discuss the two sides of stem cell research

    Ⓒ To argue that the debate over stem cells cannot be resolved

    Ⓓ To persuade lawmakers to change their position on stem cell research

2. According to the passage, stem cells

    Ⓐ have yet to be created in labs

    Ⓑ are most beneficial to young children

    Ⓒ could be used to treat many diseases

    Ⓓ have greater disadvantages than once believed

3. Which of the following is true about the ban on embryonic stem cell research?

    Ⓐ It is not in place in every country.

    Ⓑ It has encouraged research into cloning.

    Ⓒ It has lead to resolutions on the stem cell debate.

    Ⓓ It was put into effect shortly after stem cells were discovered.

4. Why would cloning be helpful for organ transplants?

    _____

5. Which of the following is NOT given as a reason some people oppose stem cell research?

    Ⓐ It is against their religious beliefs.

    Ⓑ It requires great amounts of money.

    Ⓒ It necessitates the early termination of a life.

    Ⓓ It could eventually lead to people being cloned.

6. It can be inferred from the passage that

    Ⓐ embryonic stem cell research will be completely banned in almost every country

    Ⓑ a consensus on allowing stem cell research will be reached soon among countries

    Ⓒ not enough research has been done with stem cells to know how effective they are

    Ⓓ more countries are likely to allow embryonic stem cell research in the future

Organizing & Summarizing

A Complete the following table to summarize the information about stem cell research.

Stem Cell Research

Types of Stem Cells	Advocates	Opponents	Current Situation

• Adult stem cells
  - isolated from
  (1)_____
• Embryonic stem cells
  - taken from
  (2)_____
	• Potential cure/ treatment for fatal diseases
	  - embryo is not life
	• Could be used to create (3)_____
	  - no chance of rejection
		• Destroys human embryos
		  - increases number of (4)_____
		• Could be used to create (5)_____
			• Ban on embryonic stem cell research in many countries
			• Possible (6)_____
			_____
			→ must resolve the debate over the ethics of stem cell research ASAP

B Based on the information above, complete the following summary.

abortion	human cloning	any type of cell
clone organs	a ban on the creation	embryonic stem cells

Stem cells have the potential to become (1)_____. In particular, initial research on (2)_____ has shown they have the potential to cure a number of diseases. However, whether such research should be permitted remains a controversy for many people for ethical and practical reasons. The main argument posed by opponents is that the harvesting of embryonic stem cells is the same as (3)_____. Supporters argue that the potential benefits outweigh the negative aspects of the technology. This disagreement has led to (4)_____ of new embryonic stem cell lines in many countries. This has also affected researching into cloning. Scientists want to (5)_____ for sick people needing transplants. However, opponents argue this would destroy a life and could lead to (6)_____. The ban is currently being debated within a number of countries and has yet to be resolved.

Vocabulary Expansion

Part A

A Complete the diagrams with the words from the box.

- shroud → **COVER** ← ___ / ___ / ___
- discover → **FIND** ← ___ / ___ / ___

| cloak | conceal | ~~discover~~ | expose | hide | locate |
| mask | obscure | ~~shroud~~ | spot | unearth | unmask |

B For each group of words, circle the concept that can include the others.

1. gosling   cub   foal   offspring   kitten
2. birch   elm   ginkgo   cherry   tree
3. nucleus   cell   mitochondria   membrane   chromosome
4. crop   corn   wheat   rice   barley
5. generation   year   time   decade   century

C Complete the sentences using the best words from the above exercises.

1. The bear will attack anyone who comes near its _____.
2. The _____ existed on the Earth before the evolution of flowering plants.
3. Due to increases in _____ prices, the cost of bread skyrocketed.
4. The 1960s were a _____ filled with conflict over the Vietnam War.
5. The scientist is known for _____ a possible cure for cancer.
6. The pirate decided to _____ his treasure in the cave.
7. My parents think that younger _____ are not as polite.
8. The history of the ancient civilization has been _____ in mystery.
9. Meiosis produces cells with half the number of _____ as a regular cell.
10. _____ or young horses can be divided into colts and fillies, depending on their gender.

Part B

A Complete the diagrams with the words from the box.

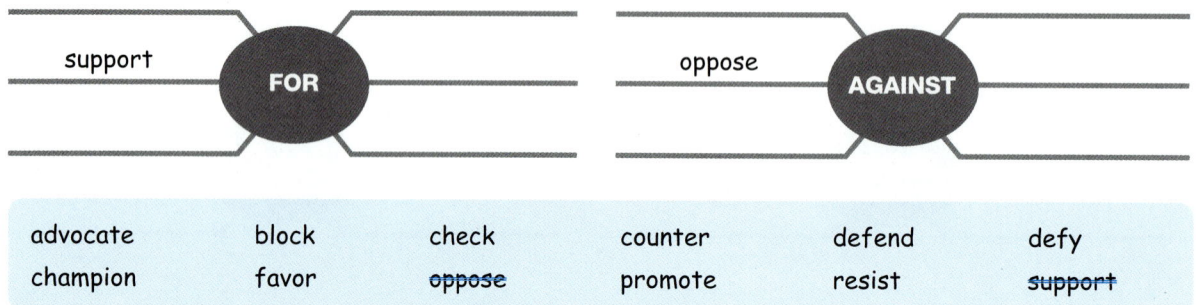

| advocate | block | check | counter | defend | defy |
| champion | favor | ~~oppose~~ | promote | resist | ~~support~~ |

B For each group of words, cross out the word that does not belong.

1. remedy — toxin — cure — antidote — treatment
2. deadlock — draw — stalemate — compromise — impasse
3. permission — suppression — prohibition — ban — restriction
4. hinder — obstruct — delay — handicap — aid
5. makeshift — temporary — necessary — improvised — stopgap

C Complete the sentences using the best words from the above exercises.

1. Mary was the only one who _____ me when I was accused of lying.
2. There is no known _____ to this poison.
3. I have trouble _____ when people offer me dessert.
4. The _____ of alcohol in the 1920s and 30s in the U.S. led to more crime.
5. The student was punished for _____ his friend during the test.
6. It is _____ to have a passport if you want to travel abroad.
7. After time ran out and the score tied, the game was ruled a _____.
8. The shortage will be _____ as we're getting new stock tomorrow.
9. You will need your parent's _____ if you want to go on the trip.
10. The actor was hired to _____ the new line of soft drinks.

Political Science

Overview
Basic Knowledge Building
Unit 07 Tyranny in Ancient Greece
Unit 08 The Patricians and the Plebeians of Republican Rome
Vocabulary Expansion

Overview

What Is Political Science?

Political science is the study of the principles and practices involved in government and lawmaking. Political scientists explore government functions, different kinds of states, voting and election processes, and the workings of political parties. They also conduct research on the historical impact of certain types of governments and political trends. Some of the subfields of political science are:

- **comparative politics** – the study and comparison of political systems within and across geographic regions
- **political theory** – the study of political concepts and ideas, such as power, influence, and democracy
- **public policy** – the study of how governments make public decisions, such as laws affecting safety, welfare, and public health
- **national politics** – the study of a specific country's political system and processes
- **diplomacy** – the study of international relations and negotiation

The earliest ideas about politics come from Plato and Aristotle. From the Middle Ages until the Renaissance, most political dialogue concerned itself with the church and state. In the 16th century, Machiavelli's *The Prince* became an important precursor of political thought. However, the academic discipline of political science did not arise until the 19th century when it was taught at the university level for the first time. In the 20th century, war and economic turmoil furthered people's fascination with political theory and its study.

Political Science and You

Students of political science can look forward to a number of careers to choose from. These include being a legislator, government agent, attorney, journalist, lobbyist, political analyst, or university professor.

Do you want to study political science? Ask yourself these questions:

- Am I interested in how power is used in human society?
- Do I enjoy discussing political issues?
- Am I interested in forms of government?
- Am I logical and analytical?
- Do I have good social skills?
- Would I enjoy working for my community?

Basic Knowledge Building

Read the following passages and check if the given statements are true (T) or false (F).

❶ The Development of the State

Human society has evolved through several stages. Societies were initially comprised of hunter-gatherer bands. They were egalitarian in that they did not support a full-time leader. A bit more complex is the tribal organization. Tribes are distinguished by some social rank yet still remain based on family and lineage. In some cases, chiefs or elders will emerge as the leader of a tribe. In a chiefdom, one individual acts as the clear leader, and class distinctions become more visible. Kings, warriors, artisans, and slaves are typical of the chiefdom hierarchy. Finally, the modern state emerged. It is a system of political institutions through which a population in a defined region is governed. States are often divided into local, regional, and federal levels of government.

Q. Chiefs are important leaders in hunter-gatherer bands.　T☐　F☐

❷ Ostracism

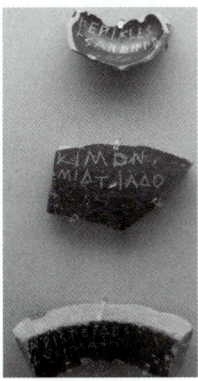

Ostracism began in ancient Athens. It was a political tool used to banish a prominent and politically threatening citizen from the city-state. The assembly voted annually to determine whether ostracism would be used that year. If a majority voted in favor of ostracism, a day was set. On that day, each voter wrote down the name of the politician he wished to be ostracized or banished on a pottery shard. The person with the most votes would then face exile. Usually, the citizen would have to leave for ten years, though some people were called back to Athens earlier. Interestingly, the ostracized person lost neither his property nor his civil rights.

Q. Ostracized citizens typically had to stay away from their homes for ten years.　T☐　F☐

❸ Autocracy, Oligarchy, and Democracy

There have been various forms of political rule in human history. An autocracy is governed by a self-appointed leader. This type of leader is termed a despot or tyrant. Often, they depend largely on their military to secure their power. In an oligarchy, an elite group holds supreme power over the country, and this group is generally determined by family or wealth. Often, children are groomed to become future oligarchs, while still being manipulated by older family members. A democracy is a form of government in which citizens hold the power and freely elect their leaders. Citizens of a democracy are entitled to a life of universal freedoms.

Q. An oligarchy is a form of government in which a small group of people rule.　T☐　F☐

❹ Niccolò Machiavelli

Niccolò Machiavelli was an Italian political philosopher who lived during the 15th and 16th centuries. Early in his career, he was a diplomat. He witnessed wars, discussed politics with prominent rulers throughout France, Germany, and Italy, and studied classical political theories. After ten years of service, Machiavelli lost his post and was imprisoned. It was then that he wrote his famous political treatise *The Prince* (1532). Drawn from Machiavelli's experiences, the text explains how rulers should gain and use their power and influence. It also explores the ideas of success and morality. Machiavelli claimed that a ruler should use the carrot and the stick appropriately to retain political power. Machiavelli's views influenced many later political leaders and thinkers.

Q. Machiavelli gained most of his ideas from reading classical political opinions. T ☐ F ☐

❺ Types of Monarchy

Historically, there are two fundamental types of monarchy: absolute and constitutional. Absolute monarchs own both the land and the people. They can rule in whatever way they see fit. Often, these monarchs attribute their authority to Divine Right, the idea that monarchs are a direct link between God and the common people. A good example from history is Louis XIV of France. In contrast is the constitutional monarchy. In this form of government, the king or queen is the head of state, yet his or her actions are bound by a constitution or set of laws set forth by a parliament. Furthermore, there is also a prime minister who functions as the head of the government. Within a constitutional monarchy, there is usually a clear balance of power unlike an absolute monarchy.

Q. An absolute monarchy is a modern example of government. T ☐ F ☐

❻ Forms of Government

Governments can be classified into several types. A kingdom is an organized society with a king or queen at its head. A commonwealth originally denoted a state which governed for the well-being of all the people, not one particular class. Today, it also can mean a joining of nations. These nations often have historical or political ties. Next is the federation. This centralized form of government is made up of several states. However, these states govern their own internal affairs according to the federal constitution. Lastly, a republic is a state without a monarch. The power is vested with the citizens who elect representatives to administer laws.

Q. A constitution is important in a federation. T ☐ F ☐

❼ The Separation of Powers

The concept and practice of the separation of powers is the opposite of absolute power. Within the separation-of-powers system, no branch of government can be more influential than another. Thus, the system protects the nation against tyrannical rule. Today, the U.S. provides a good model of the separation of powers. The three branches of government—the judicial, legislative, and executive—are given different roles. They maintain a system of checks and balances over one another. This ensures that no government body can become more powerful than the others. But this is only at the federal level. The U.S. further separates power between the federal government and the state governments. Still, many powers do overlap between branches in some cases.

Q. The separation of powers gives an elected president the most influence.   T ☐   F ☐

❽ Voting Systems

When it comes to elections, there are three main types of voting systems. The first is majority rule. Between two candidates, the one with more than half the votes is the winner. Today, it has little use in public elections but is used more in legislative votes like yes-or-no decisions by Congress. Another common voting system is proportional representation. It is common in public elections where the number of seats a party receives equates to how much public support it has. The more support, the more seats it attains and vice versa. In this voting system, winning is the most important. The final system is plurality voting. In this system, the person with the most votes is the winner, and a majority is not usually necessary or even possible.

Q. Of the three voting systems, majority rule is used most often in a legislature.   T ☐   F ☐

❾ Women's Suffrage in the U.S.

When it was first written, the Constitution of the United States did not specifically address the right of women to vote. By the end of the Civil War in the mid-1800s, the movement supporting female voting rights or women's suffrage had gained momentum. It was led by women's rights advocate Susan B. Anthony. By the early 1900s, large demonstrations were being held in Washington, D.C. and other cities as the movement pressed for an amendment to the Constitution. Some western states finally gave women the right to vote in state elections. However, it was not until 1920 that Congress ultimately passed the Nineteenth Amendment which granted women voting rights at both the state and federal level.

Q. The first states to grant women's suffrage were in the eastern U.S.   T ☐   F ☐

⑩ The Bandwagon Effect

The bandwagon effect is a social phenomenon which proposes that people will make a certain decision or act in a certain way simply because others already have. In essence, it shows that people have a tendency to follow the crowd. It is especially recognizable in political elections. In fact, the phrase originated in the U.S. during the 1848 presidential elections. In other instances, voters have sometimes shown a tendency to vote for a leading candidate because they want to be on the winning side. Early television polls might even influence voters' decisions and perhaps increase the bandwagon effect, according to some studies.

Q. The bandwagon effect only occurs during political elections.   T ☐   F ☐

⑪ The Process of the U.S. Presidential Election

Presidential elections in America occur every four years, and they are a long, complex process. Early on, after candidates are nominated, they must gather support and raise money for their election campaign. The next stage is the state caucuses and primaries where candidates are voted for by their party. In June of the election year, the main parties have conventions where they nominate their best hope for winning the White House. In November, the presidential election is held and citizens go to the polls to vote. Depending on its population, each state has a set number of electors in the Electoral College. If a candidate wins a state, he or she captures that state's electoral votes. Thus, the candidate who receives at least 270 electoral votes becomes U.S. president.

Q. American presidents are decided by an overall popular vote.   T ☐   F ☐

⑫ Local Autonomy

Autonomy in general is the concept of self-government. Local autonomy is a further extension of this idea. The term implies that a smaller, local area has been granted more control. Typically a larger, central authority will set rules for the operation of the smaller, local area. However, the local area is given room to govern itself. In some aspects, local autonomy suggests a greater level of democracy. Federal control becomes decentralized and less prevalent while local supervision increases. Benefits of local autonomy include the local authority's ability to better address the citizens' needs.

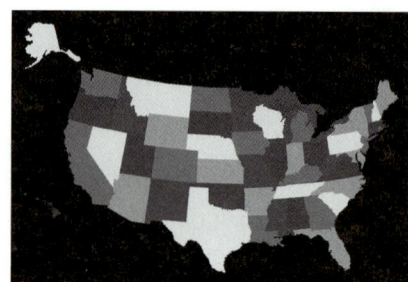

Q. Local autonomies are not completely separated from their parent governments.   T ☐   F ☐

UNIT 07 Tyranny in Ancient Greece

Thinking about the Topic

1 Look at the above pictures. Who are some notorious tyrants or dictators in history?
2 Look at the title of this unit and the word list below. What do you predict the passage will be about?

Vocabulary Focus

A The following words are from the reading. Check (√) the ones that you already know.

Noun	Verb	Adjective	Adverb
☐ despot	☐ bolster	☐ commonplace	☐ desperately
☐ oppression	☐ redistribute		
☐ prosperity	☐ restrict		
☐ void	☐ subdue		

B Write the words next to their matching definitions.

1 _____ to suppress; to pacify
2 _____ a good economic period; wealth; affluence
3 _____ an empty space
4 _____ normal; average
5 _____ to strengthen; to support; to boost
6 _____ a ruler with absolute power
7 _____ seriously; gravely
8 _____ the cruel and unfair treatment of a group of people
9 _____ to apportion differently
10 _____ to limit; to restrain

Tyranny in Ancient Greece

Time Limit: 2 min. 50 sec.

During the 7th century B.C., Greece began to experience major social unrest. A large divide between the aristocracy and general populace developed. Economic, political, and social conflict became commonplace. More and more average citizens refused to place their trust in their wealthy leaders. The noble class even began to fight among themselves. Therefore, the poor citizens began to look for an alternative figurehead. They desperately wanted a new kind of leader who would take care of their needs and challenge the aristocracy. Before long, a new ruler known as the tyrant began to come to power in various city-states in ancient Greece, forming a new type of government called a tyranny.

Tyrants were individual rulers who seized power through non-traditional means. They typically had no official right to rule via mediums such as a constitution or heredity. Often, force and violence were necessary for them to successfully gain control. Also, tyrants usually came from the middle class. They promised hope and prosperity to the lower classes and quickly gained their support. However, it should be noted that the tyrants of ancient Greece were not despots. Rather, they were widely considered to be "good" rulers, not blood-thirsty slave drivers.

Tyrannical rule lasted in Greece from about 650 to 500 B.C. In general, tyrants made many positive contributions to Greek society. First and foremost, the power of the nobility was greatly restricted. This helped subdue the class conflicts of the time. Moreover, the lower classes saw their condition improve. Farm production was encouraged, and oppression lessened. In many cases, taxes were reduced, and land was redistributed from the aristocrats to the poor. Manufacturing and trade were also promoted by tyrants, which in turn led to more jobs and greater production numbers. Finally, Greek culture benefited from tyrannical rule. Tyrants were often major patrons to the arts. Thus, greater developments and improvements in religion, art, literature, and architecture were also witnessed under tyrannies.

Tyranny did not only fill a political void and bolster the middle and lower classes in ancient Greece. It also became a stepping stone for more developed forms of government. The codification of laws became another important consequence of tyranny. As more laws became recorded, a new sense of equality between people became realized. In Athens, this eventually developed into the democratic spirit which influenced the form of government to follow tyranny. Around 510 B.C., Athens became the first political entity to ever be ruled by a democratic government.

Your Time: _____ min. _____ sec.

| Glossary | codification: (n) the reducing of unwritten customs or case law to statutory form |

Reading Comprehension

1. Why is this passage written?

   A To contrast the different classes of ancient Greece
   B To define tyranny and illustrate some of its benefits
   C To explore major examples of tyranny in ancient Greece
   D To compare despotism with tyrannical forms of government

2. What is a main reason for the development of tyranny?

   A Previous democracies had failed.
   B Greek monarchs had little power.
   C The lower classes were being ignored.
   D The noble class needed more leaders.

3. How did tyrants usually gain power?

   A They were born into their role.
   B They were elected by the people.
   C They used their fortunes to become rulers.
   D They overthrew the existing government.

4. What did tyrants promise the Greek citizens, and how were they viewed?

   ① Promise: _____
   ② View: _____

5. Which of the following was NOT a contribution of tyranny to Greek society?

   A Tax burdens were relieved.
   B People faced less oppression.
   C Productivity in society improved.
   D Class conflict totally disappeared.

6. The author implies that tyrants

   A appreciated artistic endeavors
   B usually came from the noble class
   C were completely peaceful people
   D attempted to unify the country

Organizing & Summarizing

A Complete the following table to arrange the information about tyranny in ancient Greece.

Tyranny in Ancient Greece

Background	Benefits

• Time period – (1)_____
• Class conflict
  - wealthy ruling aristocracy
  - poor lower classes
    → wanted to replace wealthy rulers
• Advent of the tyrant
  - self-made ruler from (2)_____
  - used force to seize control
  - not considered despots but good rulers
  - promised (3)_____ for the lower classes
	• Social
	  - reduced the power of the nobility
	  - reduced (4)_____ & stabilized society
	• Economic
	  - increased (5)_____
	  - promoted manufacturing & trade
	  - reduced taxes & (6)_____
	• Cultural
	  - promoted the arts & developed culture
	• Political
	  - (7)_____
	    → more equality & social balance
	  - bridge to better government
	    → (8)_____

B Based on the information above, complete the following summary.

good and fair rulers	manufacturing and agriculture	the middle class
the earliest form of democracy	600 to about 500 B.C.	the codification of laws

Tyranny was a form of government in ancient Greece that lasted from (1)_____. Tyrants were self-made rulers. Most often, they came from (2)_____. They sometimes gained power through force, and they promised peace and prosperity to the neglected lower classes. This pleased the lower classes who had long wanted to replace their wealthy noble leaders. Tyrants were the perfect answer to the problems of the lower classes. Tyrants were not despots. Instead, they were seen as (3)_____. Ancient Greece benefited from tyrannical rule in many ways. First, the power of the nobility was reduced. As class conflict decreased, society stabilized though only temporarily. Also, an increase in jobs and heightened productivity in (4)_____ was observed. Taxes were reduced, and land was redistributed. In addition, tyrants often promoted culture through the arts. Finally, better forms of government followed this period of rule. (5)_____ became more prevalent. In Athens, this led to (6)_____ being developed. Equality and social balance became more likely following the rule of the tyrants.

UNIT 08 The Patricians and the Plebeians of Republican Rome

Thinking about the Topic

1 Look at the above pictures. What different social classes have existed in different societies in history?

2 Look at the title of this unit and the word list below. What do you predict the passage will be about?

Vocabulary Focus

A The following words are from the reading. Check (√) the ones that you already know.

Noun	Verb	Adjective
☐ conflict	☐ blend	☐ eligible
☐ extravagance	☐ exclude	☐ illiterate
☐ mobility	☐ govern	☐ privileged
☐ peasant		

B Write the words next to their matching definitions.

1 _____ having special rights or benefits
2 _____ to rule by right of authority
3 _____ unable to read and write
4 _____ to mix together
5 _____ the ability to move
6 _____ a farmer of the lowest social rank and least wealth
7 _____ wastefulness, esp. of money; overspending
8 _____ to keep out or not permit entrance
9 _____ qualified; appropriate; suitable
10 _____ a difference; a disagreement

The Patricians and the Plebeians of Republican Rome

Time Limit: 3 min.

In ancient Rome, there were two different classes of citizens: the patricians and the plebeians. Their values contrasted, and they often came into conflict with each other. The patricians comprised the privileged ruling class while the average Roman citizen possessing fewer rights made up the plebeians. This distinction was established at the beginning of the Roman Republic in the early sixth century B.C. There was little mobility between the two classes. By the third century B.C., however, both classes began to blend together as the plebeians gained more rights and influence and the patricians lost much of their power.

During its peak, the patrician class enjoyed a number of privileges. Originally, the patricians were descendents of the most powerful Roman families. Their ancestors were the Founding Fathers of Rome. Thus, they had significant political influence as the holders of seats in the Roman Senate. This enabled them to exclusively govern Rome for centuries. Also, the patricians could hold all the civil and religious offices. They could become magistrates, interim heads of state, and priests. Interestingly, only patricians were allowed to enter the priesthood because it was believed that they could communicate better with the gods. Furthermore, the patricians led a life of luxury and extravagance as wealthy landowners. Many of them possessed a house in Rome and a villa in the country. However, the most unique privilege that the patricians came to enjoy occurred during the Roman Empire: only they were eligible to become the emperor.

In contrast, the plebeians were excluded from many rights although they constituted the majority of Roman citizens. Typically, they were peasants and artisans who worked for the patricians in a number of capacities. They had no access to formal education and were in large part illiterate. Also, though they paid taxes to the patrician government, the plebeians had no political rights. They were not allowed to hold public office except as a military tribune or to appeal decisions made by patrician rulers. Moreover, they were forbidden to marry a patrician. The plebeians had no hope of ever ascending the social ladder. However, the plebeians eventually massed together in 494 B.C. in what was called the Conflict of Orders.

The Conflict of Orders was the push for change and political equality by the plebeians. By not helping Rome during times of war, the plebeians gradually gained more political power and, finally, their freedom. A milestone was reached with the acquisition of the right to become elected officials in the Senate. The office of Plebeian Tribune was also established. Tribunes had the power to protect plebeians from patrician magistrates. By the end of the Conflict of Orders in 287 B.C., official equality between the patrician and plebeian classes had been established.

Your Time: _____ min. _____ sec.

Glossary

interim: (adj) serving during an intermediate interval of time; temporary

Reading Comprehension

1. What is the main purpose of the passage?

    Ⓐ To describe the luxurious lifestyle of the patrician class
    Ⓑ To illustrate how the plebeians struggled in their daily lives
    Ⓒ To contrast two major social classes of ancient Rome
    Ⓓ To note social changes in ancient Rome in the fifth century B.C.

2. Which of the following is true of the patrician class?

    Ⓐ They ruled the plebeians by the power of sheer numbers.
    Ⓑ They were not allowed to marry with the plebeian class.
    Ⓒ They were the offspring of ancient emperors of Rome.
    Ⓓ They exclusively monopolized military offices for many years.

3. Which of the following adjectives characterizes the plebeian class best?

    Ⓐ Oppressed
    Ⓑ Extravagant
    Ⓒ Outnumbered
    Ⓓ Educated

4. What major change granted the plebeians more power, and when did it happen?
    ① Change: _____
    ② When: _____

5. Which of the following is NOT true about the plebeians before the Conflict of Orders?

    Ⓐ They had no political rights.
    Ⓑ Most of them could not read or write.
    Ⓒ Many of them engaged in agriculture.
    Ⓓ They did not have to pay taxes.

6. It can be inferred from the passage that the plebeians

    Ⓐ were an important military resource
    Ⓑ were eventually outnumbered by the patricians
    Ⓒ were not a very ambitious group of people
    Ⓓ owned their own houses and cultivated their own land

Organizing & Summarizing

A Complete the following table to arrange the information about the patricians and the plebeians.

The Patricians and the Plebeians

Class	Characteristics	Other Information

Patricians	• Descendents of the Roman founders
	• Ruling class of ancient Rome
	  - major political power
	  → (1)_____, magistrates, priests & emperors
	  - (2)_____
	  → had a house in Rome & a villa in the country
		• (6)_____, patricians had lost much of their power
		• (7)_____ (494 -287 B.C.)
		  - plebeians gained a significant political & social presence
		  → could be elected to the Senate
		  → (8)_____ established
		  - equality between the classes clearly evident

Plebeians	• General citizens
	  - (3)_____ working for patricians
	  - poor & uneducated
	  → mostly (4)_____
	  - no political influence
	  → could not hold major public office (exception: (5)_____)
	  - could not marry patricians
	  - greater in number than patricians	

B Based on the information above, complete the following summary.

outnumbered the patricians	the Roman founders	elected into the Senate
the early 6th century B.C.	the Conflict of Orders	Senators, magistrates, and priests

The patrician and the plebeian classes of Rome were established in (1)_____. The patricians were a smaller, privileged class made up of descendents of (2)_____. They were wealthy and held all of the political power and influence. They monopolized public offices as (3)_____. These educated rulers controlled Roman civilization for the next three hundred years. In contrast, the plebeians were the class of poor and uneducated citizens. They possessed no political influence and could not hold any major public office. They also had few civil rights. However, they easily (4)_____. In 494 B.C., they started (5)_____ in order to achieve more rights and political power. Before long, they had gained more political control and were eventually allowed to be (6)_____. The patricians gradually lost their political upper hand. By the end of the Conflict of Orders in 287 B.C., equality between the classes was much more evident.

Vocabulary Expansion

Part A

A Complete the diagrams with the words from the box.

DEMOCRACY: president, _____, _____, _____

DESPOTISM: oppression, _____, _____, _____

| absolute power | authoritarian | civil rights | dictator | election | equality |
| freedom | imbalance | majority | oppression | president | unchallenged |

B For each group of words, circle the concept that can include the others.

1	wrench	hammer	screwdriver	saw	tool
2	mayor	career	lawyer	politician	priest
3	electorate	campaign	election	candidate	ballot
4	diplomat	ambassador	consul	minister	envoy
5	oligarchy	federation	tyranny	government	democracy

C Complete the sentences using the best words from the above exercises.

1 In an _____, an elite group holds supreme power over a country.
2 There were over one hundred _____ for the new office position.
3 The President will send a special _____ to the trade talks.
4 On a(n) _____ day everyone must go down to the courthouse and vote.
5 Because the citizens were tired of their _____, they ousted the ruler.
6 The U.S. withdrew its _____ and embassy staff from Brazil.
7 Martin Luther King, Jr. fought for the _____ of African-American people.
8 The _____ of the city gave a speech last Sunday that was well received.
9 The carpenter used a small _____ to cut the long piece of wood into two pieces.
10 Before the advent of the electronic voting system, people had to count _____ by hand.

Part B

A Complete the diagrams with the words from the box.

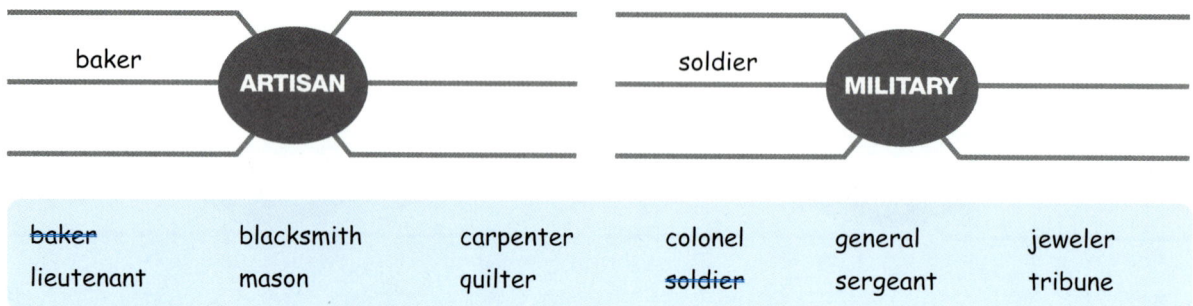

| baker | blacksmith | carpenter | colonel | general | jeweler |
| lieutenant | mason | quilter | soldier | sergeant | tribune |

(baker and soldier are crossed out)

B For each group of words, cross out the word that does not belong.

1	observe	watch	view	deny	witness
2	fortune	opulence	affluence	prosperity	dependence
3	result	consequence	foundation	outcome	upshot
4	aristocrat	monk	priest	pastor	clergyman
5	selected	fake	elite	special	choice

C Complete the sentences using the best words from the above exercises.

1 Though they are usually cheap, _____ goods do not last for a very long time.
2 Claudia Kennedy is the first female three-star _____ in the U.S. army.
3 A neighbor _____ the crime and was able to rescue the child from the kidnapper.
4 The _____ of the house began to sink into the ground due to its poor quality.
5 A _____ makes things by hand out of metal that has been heated to a high temperature.
6 The young couple was _____ a loan from the bank because they had a bad credit rating.
7 Tyrants in ancient Greece took land from the _____ and redistributed it to the poor.
8 After _____ the football game on television, the family went out for a celebratory pizza.
9 The plebeians were not allowed to hold public office except that of military _____.
10 Many countries are developing alternative energy sources to reduce their _____ on fossil fuels.

Geography

Overview
Basic Knowledge Building
Unit 09 Greenland
Unit 10 The Mississippi River and Its Dams
Vocabulary Expansion

Overview

What Is Geography?

Geography is the study of the Earth's surfaces. Typically, geographers are interested in how these surfaces change over time and why they differ from one another. Both natural and human influences are considered in geographical research. Today, there are numerous subfields of geography. They include:

- **physical geography** – the study of landforms and other physical environments
- **human geography** – the study of the patterns between humans and various Earth environments
- **environmental geography** – the study of the impact of human beings on natural landscapes
- **geomatics** – the study of gathering and processing geographical information
- **cartography** – the study of map making

The earliest research in geography can be traced back to the ancient Greeks and Romans. Ptolemy incorporated both Greek and Roman data in his book *Geographia*. During the Renaissance, explorers such as Portugal's Vasco da Gama extended the previously limited scope of the world. Interest in geography continued to increase. In the 1800s, certain geographers began to propose the idea that human activity also shapes the Earth. Today, many modern fields of geography attempt to reduce the harmful effects populations have on nature.

Geography and You

Students of geography enter a number of careers. These include being a geologist, librarian, land use planner, professor, urban planner, surveyor, and cartographer.

Do you want to be a geographer? Ask yourself these questions:

- Do I enjoy studying landforms?
- Am I concerned about the environment?
- Do I pay close attention to detail?
- Do I have strong organizational skills?
- Do I like traveling and field trips?
- Do I like to work with advanced technology?

Basic Knowledge Building

Read the following passages and check if the given statements are true (T) or false (F).

❶ Physical Geography

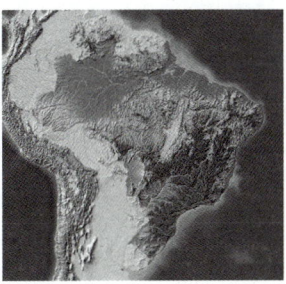

Physical geography is a branch of geography. It examines the Earth's natural features as interactive entities. It emphasizes research in the processes of the world's natural environments and how they relate to one another. One of the important subfields of physical geography is geomorphology. It studies the surface of the Earth and the processes by which it is shaped. Another is climatology, the study of how climate and weather affect the Earth. Also in hydrology, experts explore how different types of water bodies like rivers or oceans influence the environment. Key to physical geography is the integration of various concepts to better understand how and why the features of the Earth form.

Q. Physical geography is an interdisciplinary field of study. T ☐ F ☐

❷ Human Geography

Human geography is a popular branch of geography. It explores the link between people and the physical environment. How human activity affects the physical world is of special concern. Politics, society, economics, and government are all important influences. Experts look for patterns in these factors when comparing and contrasting different regions or time periods. Statistical analysis and model building also play an integral role in human geography research. More recently, with expansive urbanization, overcrowding, and pollution, urban geography has become a critical subfield of human geography. It can help increase the quality of life man enjoys in the future.

Q. Human geography is mainly the study of urbanization and its effects. T ☐ F ☐

❸ Types of Regions

A region is an area sharing some characteristics that distinguish it from other areas. Regions may be divided into two further subtypes: formal and functional regions. A formal region is distinguished by how people share common traits, such as language, religion, or nationality. It can also be categorized by environmental features, such as climate, landform, or vegetation. Climate and landform regions as well as states and provinces are typical examples of formal regions. A functional region is based on a node or central area that is connected to surrounding areas through business or economic activity. For example, a metropolitan area is linked to its surrounding areas by transportation and communication systems.

Q. An area can be part of both a formal and functional region. T ☐ F ☐

❹ Tundra

Tundra is a geographical area which is usually cold, treeless, and flat. It is typically an extreme environment that has little animal life. Due to the minimal food chain, tundra ecosystems are highly fragile. There are two types of tundra: Arctic and Alpine. Arctic tundra is found in the polar regions of the Earth, and Alpine tundra exists in the high mountain regions above the tree line. Arctic tundra receives less rainfall than Alpine tundra. Also, permafrost is found in Arctic tundra due to the freezing temperatures. Permafrost is a permanently frozen layer of soil. In contrast, Alpine tundra does not contain permafrost because its climate is not as cold as that of Arctic tundra.

Q. Alpine tundra receives more precipitation than Arctic tundra.   T ☐   F ☐

❺ The Canary Islands

The Canary Islands lie off the northwest coast of Africa. They consist of seven islands that were formed by ancient volcanoes. Mount Teide on the island of Tenerife is the third largest volcano in the world. It is over 3,700 meters above sea level and is dormant. Its last eruption occurred in the early 20th century. The Canary Islands enjoy a constant warm temperature year round. Furthermore, they fall in the path of the trade winds, which allows them to experience both wet and dry climates. The Canary Islands played an important role in human exploration as well. Once colonized by Spain in the 15th century, the islands were used as an important stopover for Spaniards on their way to the Americas, including Columbus's expedition.

Q. The volcano Teide in the Canary Islands no longer poses a threat to people.   T ☐   F ☐

❻ Urbanization

Urbanization is the process in which more and more people come to live in cities or their suburbs. It is mainly due to the influx of residents from rural areas. Urbanization occurs as individuals and families look to cities for economic opportunity and a better way of life. They leave behind a restrictive standard of living as found, for example, in farming communities, in the hopes of exploiting the seemingly unlimited potential of urban areas. One of the main attractions of urban centers is the possibility of social mobility. People believe they can move up the social ladder if only they work hard in the city. Today, more and more people are abandoning their old ways of life and going urban. Better jobs are not the only attraction. Modern health care, quality education, and even entertainment entice people to consider the move.

Q. Urbanization happens as people choose to live in cities instead of the country.   T ☐   F ☐

❼ White Flight

White flight is a demographic term. It refers to the shift or migration of white middle and working-class people from cities to the suburbs. White flight first occurred in the United States during the 1950s. The desegregation of schools in America was tagged as an early spark. However, there are other factors which are considered to cause white flight. The decay of urban areas due to crime and overcrowding is one. Another is blockbusting which plays upon the racial tensions in a neighborhood. In it, realtors pressure white property owners to sell their homes by implying that black families will soon be moving into the neighborhood. Also, the improvement of transportation infrastructure has allowed more white people to commute to work in hectic cities and live a more comfortable life on the outskirts.

Q. The poor quality of urban life is often a major cause of white flight.   T ☐   F ☐

❽ Satellite Cities

A satellite city is a small or medium-sized city that is directly adjacent to a larger one. Usually, satellite cities were independent entities before the urban expansion of the big city adjoining them occurred. Therefore, they tend to have their own form of local government and do not rely completely on their urban neighbor for survival. They have their own downtown and city hall as well. The historically self-sufficient character of many satellite cities is changing, however. Continued expansion of the nearby metropolis has caused some to become more heavily reliant on the adjacent major city. A good example is Oakland, California. While Oakland is still a major port city, many citizens living there commute to their jobs in San Francisco.

Q. Satellite cities depend completely on the neighboring major city for survival.   T ☐   F ☐

❾ Cartography

The field of cartography is involved with the depiction of geographic areas through maps and charts. Cartography allows human beings to view the Earth on a flat surface. The earliest maps were hardly accurate or durable. Much of their design relied on guesswork. However, the advent of navigational devices such as the compass changed everything. Maps improved and a truer representation of the  world began to emerge. Further advances such as the telescope were also beneficial in cartography. Today, computer technology and satellites allow instant imaging of the Earth's surface.

Q. Early ocean explorers might be important contributors to cartography's development.   T ☐   F ☐

⑩ Alexander von Humboldt

Alexander von Humboldt was a German explorer and naturalist who lived during the 18th and 19th centuries. He was one of the most acclaimed scientists of his generation. His explorations and discoveries in South America did much to lay the framework for future geographical fields. On his five-year journey through South America, Humboldt made major discoveries about plant life, volcanic activity, and ocean currents. He even documented his early notes on the makeup of the Andes. Also, his work contributed to the field of meteorology. For example, he discovered that the intensity of Earth's magnetic field decreases from the poles to the equator. Once back in Europe, Humboldt continued to do major research in geomagnetism.

Q. Humboldt's achievements were not recognized until after his death.　T ☐　F ☐

⑪ The Panama Canal

The Panama Canal is a waterway in Central America which connects the Pacific and Atlantic Oceans. The immense project was initially begun by the French in 1881. However, due to numerous setbacks, it was abandoned eight years later. The United States next undertook its construction and finally opened the canal in 1914. The canal comprises a system of locks. This was an engineering milestone at the time as the locks allow different levels of waterways to merge seamlessly together. The canal helped to create an explosion in ocean trade and commerce because ships no longer had to make the endless trek around South America.

Q. Without a lock system, the Panama Canal could not have been built.　T ☐　F ☐

⑫ The Global Positioning System (GPS)

GPS is a network of satellites which allows precise navigation and location of objects on Earth. The system is based on trilateration. This is a method of using the geometry of triangles to find positions. The basic process is that receivers measure the travel time of signals from three or more satellites to determine the distance between the satellites and Earth. The exact location of the satellites must be continually monitored for accuracy. This way, one of the intersection points will always be located on Earth for accurate positioning. GPS was originally developed by the U.S. Department of Defense for their sole use. However, it was made available to the global public in the 1980s. Since then, GPS has become an invaluable aid for everyone from map-making companies to hikers in the Himalayas to soccer moms.

Q. Initially, GPS was developed for military purposes.　T ☐　F ☐

UNIT 09 Greenland

Thinking about the Topic

1 Look at the above photos. What characteristics do you think islands have?
2 Look at the title of this unit and the word list below. What do you predict the passage will be about?

Vocabulary Focus

A The following words are from the reading. Check (√) the ones that you already know.

Noun	Verb	Adjective
☐ estimate	☐ dominate	☐ aquatic
☐ terrain	☐ hover	☐ unadulterated
☐ optimism	☐ illuminate	☐ harsh
☐ misnomer		

B Write the words next to their matching definitions.

1 _____ pure; natural
2 _____ confidence; positive thinking
3 _____ occurring in water
4 _____ a wrongly applied name
5 _____ an approximate calculation; a judgment
6 _____ to lighten
7 _____ land; ground
8 _____ to be the most important or powerful person or thing
9 _____ to float over or around
10 _____ severe; cruel

Greenland

Lying in the northern Arctic Ocean, Greenland is the world's largest island. The island was first explored by the Vikings around the 10th century. Denmark became the first country to colonize this huge terrain much later in the 1700s. Today, Greenland has been granted self-rule as an extension of Denmark. However, the population of Greenland is very small. Estimates indicate that it is just over 55,000. The majority of the population is Inuit with the rest being of Scandinavian decent. Most inhabitants live along the coast and near the capital of Nuuk. The dispersal of settlements is due to the fact that over 80 percent of the island is ice-capped.

The climate of Greenland is rather harsh. The summers are short, and the average temperature hovers just around 10 degrees Celsius. During the winter, temperatures often fall below -50 degrees Celsius. As most of the island is covered in ice sheets, there are no forests. Nevertheless, a unique ecosystem can be found in Greenland. There are various species of plant life which include moss, lichen, ferns, small shrubs, and small trees. These are typical Arctic tundra plants. Also, Greenland is home to animals such as polar bears, wolves, reindeer, and the Arctic fox. They have adapted well to the island's frigid environment. Aquatic mammals such as whales and seals also frequent the waters around Greenland.

Greenland shares similarities with other island nations because its economy and livelihood is completely dependent on the ocean. Fishing dominates most ways of life. Shrimp, salmon, and cod are the primary kinds of fish caught. Of these, shrimp is the industry's leading money-earner. Fish processing leads the manufacturing field. Most seafood exports head directly to Denmark and the rest of the European Union. Recently, the Greenland government has attempted to diversify its economy. Geological surveys have provided data that parts of the island might have rich mineral resources. Offshore petroleum could be a major boost to the economy. Precious minerals such as gold and diamonds also feed the optimism of Greenlanders.

While the name Greenland is somewhat of a misnomer, the land is full of wild, unadulterated natural beauty. For this reason, there has been a push to make it a popular tourist destination. Some cruise lines now make regular calls in various ports. One of the biggest attractions is the Ilulissat Icefjord, an immense glacier located on the west coast of Greenland. It was designated a UNESCO World Heritage Site in 2004. Another attraction is the northern lights called aurora borealis. The atmospheric phenomenon regularly illuminates the skies above the tundra of Greenland.

Glossary

UNESCO: (n) the United Nations Educational, Scientific and Cultural Organization

Reading Comprehension

1. Why is this passage written?

   Ⓐ To discuss the economy of Greenland
   Ⓑ To explore the wildlife found on Greenland
   Ⓒ To illustrate the natural features of Greenland
   Ⓓ To describe the island nation of Greenland

2. Which of the following cannot be found on the island of Greenland?

   Ⓐ Moss
   Ⓑ Forests
   Ⓒ Reindeer
   Ⓓ Trees

3. According to the passage, which of the following is true about Greenland?

   Ⓐ Greenland is the Arctic habitat of many different kinds of animals.
   Ⓑ Its ecosystem is almost non-existent because of the cold conditions.
   Ⓒ Greenlanders are famous for their history of being skilled whalers.
   Ⓓ Northern Europeans make up the majority of the population.

4. What industry drives the economy of Greenland, and what is its biggest earner?
   ① Industry: _____
   ② Biggest: _____

5. Which of the following is NOT true about Greenland?

   Ⓐ It is the biggest island on Earth.
   Ⓑ It has close relations with Denmark.
   Ⓒ The country has no indigenous plant life.
   Ⓓ The island may be rich in mineral resources.

6. What does the author imply about Greenland?

   Ⓐ Its name is a paradox.
   Ⓑ Its population is growing.
   Ⓒ It is part of the European Union.
   Ⓓ Greenlanders are mostly vegetarian.

Organizing & Summarizing

A Complete the following table to arrange the information about Greenland.

Greenland

Geography	History	People	Environment	Economy
• Northern Arctic Ocean • World's largest island • (1)_____ covered in ice • Mainly coastal settlements	• First colonized by (2)_____ in the 1700s - close economic and political ties	• Vikings first to settle • Majority (3)_____ with some Scandinavian descendents • Total population: (4)_____	• Frigid & severe - summers: average of 10℃ - winters: (5)_____ • Arctic tundra plant life - (6)_____ & small trees • Arctic wildlife - polar bears, wolves, reindeer & whales	• Fishing - (7)_____ : highest earner • Search for (8)_____ • Tourism - cruises - glaciers - aurora borealis

B Based on the information above, complete the following summary.

the aurora borealis	Arctic tundra plant life	the fishing industry
Inuit descent	oil and precious minerals	Denmark in the 1700s

First explored by the Vikings, Greenland is the world's largest island. It was colonized by (1)_____. Greenland is located in the northern Arctic Ocean. Because more than 80 percent of the land is covered in ice, most of the population lives near the coast. The majority are of (2)_____. The climate is very frigid with summers averaging about 10 degrees Celsius and winter temperatures reaching minus 50 degrees Celsius. Greenland has (3)_____ such as moss, lichen, ferns, small shrubs and trees. Also, different species of wildlife like polar bears, wolves, reindeer, whales, and seals live in and around Greenland. The economy is almost completely dependent on the ocean via (4)_____ with shrimp being the highest earner. However, economic diversification is in the works. The search for (5)_____ is ongoing. Also, tourism is beginning to open up as tourists arrive on cruise ships to view the awesome glaciers and possibly catch (6)_____ in the northern night sky.

UNIT 10
The Mississippi River and Its Dams

Thinking about the Topic

1. Look at the above photos. What are some famous dams in your country? What are they used for?
2. Look at the title of this unit and the word list below. What do you predict the passage will be about?

Vocabulary Focus

A The following words are from the reading. Check (√) the ones that you already know.

Noun	Verb	Adjective
☐ artery	☐ oppose	☐ commercial
☐ habitat	☐ utilize	☐ crucial
☐ modernization	☐ navigate	☐ migratory
		☐ precious

B Write the words next to their matching definitions.

1. _____ to take advantage of
2. _____ innovation; making new and up-to-date
3. _____ extremely important
4. _____ moving from one habitat to another
5. _____ concerning business
6. _____ rare; expensive
7. _____ to dispute; to resist
8. _____ home; territory
9. _____ a main channel or route; a blood vessel going from the heart
10. _____ to sail on or across an area of water

The Mississippi River and Its Dams

Time Limit: 2 min. 40 sec.

The Mississippi River is the largest river in the United States and a crucial waterway. It runs from Lake Itasca, Minnesota in the north to the Gulf of Mexico in the south and is approximately 2,340 miles long. The river has played a key role in the development and growth of America. In the early days of American history, it quickly became a main artery for commerce and trade. Today, the river is divided into two sections: the upper and lower Mississippi. The upper extends from its origins in Minnesota south to the Ohio River. The lower Mississippi is designated from the Ohio River to its mouth near New Orleans, Louisiana. A series of locks and dams were implemented in the upper section of the river. These were necessary to deepen the river to allow for commercial shipping.

In the 1930s, the U.S. government recognized a need to better utilize the upper Mississippi River as a shipping route and enacted a project to construct a series of dams. A total of 29 locks and dams were built by the early 1940s. The primary intention behind their construction was the regulation of water levels in the upper section of the river. The dams created a series of pools to allow for better barge transport. This added depth made commercial navigation of the river possible. Without the lock-and-dam system, the river would have been too shallow to navigate. At its completion, the project created a uniform nine-foot depth in the upper Mississippi River.

However, the Mississippi River's importance is not limited to shipping and commerce. Hundreds of species of animals live in the various habitats of the Mississippi River Basin, which comprises 40 percent of the entire country. These animals include almost 300 different species of fish and about 50 different types of mammals. Experts also believe about half of America's migratory birds live near the Mississippi during certain times of the year. Therefore, the Mississippi River is a vital element of the entire American ecosystem.

Today, the U.S. Army Corps of Engineers is in charge of maintaining the dams along the Mississippi River. It is also responsible for protecting the river and its precious environs. Presently, the lock and dam system is showing its age. Numerous groups have called for a modernization project to make it more efficient at flood control. Still, various environmental groups oppose such a project, claiming that it will destroy the natural wetlands of the Mississippi River.

Your Time: _____ min. _____ sec.

Glossary	**commerce:** (n) buying and selling of goods, esp. on a large scale **barge:** (n) a long, narrow boat with a flat bottom

Reading Comprehension

1 Why is this passage written?

   Ⓐ To discuss how the Mississippi River dams were built by engineers

   Ⓑ To illustrate the importance of the Mississippi River and its dams

   Ⓒ To show how dams are environmentally friendly and preserve wildlife

   Ⓓ To trace the history of the Mississippi River dams and locks

2 Where are the majority of Mississippi locks and dams located?

   Ⓐ Near the mouth of the river

   Ⓑ In the lower Mississippi River

   Ⓒ In the middle section of the river

   Ⓓ In the upper Mississippi River

3 Which of the following is true about the Mississippi River dams?

   Ⓐ They have all been recently upgraded and modernized.

   Ⓑ They create a uniform depth of eight feet along the river.

   Ⓒ They increase the depth of the river for shipping.

   Ⓓ They provide recreational and commercial benefits

4 How many species of fish and mammals call the Mississippi River and its environs home?

   ① Fish: _____

   ② Mammals: _____

5 Which of the following is NOT true about the Mississippi River?

   Ⓐ It is an important commercial artery.

   Ⓑ It starts from Minnesota and ends in Ohio.

   Ⓒ It is a critical component of the American ecosystem.

   Ⓓ It is maintained by the U.S. Army Corps of Engineers.

6 Without the Mississippi River, the United States

   Ⓐ would not have expanded as quickly as it did

   Ⓑ could not have developed high-tech locks and dams

   Ⓒ would probably trade more with neighboring countries

   Ⓓ could still rely on smaller stream networks for commerce

Organizing & Summarizing

A Complete the following table to arrange the information about the Mississippi River and its dams.

The Mississippi River & Its Dams

Role & Layout	Locks and Dams	Habitat	Maintenance
• Crucial (1)_____ _____ - instrumental in the development & expansion of the U.S. • Runs north to south - upper and lower sections - about (2)_____ _____ in length	• 29 locks & dams altogether • Built to maximize commerce early 1940s • Dams deepen river to consistent (3)_____ _____ in upper section - allows barges to navigate • Becoming outdated - need upgrades for better (4)_____ _____ - environmental concern about destruction of wetlands	• Critical to American wildlife - (5)_____ comprises 40% of entire country - 300 species of fish - over (6)_____ _____ of mammals - half of America's (7)_____	• Implemented by (8)_____ - maintain locks & dams - protect environment

B Based on the information above, complete the following summary.

40 percent of the U.S.	about 2,340 miles	migratory birds
By the 1940s	better flood control	barge navigation

The Mississippi River runs (1)_____ from north to south in the U.S. The river was instrumental in the development of the U.S. (2)_____, a series of locks and dams were built in the upper Mississippi River region. This system created a consistent depth of nine feet, which is ideal for (3)_____. This helped maximize commerce and trade on the river. Today, however, the system is becoming outdated and needs to be upgraded for (4)_____. However, environmentalists fear this will damage the habitats of wildlife in the region. As the basin comprises over (5)_____, hundreds of species of fish and about 50 different kinds of mammals call it home. Also, a half of America's (6)_____ spend time in the region. The upkeep of the locks and dams as well as the protection of the surrounding environment are the responsibilities of the U.S. Army Corps of Engineers.

Vocabulary Expansion

Part A

A Complete the diagrams with the words from the box.

desert — TERRAIN

river — WATERWAY

| channel | desert | dune | glacier | gorge | lake |
| mountain | ocean | river | sea | strait | valley |

B For each group of words, circle the concept that can include the others.

1. mouth · lips · tongue · teeth · gums
2. scavenger · habitat · ecosystem · prey · predator
3. sleet · hail · tornado · weather · typhoon
4. car · train · bus · subway · commute
5. railroad · milestone · electricity · wheel · radio

C Complete the sentences using the best words from the above exercises.

1. One of the biggest _____ in recent years is the Internet.
2. The _____ crossed from the Philippines and struck the island of Guam.
3. Each morning millions of people make their daily _____ to work.
4. _____ tours are very popular in Patagonia due to the natural beauty of the ice.
5. The key to healthy teeth and _____ is regular flossing and brushing.
6. The city proposed a new _____ system much like the London Tube.
7. The swamp and its plants, animals, and water supply form an _____.
8. Before television, listening to the _____ was a common pastime for families.
9. _____ can be very deadly, though they do not last as long as hurricanes.
10. _____ such as vultures and hyenas eat the meat of dead animals instead of killing their own food.

Part B

A Complete the diagrams with the words from the box.

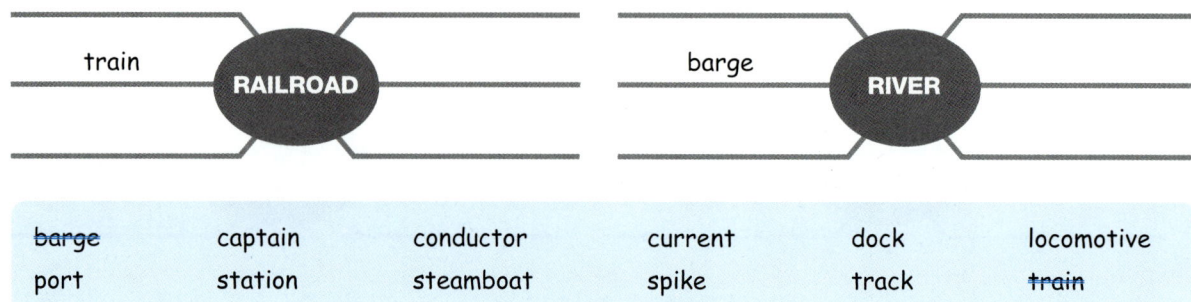

~~barge~~	captain	conductor	current	dock	locomotive
port	station	steamboat	spike	track	~~train~~

B For each group of words, cross out the word that does not belong.

1. bordering   adjoining   neighboring   adjacent   separating
2. strong   durable   sturdy   limp   firm
3. habitat   abode   ceiling   domicile   home
4. concrete   forest   urban   highway   skyscraper
5. coarse   damp   moist   wet   soaked

C Complete the sentences using the best words from the above exercises.

1. The _____ showed the passengers to their seats then took their tickets.
2. The workers drove the steel _____ into the wood in the hot sun.
3. We live in a large three-bedroom detached house _____ to the park.
4. Strong _____ prevent fishermen from entering the dangerous river.
5. After they tied the boat to the _____, they went into the restaurant for lunch.
6. _____ allows contractors to build big buildings relatively inexpensively.
7. The cow stumbled into the electric wire and fell down _____.
8. One of the most important _____ cities in the United States is New Orleans.
9. _____ crowd the cityscapes of large metropolises like New York and Chicago.
10. They were so poor that they could only afford _____ clothing.

Mass Communication

Overview
Basic Knowledge Building
Unit 11 Joseph Pulitzer
Unit 12 The History of Magazines
Vocabulary Expansion

Overview

What Is Mass Communication?

Mass communication is the study of how information is relayed to large groups of people at the same time. Television, radio, newspapers, magazines, and the Internet are the most common media of mass communication. Mass communication is a vast discipline covering many areas. Major study areas include:

- **print journalism** – the study of magazine and newspaper writing, reporting, and editing
- **electronic journalism** – the study of writing, reporting, and producing news for radio, TV, and the Internet
- **film** – the study of the principles and methods used to produce movies as well as the purposes for which they are made
- **advertising** – the study of the principles and techniques used to make the public aware of goods and services
- **public relations** – the study of the methods and activities used to create a good public image

Mass communication in the modern sense started with the invention of printing in the 15th century. Later, modern journalism began with the publication of newspapers in the 18th century. By the late 19th and 20th centuries, journalism exploded in the forms of magazines and newspapers. The advent of the radio, television, film, and the Internet since then has expanded the territories of mass communication.

Mass Communication and You

Students of mass communication work in a broad range of fields. They may work in newspaper and magazine companies, radio and television companies, publishing houses, advertising agencies, public relations agencies, government organizations, or in the entertainment industry.

Do you want to study one of the fields of mass communication? Ask yourself these questions:

- Do I have good communication skills?
- Am I good at writing about different topics?
- Can I convey strong emotion with words or photos?
- Am I a good team player?
- Am I creative and hard-working?
- Do I have strong physical stamina and will power?

Basic Knowledge Building

Read the following passages and check if the given statements are true (T) or false (F).

❶ Johannes Gutenberg

Johannes Gutenberg was a German printer and goldsmith who lived in the 15th century. He is usually recognized as the inventor of moveable metal type printing in the west. As metal type produced high-quality printing, the innovation rapidly spread through Europe. It also allowed printing to be done more quickly and efficiently. For example, prior to metal type, books had to be copied by hand or with wooden blocks carved by hand. These books were not as durable as press-printed material, either. Gutenberg's invention made books affordable and accessible, and it increased literacy among the common people. Thanks to metal type, the book industry was forever changed.

Q. Metal type printing was faster than wood-block printing. T ☐ F ☐

❷ Mass Society

Mass society is a term that has been used since the Industrial Revolution to describe the atmosphere of industrialized societies. Generally speaking, it describes the inhabitants of industrialized societies as people who have lost their individuality. Capitalism and consumerism dominate mass societies. In this way, a mass society is considered faceless. Consumers rarely meet the producers of goods. People work at similar jobs and build look-alike homes filled with act-alike families. Mass society might also be marked by a decline in high culture. People often prefer mass media such as television to the arts like literature and painting.

Q. Mass society is a term which describes society as full of unique individuals. T ☐ F ☐

❸ The Penny Press

Penny Press newspapers were popular in the U.S. in the 19th century. They were sold on the street for one cent and helped broaden the readership of newspapers. Prior to the Penny Press, newspapers were purchased through subscription only and were rather expensive compared to Penny Press publications. Penny Press newspapers catered to everyday people with their direct, understandable writing style. The language was more colorful, and human-interest stories began to appear in mass print for the first time. The booming populations of urban areas like New York City and Chicago helped fuel the popularity of the Penny Press.

Q. Penny Press publications could be purchased on the street. T ☐ F ☐

❹ William Randolph Hearst I

William Randolph Hearst I was an influential American media mogul during the late 19th and 20th centuries. He was born into an elite millionaire family. He enrolled in Harvard, after which his father gave him control of the *San Francisco Examiner*. Hearst invested much of his fortune and effort in making the newspaper successful. He later bought the New York City paper the *Morning Journal*. Hearst was a different breed of newspaper man. He targeted the working class and slashed the costs of his publications, forcing other newspapers to follow his lead. Hearst continued to extend his empire by purchasing more newspapers, magazines, and a film company. However, at the end of his life in the early 1950s, most of these ventures had become failures.

Q. William Randolph Hearst I built his wealth by investing in the film industry.   T ☐   F ☐

❺ A Brief History of Telegraphy

Primitive forms of telegraphy occurred as far back as ancient times in the form of drums or even fire. However, not until the advent of electricity did modern telegraphy come into being. In the 19th century, European scientists realized messages could be sent through electrical wires. In America in the 1820s, Samuel Morse used electromagnets to send messages across great distances. He developed the Morse Code, a code of dots and dashes, to render the alphabet electrically. Soon, long telegraph cables were laid that connected cities, countries, and continents. Europe and the U.S. became linked by an underwater cable in the late 1860s. Telegraphy was used for a century until it was replaced by more modern forms of computer technology.

Q. Telegraphy is a modern invention made popular by Samuel Morse.   T ☐   F ☐

❻ News Agencies

News agencies are organizations which collect and provide information to media outlets such as newspapers, radio, and television. Two of the largest in the world are Reuters and the Associated Press (AP). Reuters was founded in London in 1851. It is a global news agency which specializes in providing financial and economic information to subscribers. Yet, its reporters also cover a range of news stories throughout the world. Across the Atlantic, the AP was formed in 1846 in the United States. It operates over 200 news bureaus and serves about 120 countries worldwide in its role as a leading international news agency. Today, the AP is owned by other U.S. media companies.

Q. Reuters has traditionally focused on world money matters.   T ☐   F ☐

❼ The Radio and Nikola Tesla

The invention of the radio was more of a process of key discoveries by many inventors and engineers. Their contributions eventually allowed the wireless transmission of information. Arguably, Guglielmo Marconi has been thought of as the "father of radio." However, a more obscure inventor, Nikola Tesla made many important discoveries earlier that aided in the eventual development of the modern radio. Tesla first patented the process of creating radio waves in the very late 1800s. It was his research in alternating currents, however, that paved the way for the radio. Furthermore, Tesla developed multi-frequency transmission, a four-tuned circuit, and an advanced receiver of radio waves. He also designed and patented the Tesla Coil, an energy transformer which is still used in many modern electronic products.

Q. Nikola Tesla borrowed from Marconi's ideas to create the modern radio.   T ☐   F ☐

❽ Reportage

In journalism, reportage usually refers to the overall style and point of view of an entire news report on a particular topic or event. One of the major facets of reportage is criticism of how the media portrays a certain event. Another is techniques employed to write and film the news coverage. However, reportage can also take on another meaning. It can refer to a journalist's eyewitness account of an event. Often, journalists immerse themselves in a topic and become expert witnesses on specific events by being on location. They later express their impressions and slant through various media outlets.

Q. Reportage is simply eyewitness accounts of news events in the world.   T ☐   F ☐

❾ War Correspondence

War correspondents are journalists who place themselves right in the middle of conflict. The first ones probably emerged during wars in antiquity. This type of journalism is the most dangerous in the field, yet it is often one of the most successful, too. The deeper reporters go into the action, the higher the newspaper sales and television ratings. Recently, wars in Vietnam, Kosovo, and Iraq have witnessed an increased presence of journalists roaming battle zones alongside soldiers. Many war reporters throughout history have paid the ultimate price for attempting to gather their war reports.

Q. Many war correspondents have died while gathering news on the battlefield.   T ☐   F ☐

⑩ Photojournalism

Photojournalism is a kind of journalism which tells a story through pictures. It usually contains still photographs though some video might also be used. A unique aspect of the field is that it can be highly objective and accurate. That is, the photos tell the story themselves. Usually, the pictures cannot be disputed. With the advent of high-tech digital cameras and the Internet, photojournalism has blossomed. Photographers no longer have to spend valuable time developing film or mailing images back to a news corporation. Their images can be uploaded instantaneously. Thus, pictures can find their way onto the Web moments after an actual event has taken place. Often, the text or actual story comes a bit later.

Q. Text is crucial to photojournalism and the events being depicted.   T ☐ F ☐

⑪ Digital Communications

Digital communications are a fast, popular form of sending and receiving information. Data can be exchanged electronically via email, cell phones, and the Web. These forms of communication have drastically changed how people communicate with one another. Individuals can now keep in contact almost free of time and space constraints through digital media. The Internet allows almost any type of data to be accessed at any time from any place. Instant access and contact have created a high demand in the field of digital communications in recent years. Another benefit is easy storage. Information can be stored and reviewed whenever needed. Convenience has thus become another tenet of the digital age.

Q. The Internet is mandatory for any form of digital communications.   T ☐ F ☐

⑫ Citizen Journalism

Citizen journalism is the concept that non-professionals can criticize as well as create news content. Common people without journalism experience have access to technology today which allows them to produce news material. Uploaded videos or photos of newsworthy events posted on a blog are but one example. Checking the validity of a magazine article through other media resources is another. The crux of citizen journalism is that anyone can do it. A person does not have to be a professional journalist to play an active role in what happens in the world. Furthermore, citizen journalism creates a broader range and depth of information. It is independent and often unbiased compared to mainstream media.

Q. Citizen journalism can create more variety in the reporting of news.   T ☐ F ☐

UNIT 11 Joseph Pulitzer

Thinking about the Topic

1 Look at the above photos. What are some famous newspapers in your country and abroad?
2 Look at the title of this unit and the word list below. What do you predict the passage will be about?

Vocabulary Focus

A The following words are from the reading. Check (√) the ones that you already know.

Noun	Verb	Adjective
☐ acquisition	☐ emigrate	☐ monetary
☐ immortality	☐ overhaul	☐ prestigious
☐ legacy	☐ revive	☐ viable
☐ prosperity		

B Write the words next to their matching definitions.

1 _____ the act or process of gaining ownership of something
2 _____ to move to another country in order to live there
3 _____ relating to money; financial
4 _____ capable of success or continuing effectiveness
5 _____ a successful condition
6 _____ influential; famous or important
7 _____ to bring back to life
8 _____ eternal fame
9 _____ heritage; tradition
10 _____ to examine carefully for needed repairs

Joseph Pulitzer

Joseph Pulitzer was an American publisher as well as politician. He was originally born in Hungary and emigrated to the U.S. to fight in the Civil War. After the war, he became a reporter. Before long, his vision and ambition would make him an early pioneer in the world of American mass media. His acquisition of various newspapers during the course of his life made him wealthy and powerful. After his death, the Pulitzer Prizes were endowed in his name. They are amongst the most prestigious awards possible in the U.S. for journalists, writers, and musicians.

Pulitzer began his march to the top of American media by buying failing newspapers, overhauling them, and selling them for a profit. In 1883, he bought the *New York World* and revived it with aggressive journalism. Pulitzer turned the angle of the paper to human-interest stories and sensationalism. He then employed yellow journalism to increase its circulation. This technique used scare tactics, largely-misleading headlines, comic strips, and false facts to boost sales. Scandal-inducing articles also became an important feature of yellow journalism. Pulitzer's strategies were hugely successful. By 1895, the *New York World* was the largest paper in the entire country. More importantly, Pulitzer had forever altered the future of the newspaper business in the United States.

However, Joseph Pulitzer did not only seek his own fortune and fame. He was also concerned with making journalism a viable profession for years to come. Pulitzer established lasting ties with Columbia University in New York City over the course of his life. Pulitzer's large monetary gifts helped the university establish the first journalism school in the world. But that was not all. In his will, Pulitzer endowed the university with half a million dollars for the Pulitzer Prizes. A Pulitzer Prize is one of the highest honors in America. It recognizes achievements in journalism and literature as well as music. The first Pulitzer Prize was awarded in 1917 six years after Pulitzer's death.

Joseph Pulitzer's life and achievements epitomize a successful realization of the American dream. A man who came from virtually nothing was able to rise above the masses to wealth and prosperity. Yet, he was also clearly aware of his own legacy as well. He wanted to be remembered not just for his exploits as a newspaper man. Record-breaking circulation numbers and a fat bank account were not a sufficiently satisfying record. Through the establishment of the first journalism school and the Pulitzer Prizes, however, Joseph Pulitzer was able to attain immortality.

Glossary

epitomize: (v) to be a typical example of something

Reading Comprehension

1. Why is this passage written?

   Ⓐ To highlight the different Pulitzer Prizes
   Ⓑ To discuss the influence of Joseph Pulitzer
   Ⓒ To illustrate Pulitzer's different business ventures
   Ⓓ To talk about how Pulitzer established a journalism school

2. How did Pulitzer become successful?

   Ⓐ He merged smaller newspapers together to increase efficiency.
   Ⓑ He hired top-name writers, editors, and reporters for his staff.
   Ⓒ He inherited the largest New York newspaper from his father.
   Ⓓ He bought struggling newspapers and turned them around.

3. What changed the direction of the *New York World*?

   Ⓐ It used a new type of journalism which stretched the truth.
   Ⓑ Pulitzer made the price of the paper cheaper than others.
   Ⓒ It focused on international not domestic stories.
   Ⓓ Pulitzer Prize winning journalists worked there.

4. When was the Pulitzer Prize first awarded, and what is it awarded for?
   ① When: _____
   ② What: _____

5. Which of the following is NOT true of Joseph Pulitzer?

   Ⓐ He was a soldier before becoming a millionaire.
   Ⓑ He helped establish the first school of journalism.
   Ⓒ Honesty was always a hallmark of his newspapers.
   Ⓓ He donated large sums of money to Columbia University.

6. What does the author mean by the phrase "viable profession" in paragraph 3?

   Ⓐ Work which requires little skill or knowledge
   Ⓑ A job which brings one success and respect
   Ⓒ A career which wins one a lot of friends and fame
   Ⓓ A profession which requires an advanced degree

Organizing & Summarizing

A Complete the following table to arrange the information about Joseph Pulitzer.

Joseph Pulitzer

Background	Newspapers	Contributions & Legacy

• Born in Hungary
• Fought in the U.S. (1)_____
 	
• Worked as a reporter
  - ambitious & hungry
  - pioneer of mass media
	• Purchased failing newspapers & turned them around for profit
	• (2)_____
	  - bought in 1883
	  - the largest paper in the U.S. by 1895
	  - used sensationalism & scandals to increase sales
	  → (3)_____
		• (4)_____
		  - helped establish world's first journalism school
		• (5)_____
		  - prestigious awards in journalism, literature, & music
		  - first awarded (6)_____ _____ after his death
		• Rags to riches
		  - successful embodiment of the American dream

B Based on the information above, complete the following summary.

the Civil War	Columbia University	journalism, literature, and music
New York World	yellow journalism	failing newspapers

Joseph Pulitzer was born in Hungary and later moved to the U.S., where he fought in (1)_____. After the war, he became a reporter. He was young, ambitious and hungry to learn the ins and outs of the business. Before long, he began investing in (2)_____. After successfully turning them around, he sold them for a respectable profit. One of his best decisions was his purchase of the (3)_____ in 1883. By 1895, it had the largest circulation in the country. Wealth and power soon followed his mass media success. His invention of (4)_____ contributed greatly to his success. His papers used sensationalism and scandals to increase circulation. Though many questioned the ethics or lack thereof involved, papers sold in record numbers. But Pulitzer was not just about making a profit. He helped establish the world's first school of journalism at (5)_____. After his death, the university created the Pulitzer Prizes, which recognize excellence in (6)_____. Ultimately, Pulitzer became the embodiment of the American dream by rising from rags to riches.

UNIT 12 The History of Magazines

Thinking about the Topic

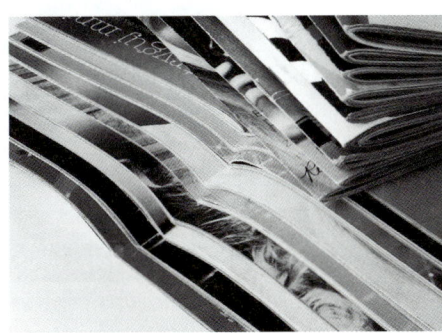

1 Look at the above photos. What kinds of magazines are there? Which of them would you like to read?
2 Look at the title of this unit and the word list below. What do you predict the passage will be about?

Vocabulary Focus

A The following words are from the reading. Check (√) the ones that you already know.

Noun	Verb	Adjective
☐ advent	☐ cater	☐ breathtaking
☐ distribution	☐ devise	☐ authoritative
☐ periodical	☐ explode	☐ inaugural
	☐ refine	

B Write the words next to their matching definitions.

1 _____ to perfect; to polish
2 _____ the act of giving out; the supplying of something
3 _____ first; initial; introductory; opening
4 _____ beginning; appearance; arrival
5 _____ reliable; dependable; trustworthy
6 _____ to think up; to invent
7 _____ to increase suddenly and rapidly in number or intensity; to blow up
8 _____ amazing; awesome; extremely beautiful
9 _____ to satisfy someone's special needs and desires; to provide
10 _____ a regular publication

The History of Magazines

Time Limit: 2 min. 50 sec.

The earliest English language magazines can be traced back to 18th-century England. *The Gentleman's Magazine* opened the field with its publication in London in 1731. It is commonly considered the first general-interest magazine of the English language. Its founder, Edward Cave initiated use of the term "magazine", and he devised a successful distribution system to get the periodical out to readers. During the same period in America, most magazines were actually reprints of British ones. It was not until the 19th century that magazines really began to make an impact in the United States.

In the early 1800s in the U.S., there were less than one hundred magazines in the entire country. Also, most had very small circulations and were short-lived. However, by the mid-19th century, the number of magazines had exploded to nearly one thousand. There were two basic reasons for this phenomenon. First, it was the time of the Civil War. The country was divided, and the magazine became an easy way to spread opinions about war issues. Second, technological advancements made printing faster and cheaper. This made magazines more accessible to the general public. By the beginning of the 20th century, there were over five thousand magazine periodicals in the U.S. alone.

Another notable reason for the magazine's popularity boom in the U.S. was due to a single publication—*National Geographic*. It was first published in 1888. Currently, *National Geographic* is one of the most popular magazines worldwide. Its early editors used cultural pieces and breathtaking photos from around the world to wow readers. The magazine took American and later international readers to places they could only dream of. No one ever had to leave their home or office. The periodical is also one of the only survivors of the many 19th-century American magazines. In the early 20th century, the advent of World War I changed the course of magazine history.

In 1923, *Time* magazine was established as one of the world's first "news-only" magazines. It was direct and authoritative. *Time* set the tone for future news magazines and other mass media. By the mid-1900s, as Americans began to refine their individual identities, so too did the magazines. They became specialized in areas of interest such as sports, hobbies, and health. Some magazines even began to cater to a specific gender. Economics and money also became popular subject matter. Modern-day magazines continue this tradition of catering to a specific target audience. However, many people are now turning from paper editions to more easily accessible online editions.

Your Time: _____ min. _____ sec.

Glossary	
	circulation: (n) the number of copies of a newspaper, magazine, etc., sold at one time

Reading Comprehension

1. Why is this passage written?

   Ⓐ To discuss the top magazines in England
   Ⓑ To compare British and American periodicals
   Ⓒ To explain the magazine boom in the U.S. in the 1920s
   Ⓓ To show how certain periodicals shaped magazine history

2. Why did magazines become more popular in the U.S. in the 19th century?

   Ⓐ They had become more specialized in nature.
   Ⓑ Citizens were becoming more highly educated.
   Ⓒ They became a medium for discussing the Civil War.
   Ⓓ Magazines were sold by subscriptions for the first time.

3. Which of the following is true of *National Geographic*?

   Ⓐ It first came out in the early 20th century.
   Ⓑ It used photography to attract readers.
   Ⓒ Early on, it focused on political issues abroad.
   Ⓓ The magazine nearly went out of business in the 1900s.

4. When was *Time* magazine first established, and what was its focus?

   ① When: _____
   ② Focus: _____

5. Which of the following is NOT true about American magazines in the 20th century?

   Ⓐ A general audience was preferred over a targeted readership.
   Ⓑ Some began to focus more on economics and money.
   Ⓒ Certain magazines explored single topics.
   Ⓓ They started to become more specialized.

6. Which of the following is probably true of the earliest American magazines?

   Ⓐ They catered to the working class.
   Ⓑ They did not require many reporters.
   Ⓒ They were more like books than magazines.
   Ⓓ They were inferior to their British counterparts.

Organizing & Summarizing

A Complete the following table to arrange the information about the history of magazines.

The History of Magazines

18th century	Early 1800s in the U.S.	Mid-1800s in the U.S.	20th century
• (1)_____ - first published by Edward Cave in London in 1731 - 1st English language magazine - 1st usage of the name "magazine" • Magazines in the U.S. - reprints of British counterparts	• Less than (2)_____ in total - very small circulations - short-lived	• Surge in circulations - nearly 1,000 magazines - opinions & discussions of (3)_____ - better technology → cheaper → reach more people • (4)_____ (1888) - photos & global stories - cultural focus	• Appearance of (5)_____ - news, hobbies, sports, gender specific • *Time* (1923) - 1st (6)_____ magazine - direct & authoritative • Present-day - cater to specific target audiences - online popularity

B Based on the information above, complete the following summary.

| their British counterparts | *Time* magazine | global stories |
| Civil War discussions | in London in 1731 | *National Geographic* |

The Gentleman's Magazine, the first English-language magazine, was published (1)_____. This was also the first time the term "magazine" was used. In America, magazines during the same period were basically reprints of (2)_____. Later during the early 1800s there were less than one hundred magazines in print in the U.S. But by the middle of the century, magazines were on the rise due to interest in (3)_____ and advanced technology. Better equipment made magazines cheaper. Circulations increased to over one thousand country-wide. (4)_____ was also established in 1888. Photos and (5)_____ with a cultural focus attracted readers. The 20th century saw magazines grow even more. They became more specialized with topics such as sports, news, and health. They even targeted audiences by gender. In 1923, (6)_____ was founded as the first news-only magazine. Its tone was direct and authoritative. Today, most print magazines have found their way online.

Vocabulary Expansion

Part A

A Complete the diagrams with the words from the box.

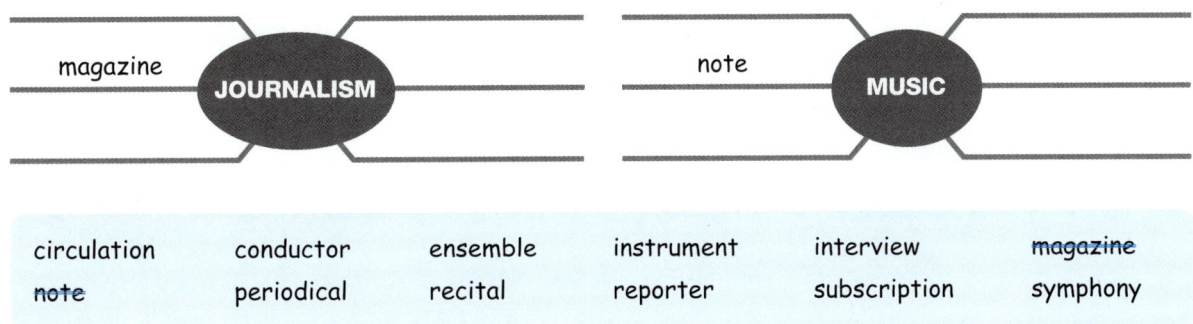

| circulation | conductor | ensemble | instrument | interview | ~~magazine~~ |
| ~~note~~ | periodical | recital | reporter | subscription | symphony |

B For each group of words, circle the concept that can include the others.

1 editor   proofreading   content   photograph   publisher
2 manufacturer   personnel   capital   corporation   stock
3 lawyer   negotiator   profession   journalist   accountant
4 media   print   news   broadcast   Internet
5 Harlem   New York   Central Park   Wall Street   Statue of Liberty

C Complete the sentences using the best words from the above exercises.

1 _____ is one of the most culturally rich cities in the United States.
2 _____ crowded around the accused man hoping for an interview.
3 When a _____ becomes bankrupt, its stock is of no value anymore.
4 By 1895, the *New York World* had the largest _____ in the United States.
5 Many people enjoy the open spaces and beauty of _____ each day.
6 The _____ told the musicians how he wanted the music to be played.
7 The student is interested in becoming a _____ because she finds court trials fascinating.
8 William Randolph Hearst I was an American _____ mogul during the late 19th and 20th centuries.
9 War correspondents are _____ who place themselves in the middle of conflict.
10 The police sent a hostage _____ to the scene where a family was being held hostage by a robber.

Part B

A Complete the diagrams with the words from the box.

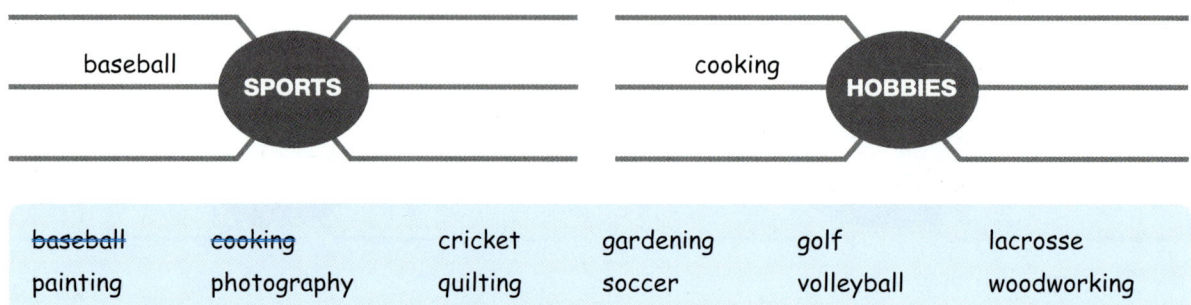

| baseball | cooking | cricket | gardening | golf | lacrosse |
| painting | photography | quilting | soccer | volleyball | woodworking |

(baseball and cooking are crossed out)

B For each group of words, cross out the word that does not belong.

1. first   inaugural   maiden   initial   final
2. monetary   financial   economical   pecuniary   fiscal
3. essence   gist   crux   pitch   core
4. collapse   boom   expansion   growth   increase
5. fans   frequency   crowd   followers   audience

C Complete the sentences using the best words from the above exercises.

1. The point of _____ is to get the ball into the hole in the least amount of strokes.
2. This car burns so much gasoline that it is not _____ to own it.
3. People exercise with less _____ when they are consumed by their career.
4. Most of the students complained that the _____ exam at the year-end was impossible.
5. The recent stock market _____ was caused by the fall in the housing marking.
6. The salesperson's _____ was so entertaining that many people bought the product.
7. The runner came in _____ place in the race and received a gold medal.
8. The angry _____ surged down Main Street to protest in front of the capital building.
9. _____ requires certain tools like a needle, yarn or thread, as well as fabric.
10. _____ is played by two teams who use long-handled rackets to catch and throw a ball.

Psychology

- **Overview**
- **Basic Knowledge Building**
- **Unit 13** Howard Gardner and Multiple Intelligences
- **Unit 14** Behaviorism, Cognitivism, and Constructivism
- **Vocabulary Expansion**

Overview

What Is Psychology?

Psychology is the science which explores the human mind and behavior. The purpose of psychology is to gain a better understanding of how human beings think and why they behave in certain ways. Psychology in general is a very broad field. More specific study areas include:

- **biological psychology** – the study of the biological bases of behavior and mental processes
- **cognitive psychology** – the study of what people know and how they come to know it
- **clinical psychology** – the study of mental dysfunction and distress and its treatment
- **developmental psychology** – the study of how human thought and behavior develop and change from conception to death
- **social psychology** – the study of how environment affects the way people interact with each other

Some experts consider the work of Aristotle to be some of the earliest explorations into the field of psychology. However, it was German psychologist Wilhelm Wundt who made psychology an independent scientific discipline. He set up the first laboratory for psychological research at Leipzig University in 1879. For that reason, he is now called the father of psychology. Today, new sub-fields in psychology are constantly being established—for example, health psychology and industrial psychology.

Psychology and You

Students of psychology work in a variety of fields. Some of the different workplaces psychologists are found are government agencies, universities, hospitals, and research labs. They also work in private practices and private industry.

Do you want to study psychology? Ask yourself these questions:

- Do I enjoy learning about the human mind and how people think?
- Am I interested in exploring human or animal behavior?
- Do I like to discover patterns in behavior?
- Do I have good reasoning skills?
- Do I enjoy doing research and performing experiments?
- Am I interested in both science and liberal arts?

Basic Knowledge Building

Read the following passages and check if the given statements are true (T) or false (F).

❶ Sensory, Short-term and Long-term Memory

Memory is the mental capacity to store information. Three levels of memory are often distinguished. Sensory memory retains impressions of sensory stimuli for brief amounts of time. These memories are made automatically and last only about a second. Short-term memory stores information for up to 20 seconds while the mind analyzes and interprets it. Typically, people can keep 7±2 units of information in their short-term memory. A common example is the seven-digit phone number. Finally, long-term memory refers to the permanent storage of information by the brain. However, a person must actively recall the information for it to last.

Q. Short-term memory requires conscious effort to process information.   T ☐   F ☐

❷ Declarative and Procedural Memory

There are two ways information is stored in long-term memory. Declarative memory is involved with remembering consciously learned facts, concepts or ideas. Thus, the information can easily be conveyed through words. A good example is remembering important dates learned in a history class. Another example is recalling the English verb tense system. In contrast, procedural memory involves the knowledge of skills and processes. Into this category fall things a person has learned how to do without being consciously aware of how they were learned. For instance, people who can swim or play the piano cannot verbally explain how they are able to swim or play the piano.

Q. An example of declarative memory is learning to type.   T ☐   F ☐

❸ The Primacy and Recency Effects

How well people can recall an item in a list depends on its position in the list. Typically, people easily recall items at the beginning of a list. This phenomenon is called the primacy effect. For example, a person is told to read a long list of names. Afterwards, they can recall the names at the beginning more easily than those in the middle. The recency effect is the opposite phenomenon. Given the same list of names, a person can best recall those that fall at the end of the list. Both the primacy and recency effects show how memory focuses on first and last impressions. The middle, however, is not as easily accessible.

Q. Items in the middle of a list are the most difficult to commit to memory.   T ☐   F ☐

❹ The Id, Ego, and Superego

According to Sigmund Freud, the id, ego, and superego are the three components of personality. He contended that people are born with the id. The id contains basic human drives like hunger and thirst. It cares for nothing except that its needs are met immediately. It does not even care whether those needs are rational or harmful. In contrast, the ego develops as a person grows after birth. The ego realizes that other people have needs as well. Therefore, it is closely associated with the reality principle. It seeks to satisfy the id's instinctual needs in realistic ways while simultaneously weighing those of other people. Last to develop is the superego. The superego functions as an individual's conscience. It distinguishes between what is right and wrong.

Q. The superego was founded on the reality principle.   T ☐   F ☐

❺ Carl Jung

Carl Jung was an influential Swiss psychologist and psychiatrist. He lived from 1875 to 1961. Early in his career, Jung worked with Sigmund Freud. Later, he came to disagree with many of Freud's theories. Jung created the field of analytic psychology. Central to Jung's theory is the idea of the unconscious. For Jung, a person's unconscious is comprised of two elements. One is the personal realm. It is filled with repressed memories. The other is the collective realm. Jung believed each individual shared certain acts and experiences with the rest of humanity, past and present. He also maintained that dreams were a kind of depository of universal archetypes.

Q. Carl Jung divided the unconscious into a personal domain and a collective domain.   T ☐   F ☐

❻ Abraham Maslow's Hierarchy of Needs

Abraham Maslow was a 20th-century American psychologist. In the 1940s he developed a theory of personality by analyzing people's needs. His hierarchy describes how some needs are more important than others. The five levels of human need are organized in pyramidal form. Basic needs like breathing and eating form the base of the pyramid. The next level is safety, satisfied, for example, by personal well-being or employment. Above safety lie love, affection, and belonging. Friends may fulfill this need. The next level is self-esteem which may be realized by personal achievement and respect. Finally, at the peak of the pyramid, Maslow placed self-actualization. This realm contains creativity and morality. Only when lower needs are met can upper ones be fulfilled.

Q. An individual must satisfy basic needs before upper needs can be addressed.   T ☐   F ☐

❼ Jean Piaget's Theory of Cognitive Development

The Swiss psychologist Jean Piaget published a groundbreaking theory in 1952 after observing children to find out how their thinking develops. He proposed that a child's knowledge is made up of schemas or networks of basic knowledge structures. Schemas help children organize previous experiences and understand new experiences. Furthermore, Piaget surmised that there are four stages to the cognitive development of children. The earliest is the sensorimotor, which lasts from birth to two years of age. The next is the preoperational stage from ages two to seven. The concrete operational stage from ages seven to eleven comes next. And last is the formal operational stage lasting from age eleven through adulthood. More complex thought occurs in the later stages. Also, the stages always occur in the same order.

Q. Piaget's sensorimotor stage represents the most sophisticated level of thought.　T ☐　F ☐

❽ Observational Learning

The theory of observational learning is based on the idea that humans learn from watching others. However, this does not imply imitation. Human beings can learn what not to do as well as what to do by observing others' actions. Observational learning is mainly associated with the Canadian psychologist Albert Bandura. He called this type of learning modeling. He noted four conditions necessary for modeling. They are attention, retention of details, motor reproduction, and motivation/opportunity. Observational learning can take place at any stage of life. However, Bandura noted it is most common during childhood. This is the time when role models often exert the most powerful influence.

Q. Observational learning is different from simple imitation.　T ☐　F ☐

❾ The Placebo Effect

A placebo is a kind of fake medication which has no medicinal value. A sugar pill is a common example. When a patient begins to get better after taking mere sugar pills, the placebo effect is said to have occurred. Clearly, the sugar pill has not done anything. Yet, because the patient believes his or her condition will improve by taking the placebo, it does. Essentially, the placebo effect is mind over matter. Simply believing a medicine or therapy will help is enough to cure some patients. Some experts even maintain that placebos are over 30 percent effective. This number implies that the mind has much to do with a person's physical health.

Q. The placebo effect explains how a patient can improve even when taking false medicine.　T ☐　F ☐

⑩ Buyer's Remorse

Buyer's remorse is a type of anxiety a buyer feels after making an excessive purchase. Soon after the purchase, the buyer begins to question or regret their actions. This regret may be rooted in a number of factors. The buyer might think they made the wrong choice. Or, they might think they paid too much. Buyer's remorse can be explained psychologically. Pre-purchase, positive emotions are linked to the situation. The person may be happy or feel envied by others, for example. Afterwards, however, negative emotions come to the fore. For instance, they might realize they will end up in debt or be unable to buy anything further.

Q. Buyer's remorse describes the guilt people can feel after purchasing something.   T ☐   F ☐

⑪ Imprinting

Imprinting is one of the most common types of learning found in many animal species. Essentially, baby animals learn the characteristics of their parents. Some studies have shown that certain birds attach themselves to whomever or whatever they see first and regard this as their mother. One of the earliest discoveries of imprinting was made in the 19th century with domestic chickens. Later, the ethologist Konrad Lorenz studied the behavior of ducklings and goslings. Lorenz discovered that within 13 to 16 hours of birth, the young birds would imprint on the first thing that moved in front of them. Often, they would imprint on Lorenz. He called this time period the "critical period".

Q. Konrad Lorenz was the first to discover the imprinting effect in some bird species.   T ☐   F ☐

⑫ Color Psychology

Color psychology is the study of the effects of color on human mood, emotion, and behavior. Proponents believe that people have similar reactions to certain colors. These reactions can be both psychological and physiological. However, color psychology is not considered a major field of science. Critics claim that different cultures view colors in different ways. Also, the meanings of various colors change over time. Still, color psychology continues to have influence. For example, practitioners believe the color red can motivate people or that pink has a calming effect. Blue is also believed to have a relaxing effect. This is a reason color psychology plays a greater role in advertising and sports today.

Q. In color psychology, the color pink is believed to help calm people.   T ☐   F ☐

UNIT 13: Howard Gardner and Multiple Intelligences

Thinking about the Topic

1 Look at the above photos. What kinds of activities are you good at doing?
2 Look at the title of this unit and the word list below. What do you predict the passage will be about?

Vocabulary Focus

A The following words are from the reading. Check (√) the ones that you already know.

Noun
- curiosity
- evaluation
- potential

Verb
- constitute
- embrace
- enroll

Adjective
- controversial
- existential
- flawed
- unitary

B Write the words next to their matching definitions.

1 _____ whole; united; not divided
2 _____ an assessment; an analysis
3 _____ to officially register or enter
4 _____ based on experience
5 _____ to include; to accept
6 _____ the unrealized capability of being or doing something
7 _____ at issue; debatable; arguable
8 _____ having imperfections; faulty
9 _____ to comprise or form; to make up
10 _____ an intense desire to know or understand

Howard Gardner and Multiple Intelligences

Time Limit: 2 min. 55 sec.

Howard Gardner was born in Pennsylvania in 1943. In his teens, he proved to be a skilled musician. Later, he enrolled at Harvard in 1961 as a history major, yet his academic curiosity quickly shifted to the social sciences and psychology. Gardner graduated with high honors in 1965 and entered Harvard graduate school. He soon became part of Project Zero, a research group that investigates the development of learning processes in children, adults, and organizations. The project allowed Gardner to explore human cognition and develop his own theory about human intelligence. Later, he published his theory in the book *Frames of Mind: The Theory of Multiple Intelligences* (1983).

Gardner's theory of multiple intelligences (MI) attempts to redefine what constitutes human intelligence and how it can be measured. Traditionally, intelligence has been thought to be a single unitary quality of the mind. The intelligence quotient (IQ) has been used to evaluate it in logical-mathematical and linguistic terms. However, Gardner believes this type of evaluation is flawed because it fails to cover the wide variety of abilities people actually possess. He argues that a student who is better at math, for example, than another student is not necessarily the one with the higher intelligence. In response, the MI theory embraces a broader range of human talents or intelligences. The core intelligence categories created by Gardner are known as interpersonal, intrapersonal, musical, spatial, linguistic, logical-mathematical, and bodily-kinesthetic. Later, a few more categories like naturalist, spiritual, existential, and moral were also proposed by Gardner as possible candidate intelligences.

Gardner believes his theory should be applied to how children are educated as well. In the U.S., the traditional focus of education has been reading, writing, and math. Gardner believes this limits students who are weaker in core subjects yet talented in others. By applying MI to education systems, teachers could use different methods to meet the unique needs of each student. MI then becomes the basis for evaluating the different intellectual needs of each child. Both weak and strong intelligences would be addressed by the instructor. Ultimately, Gardner believes this form of evaluation and education will maximize an individual's intellectual potential.

Today, Gardner's MI theory continues to be highly debated in both the fields of psychology and education. Generally, his theory has not been well received by academic psychologists, although it has been embraced by a number of educators in North America. Many schools have structured curricula and designed classroom activities according to MI. While controversial, Howard Gardner has at least forced traditionalists to take another look at the basis of how intelligence is evaluated and how students are taught.

Your Time: _____ min. _____ sec.

Glossary

cognition: (n) the mental processes involved in knowing, learning, and understanding things

Reading Comprehension

1. What is the main purpose of the passage?

   Ⓐ To reveal how traditional intelligence testing falls short of student needs
   Ⓑ To explain Gardner's theory and why it is important in education
   Ⓒ To show how Gardner came up with multiple intelligences
   Ⓓ To compare traditional IQ tests to multiple intelligences

2. Why did Gardner originally develop MI?

   Ⓐ He felt the IQ test was too difficult and ultimately inaccurate.
   Ⓑ He wanted to revolutionize the American university system.
   Ⓒ He hoped educators would focus more on the sciences than the arts.
   Ⓓ He believed that unique abilities are as important as core abilities.

3. Which of the following is true about multiple intelligences?

   Ⓐ It has been rejected by most experts and educators.
   Ⓑ It continues to be expanded by Gardner and his findings.
   Ⓒ It is nearly as limited in scope as traditional intelligence measurements.
   Ⓓ It proposes that artistically-inclined students are smarter than scientifically-inclined ones.

4. What has been the traditional educational trend in the U.S., and how does Gardner hope to change the system?
   ① Trend: _____
   ② Change: _____

5. Which of the following is NOT true about MI?

   Ⓐ It has hardly influenced the traditionalist attitude about how intelligence is measured.
   Ⓑ It continues to be a highly debatable concept for educators and psychologists.
   Ⓒ It attempts to address both the strengths and weaknesses of students.
   Ⓓ It supports a broad range of human abilities and skills.

6. Why would implementation of MI be better for students?

   Ⓐ Teachers would not have to waste their time on unmotivated students.
   Ⓑ They could direct their strengths towards a goal established by experts.
   Ⓒ They would receive a more specific and balanced education.
   Ⓓ Students could create their own curriculum and enjoy studying more.

Organizing & Summarizing

A Complete the following table to arrange the information about Howard Gardner and multiple intelligences.

Howard Gardner and Multiple Intelligences

Background	Multiple Intelligences	Educational Impact

• Educated at Harvard Univ.
• (1)_____
  - research on human learning processes
  - developed personal theories on learning
	• *Frames of Mind: The Theory of Multiple Intelligences* (1983)
	  - rethinks how intelligence is measured → traditional (2)_____ has limitations
	  - explores many factors, not just (3)_____
	• Multiple Intelligences (MI)
	  - intelligence not a uniform quality
	  - six categories: interpersonal, intrapersonal, musical, spatial, linguistic, logical-mathematical, & (4)_____
		• Traditional school system
		  - emphasizes (5)_____
		  _____
		  - restricts student potential
		• New proposal
		  - MI used to evaluate needs of each child
		  - teachers can target both the (6)_____ of students
		• Debatable
		  - not well received by traditionalists

B Based on the information above, complete the following summary.

> strengths and weaknesses   remain controversial   multiple intelligences
> cognition and intelligence   Project Zero   math and science

Howard Gardner is a Harvard-educated psychologist and social scientist. He works with (1)_____, which explores the learning process of human beings. Gardner's fascination with (2)_____ led him to develop his theory of (3)_____ or MI. MI attempts to take into account the broad range of a person's abilities. This is contrary to traditional IQ testing, which only focuses on core abilities in the fields of (4)_____. Gardner also believes MI should be applied to schooling. He feels students are restricted by the traditional system. With MI, however, teachers are able to focus on a student's (5)_____. Some schools have implemented MI in evaluating and educating students. Still, Gardner's proposals (6)_____ with traditionalists.

UNIT 14 Behaviorism, Cognitivism, and Constructivism

Thinking about the Topic

1 Look at the above images. What methods do you use to memorize or remember things easily?
2 Look at the title of this unit and the word list below. What do you predict the passage will be about?

Vocabulary Focus

A The following words are from the reading. Check (√) the ones that you already know.

Noun	Verb	Adjective	Adverb
☐ framework	☐ acknowledge	☐ external	☐ substantially
☐ theory	☐ overshadow	☐ mechanical	
	☐ alter	☐ plausible	
		☐ rigid	

B Write the words next to their matching definitions.

1 _____ done by machine; automatic
2 _____ significantly; considerably; essentially
3 _____ to rise above; to dominate
4 _____ unable to change or vary; inflexible
5 _____ believable; reasonable
6 _____ to change; to correct
7 _____ an idea or set of ideas that is intended to explain something
8 _____ to recognize; to admit; to accept
9 _____ a structure used to support other things; an organization of ideas
10 _____ coming from the outside

115

Behaviorism, Cognitivism, and Constructivism

Time Limit: 2 min. 50 sec.

The process of how human beings learn has been studied scientifically since around the 19th century. Modern learning theories attempt to describe what happens in the mind when learning occurs. Explanations usually fall into three main categories: behaviorism, cognitivism, and constructivism. These theories cannot provide clear-cut solutions to how every person learns. However, they do describe general patterns in how human beings gain knowledge and build upon it.

Behaviorism is most closely associated with American psychologist B.F. Skinner. He proposed that learning is based on what he called operant conditioning. In simple terms, an individual's behavior is reinforced by a reward or a punishment. Thus, learning behavior can change based on positive or negative responses to an individual's actions. On the surface, Skinner's proposal seems quite plausible. However, the "surface" is its fundamental flaw. Behaviorism is based on visible or external stimuli which influence actions. It does not take an individual's internal thinking or emotions into account. In the latter 20th century, the theory of cognitivism began to overshadow the limited scope of behaviorism.

Cognitivism is a divergence from the behaviorist viewpoint as it focuses on mental states. Thought, then, is central to the cognitivist camp. One of the chief opponents of behaviorism was Noam Chomsky. As a linguist, he proposed that language could not exist without an internal mechanism. This notion revealed a major flaw in the behaviorist approach. However, while cognitivism might be more complete than behaviorism, its structure is also too rigid. Many theorists see the brain as a kind of computer with mappable processes of inputs and outputs. This approach is too mechanical when dealing with the inner workings of learning and human behavior. Also, cognitivism relies too much on prior knowledge. Thus, it does not substantially address the influence of experience upon human beings and how they handle it, unlike constructivism.

Constructivism argues that human beings gain new meaning and knowledge from their own experiences. According to one of its leading proponents, Jean Piaget, people then assimilate or accommodate the experience. Assimilation places new experiences into the existing framework of their mind. This framework goes unchanged. Accommodation occurs when new experiences alter the individual's existing framework of reality. Critics contend that one of the main problems of constructivism is that every person will have a unique framework and assimilate or accommodate differently. Therefore, it cannot be a uniform theory able to be applied in a broad sense. Yet, this is also its advantage. Unlike cognitivism and behaviorism, constructivism relates the closest to how an individual shapes his or her world by acknowledging the unique experiences, socially or academically, of each person.

Your Time: _____ min. _____ sec.

Glossary	
	divergence: (n) difference; lack of agreement

Reading Comprehension

1 Why is this passage written?

　Ⓐ To compare Skinner and Chomsky
　Ⓑ To boost the popularity of behaviorism
　Ⓒ To illustrate popular learning theories
　Ⓓ To raise the need to develop new learning theories

2 Which of the following is associated with behaviorism?

　Ⓐ assimilation
　Ⓑ internal stimuli
　Ⓒ divergent theory
　Ⓓ operant conditioning

3 Which of the following is a weakness in the behaviorist theory?

　Ⓐ It does not always account for visible influences.
　Ⓑ The concept is too vague due to a lack of research evidence.
　Ⓒ Thoughts and feelings are not as important as they should be.
　Ⓓ Lab animals do not know the difference between reward and punishment.

4 Who revealed the limitations of behaviorism, and what was the main evidence used?
　① Who: _____
　② What: _____

5 Which of the following is NOT true about constructivism?

　Ⓐ It relies heavily on previous experiences.
　Ⓑ Jean Piaget was a leading supporter of the theory.
　Ⓒ It takes into account a person's individual experiences.
　Ⓓ Assimilation is an important component of the concept.

6 The passage implies that cognitivism

　Ⓐ and behaviorism are closely related to one another
　Ⓑ assumes a person's learning process is always changing
　Ⓒ was proposed before the concepts of behaviorism and constructivism
　Ⓓ is too general and does not take into account an individual's emotions

Organizing & Summarizing

A Complete the following table to arrange the information about major learning theories.

Behaviorism, Cognitivism, & Constructivism

Theory	Proponent	Traits

Behaviorism	(1)_____	• (2)_____
		  - stimuli & response
		  - (3)_____ by rewards & punishments
		• Does not account for internal states

Cognitivism	Noam Chomsky	• Focuses on mental states - study of (4)_____ • Human brain – processing information like a computer • Sees (5)_____ as important • Does not account enough for the effects of new experiences
Constructivism	(6)_____	• Importance of individual experience • (7)_____ - the existing framework is unchanged • Accommodation - the existing framework is changed • (8)_____: focuses on unique experiences of each individual

B Based on the information above, complete the following summary.

> operant conditioning   assimilate and accommodate   like a computer
> B.F. Skinner   the individuality of each person   Jean Piaget

Behaviorism, cognitivism, and constructivism are three major learning theories. Behaviorism was popularized by (1)_____. It is based on reinforcement by rewards and punishments. Skinner called this (2)_____. Yet, this concept mainly relies on external stimuli and not internal states. In contrast, cognitivism relies on mental states. The linguist Noam Chomsky is a major proponent. Cognitivism sees the human brain as processing information (3)_____. In this processing, prior experience is also crucial. But this learning theory does not substantially account for how learning relates to new experiences. Constructivism does. (4)_____ was a major supporter. He believed human beings (5)_____ new experiences. Assimilation stores new experiences in the framework of the mind. Accommodation does as well, yet the new experiences alter the entire mental reality. Ultimately, constructivism takes into account (6)_____, unlike the previous concepts.

Vocabulary Expansion

Part A

A Complete the diagrams with the words from the box.

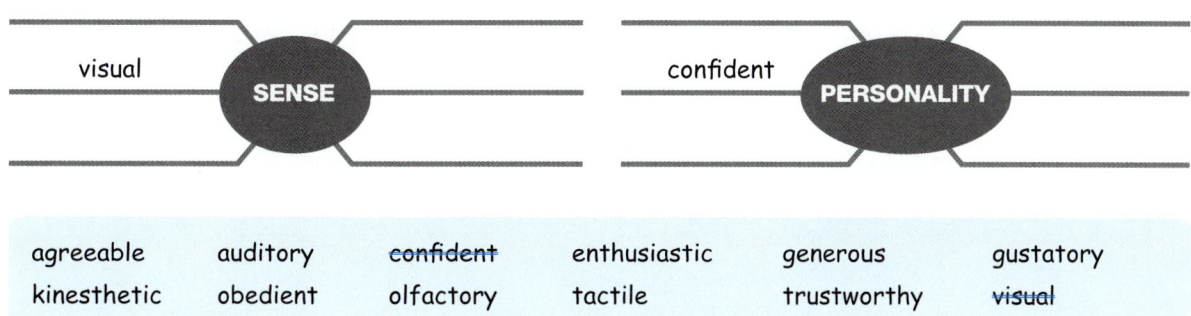

| agreeable | auditory | confident | enthusiastic | generous | gustatory |
| kinesthetic | obedient | olfactory | tactile | trustworthy | visual |

B For each group of words, circle the concept that can include the others.

1 geologist   scholar   biologist   psychologist   economist
2 dentist   surgeon   psychiatrist   lawyer   practitioner
3 human   physical   emotional   spiritual   mental
4 suppose   infer   guess   surmise   conjecture
5 appraise   assess   estimate   judge   evaluate

C Complete the sentences using the best words from the above exercises.

1 Visit your _____ twice a year for a check-up of your teeth.
2 Jim is very _____; he donated $50,000 to a charity last month.
3 _____ study the nature, composition, and structure of the earth.
4 She was highly motivated, positive, and _____ about her teaching job.
5 The _____ operated on the compound fracture in Jimmy's left leg.
6 If you are a _____ person, you like to learn by touching or manipulating things.
7 People with mental problems often seek a good _____ for therapy.
8 The _____ sense is able to distinguish among a large number of different smells.
9 They got married in a cathedral, because they wanted the wedding to be a _____ experience.
10 An _____ 25 million American adults experienced serious psychological distress last year.

Part B

A Complete the diagrams with the words from the box.

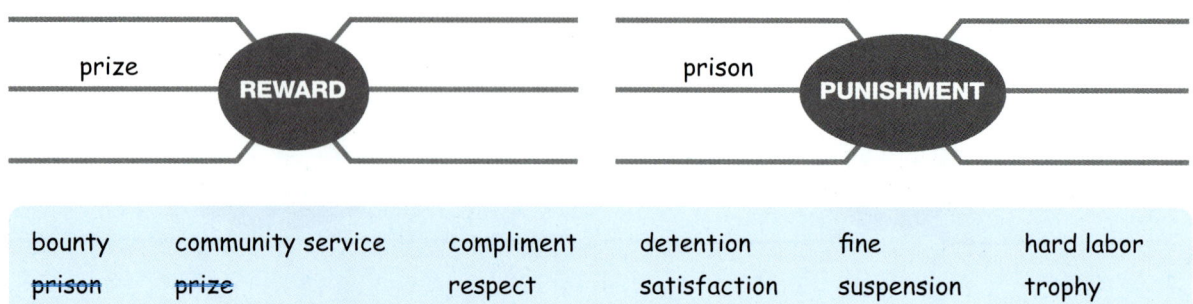

| bounty | community service | compliment | detention | fine | hard labor |
| prison | prize | | respect | satisfaction | suspension | trophy |

B For each group of words, cross out the word that does not belong.

1 recall   reminisce   recur   remember   recollect
2 agitate   ease   calm   relax   soothe
3 hierarchy   order   pyramid   president   scale
4 supporter   champion   proponent   advocate   critic
5 anxiety   debut   stress   worry   tension

C Complete the sentences using the best words from the above exercises.

1 My grandmother often _____ about the good times of her youth.
2 She has been suffering from _____ nightmares that are very scary.
3 After reading my essay, my writing teacher paid me _____ on my analysis.
4 The _____ hunter was given $1,000 for bringing the fugitive to justice.
5 The rock star _____ the crowd by refusing to go on stage for over an hour.
6 Some of the _____ in Egypt will require heavy restoration in order to survive.
7 On its release some _____ accused the movie of being nothing more than a fairy tale.
8 Many criminals avoid jail time in the U.S. because the _____ system is so overcrowded.
9 Teachers sometimes threaten students with after-school _____ if they are late to class too often.
10 The speeding driver was stopped by the police and given a heavy _____ of $200.

Economics

Overview
Basic Knowledge Building
Unit 15 John Ruskin
Unit 16 The Theory of Marginal Utility
Vocabulary Expansion

What Is Economics?

Economics is the study of how the distribution, production, and consumption of goods and services impact society. The laws of supply and demand are explored in classical economics. Other important factors include resources, wants, needs, and scarcity. Some major study areas of economics are:

- **macroeconomics** – the study of national economies as well as the global economy
- **microeconomics** – the study of a specific economic sector such as companies and households
- **financial economics** – the study of how companies and individuals invest and profit
- **monetary economics** – the study of the supply and demand of money and factors which influence it
- **behavioral economics** – the study of how psychology influences economic decisions

Some of the earliest economic concepts were developed by the ancient Greeks. For example, Plato wrote of the importance of the division of labor in the *Republic*. Mercantilism dominated the 16th through mid-18th centuries as the world expanded. After that, the foundation of classical economics was laid by Adam Smith who explored the importance of self-interest in his *Wealth of Nations* (1776). In the 20th century, John Maynard Keynes became a strong proponent of direct government involvement in faltering economies as happened during the Great Depression.

Economics and You

People who study economics face a great number of career choices. They include being a loan officer, credit analyst, financial advisor, consultant, auditor, professor, and lobbyist.

Do you want to study economics? Ask yourself these questions:

- Am I logical and analytical?
- Do I like working with numbers and graphs?
- Am I good at recognizing trends?
- Do I enjoy discovering patterns in the economy?
- Do I like to explain things based on principles and models?
- Do I enjoy working with different types of people?

Basic Knowledge Building

Read the following passages and check if the given statements are true (T) or false (F).

❶ Adam Smith

Adam Smith was a Scottish political economist and sociologist. In 1776, he published his masterpiece *The Wealth of Nations*. The book laid the foundation for modern capitalist society. It is considered the first book on modern economics in general. Smith believed that competition and a free market benefit everyone, including consumers, businesses, and governments. He contended that a free market not only keeps prices down but also ensures a diversity of services and goods. The concept of a free market with little government regulation was groundbreaking. It would later become known as laissez-faire economics in the 19th century.

Q. Adam Smith was able to popularize socialism in the 18th century.　T ☐　F ☐

❷ Thomas Malthus

Thomas Malthus was an English political economist who lived during the 18th and 19th centuries. In his book *An Essay on the Principle of Population* (1798), Malthus maintained that human society would ultimately return to a subsistence economy because of population growth and lack of food. This theory is known as the Malthusian catastrophe. According to this theory, populations grow exponentially but agricultural resources grow arithmetically. Eventually, food sources will not be able to support human populations. Therefore, if major emergency plans are not formed, societies will shrink, resulting in a very bleak social scene.

Q. Malthus believed that societies would be in trouble due to overcrowding.　T ☐　F ☐

❸ GDP and GNP

GDP and GNP are both critical measures of a country's economy. Still, they are often confused by many people. GDP stands for gross domestic product. It represents the value of all goods and services produced in a country in one year. However, GNP stands for gross national product. It is the same as GDP with the addition of the earnings of that country's citizens abroad. Also, GNP subtracts foreigner income in a given country. Put more simply, GDP is the regional value of all production in a year while GNP is the total production of its citizens regardless of where they live.

Q. GDP includes the income of foreigner production.　T ☐　F ☐

123

❹ Supply and Demand

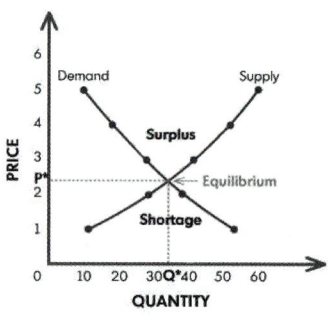

The law of supply and demand is the basis of all market economies. Supply is the willingness and ability of a supplier to provide a good or service during a certain time period. Demand is the willingness and ability of a consumer to buy a good or service in a given period of time. In a competitive market, if demand is greater than supply, price increases. If, on the contrary, supply is greater than demand, price decreases. Thus, the role of the market is to balance supply and demand so that price is kept stable.

Q. In a competitive market, price decreases when supply is smaller than demand.   T ☐   F ☐

❺ Karl Marx

Karl Marx was a revolutionary German thinker. Notable among his achievements was Marxist economics. This theory is based on the concept of class struggle. Marx termed the two chief classes the bourgeoisie and the proletariat. The first is the ruling or dominant class, and the second the working class. For Marx, the proletariat is most crucial to society because they are the producers. Products are made with their labor. The bourgeoisie or capitalists simply take advantage of workers. According to Marxist economics, in capitalist societies, technology tends to replace the worker. This causes the proletariat  to revolt. The workers should emerge victorious from the struggle and seize the power of production. Ultimately, economic divisions dissolve.

Q. Karl Marx believed workers were the most important segment in an economy.   T ☐   F ☐

❻ Alfred Marshall

Alfred Marshall lived from 1842 to 1924. He was a leading English economist and taught at Cambridge University for over 20 years. Marshall contributed to economics with his new way of explaining how the price of a good or service is determined. Before Marshall, some economists considered production costs the major factor in the determination of price. Others thought marginal utility was the most important, claiming that the more someone had of something, the less they would pay for even more. However, Marshall fused these ideas to describe how price changes according to the interaction of supply and demand. This fusion clarified modern economic thought.

Q. Marshall believed marginal utility has little to do with a product's value.   T ☐   F ☐

❼ Keynesian Theory

British economist John Maynard Keynes developed his theory in the first half of the 20th century. It was created during the Great Depression. Keynes went against classical economic theory. For example, he disagreed with Adam Smith's principles. Smith believed that markets should be left alone. Governments should intervene only when absolutely necessary. Keynes, on the other hand, believed that it was a government's duty to stimulate economic growth. A government's adjustment of interest rates, taxes, and spending could thwart economic downturns and stabilize the private sector. Keynesian theory proved to be effective in coping with the Great Depression and has since been the backbone of many world economies.

Q. Keynesianism was probably a reaction to the Great Depression. T ☐ F ☐

❽ Friedrich Hayek

Friedrich Hayek was a crucial economist during the 20th century. He was born in Austria. After formal education in his homeland, he later held professorships in both England and the U.S. He was a strong critic of socialism. His economic views also opposed Keynesian theory. Hayek believed that any type of government meddling was futile. State action could not protect society from high unemployment or recession. Furthermore, Hayek believed that government intervention was dangerous to the individual. It could rob people of their freedom and liberty. In 1974, Hayek received the Nobel Prize in Economic Sciences.

Q. Hayek and Keynes both supported government intervention in the market. T ☐ F ☐

❾ Milton Friedman and Monetarism

Milton Friedman was an American economist. He is the 20th-century founder of monetarism. This theory contends that a nation's money supply is critical because it influences inflation and growth. Therefore, monetary authorities such as a central bank should focus on keeping prices stable by adjusting the money supply. In general, monetarists believe an increase in the money supply each year is necessary. According to Friedman and proponents of his theory, an injection of around 3 to 4 percent creates price stability. The "velocity of money" is also important. Velocity measures how many times each dollar is spent each year. Thus, the velocity dictates how much money should be added each year.

Q. Monetarism supporters believe in control of the money supply. T ☐ F ☐

⑩ The History of Banknotes

Banknotes or paper money were probably first used in ancient China between the 6th and 9th century A.D. They were created because of a shortage of metal for coins. The first true banknotes in Europe did not come about until the 16th or 17th century. They were produced by private institutions, and there were not many in circulation. It was not until the 18th century in Europe that banknotes were supported by governments. In the U.S., however, printed banknotes issued by the state were introduced for the first time in the 1700s. In many countries today, banknotes or bills have replaced coin currency completely.

Q. The first banknotes in Europe were created by a government.   T ☐   F ☐

⑪ Sunk Costs

In economics, sunk costs simply refer to costs which cannot be recovered. Often, sunk costs are equated with economic loss, yet there is a major distinction between the two. Sunk costs are a price paid in the past. With sunk costs, the original price is no longer relevant. Economic loss, on the other hand, refers to the difference between the first price and a later price. For example, when a person buys a car, the price paid is the sunk cost. That price will never change, and the car will depreciate in value with the passing of time. Perhaps, a couple of years later, the person decides to sell the car for less than what was paid for it. This difference in price accurately describes the person's economic loss.

Q. Sunk costs mean the same thing as economic loss on a product or service.   T ☐   F ☐

⑫ The World Trade Organization

The World Trade Organization (WTO) was established in 1995. It is based in Geneva, Switzerland. Today, there are over 140 active member countries. The WTO serves a number of international purposes. First on the list, of course, is trade. The WTO attempts to make trade and commerce easier between countries.

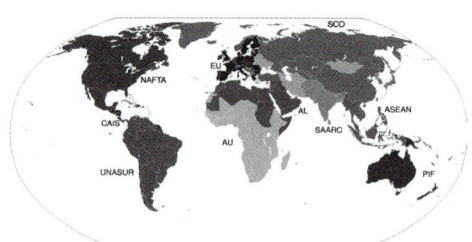

Furthermore, it hopes to expand free trade in a more globalized world. The WTO also serves a judicial role. When there are disputes between countries, the WTO rules over the disagreements. In many ways, the WTO might seem to exist only for rich countries. However, the organization also helps developing countries with technology and advanced economic strategy.

Q. The WTO is the world's leading monitor of international trade and commerce.   T ☐   F ☐

UNIT 15 John Ruskin

Thinking about the Topic

1 Look at the above pictures. What changes did the Industrial Revolution bring about?
2 Look at the title of this unit and the word list below. What do you predict the passage will be about?

Vocabulary Focus

A The following words are from the reading. Check (√) the ones that you already know.

Noun	Verb	Adjective	Adverb
☐ decline	☐ accumulate	☐ enormous	☐ ultimately
☐ realm	☐ advocate	☐ rational	
☐ reformer	☐ intervene		
	☐ subsist		

B Write the words next to their matching definitions.

1 _____ sensible or reasonable
2 _____ large; huge in size
3 _____ to collect or gather gradually
4 _____ one who works for change
5 _____ to support; to argue for
6 _____ downward movement
7 _____ to become involved in
8 _____ an area of activity, interest, or thought; a domain
9 _____ in the end; after all
10 _____ to live or exist

John Ruskin

Reading Time: 3 min.

In the 19th century, the United Kingdom witnessed great prosperity and change under the reign of Queen Victoria. The country accumulated enormous wealth through overseas colonization. The number of city dwellers increased rapidly due to the Industrial Revolution. Also, many thinkers, artists, and scientists advocated various cultural movements and social reforms. Among those intellectuals was John Ruskin.

Ruskin was an influential art critic and social thinker during the Victorian era. He was born in London in 1819 and lived until 1900. He was a man of many interests and was influential in a variety of realms, including literature, art, and architecture. He believed art to be an expression of society's values and morality. He felt it was closely related to social justice. Thus, the decline of art signified social, as well as cultural, crisis. This view of art naturally led Ruskin to pay attention to social conditions.

At the time, Britain was experiencing significant changes in the composition of its social classes. A large educated middle class was growing steadily, and a new wealthy commercial class was integrating into the upper class. However, the working class was still suffering from poverty. Great numbers of laborers had to subsist on very small wages. Many young children were forced to work in factories and mines. They were also afflicted by the lack of housing. These tragic conditions resulted from the rapid development of laissez-faire capitalism after the Industrial Revolution.

Opposed to these social conditions, John Ruskin published a series of essays in 1860 that attacked laissez-faire capitalism. These essays he later compiled into a book called *Unto This Last* (1862). In them, Ruskin harshly criticizes the standardized labor that accompanied the Industrial Revolution. He also argues that all workers, whether skilled or not, must be paid a fixed rate. Differential rates only result in workers suppressing their wages to get jobs. This competition is harmful to all laborers and society as a whole.

Ruskin's views were in direct contrast with those of Adam Smith, who is known as the founder of laissez-faire economics. In his book *The Wealth of Nations* (1776), Smith argues that competition among individuals and businesses in a free market ultimately benefits the whole of society. Thus, governments should not intervene in the market. It will be guided by the rational choices and decisions of consumers and producers.

However, Ruskin believed free competition merely allowed the poor to be used as tools to make the rich richer. He thought all production in society should serve the greater good of humanity. Thus, he advocated social reforms, such as better housing, free universal education, and old-age pensions. He also suggested that income tax be graduated. In many ways, Ruskin was a pioneering social reformer.

Your Time: _____ min. _____ sec.

> **Glossary**
> **laissez-faire:** (adj) based on the policy of allowing private businesses to develop without government control

Reading Comprehension

1. What is the purpose of the passage?

   Ⓐ To show how Ruskin's art affected capitalism
   Ⓑ To summarize Ruskin's most important economic essays
   Ⓒ To contrast Ruskin's and Smith's main economic concepts
   Ⓓ To discuss Ruskin's opposition to laissez-faire capitalism

2. How did art affect Ruskin's views of society as a whole?

   Ⓐ He thought a decline in artistic appreciation was a symptom of social crisis.
   Ⓑ He considered the current economy a better indicator of social progress.
   Ⓒ He considered the arts a heavy burden on any industrialized society.
   Ⓓ He believed people should not waste their money on art.

3. What was Ruskin's main intention in publishing *Unto This Last*?

   Ⓐ To show his support for standardized labor practices
   Ⓑ To champion fair treatment of all workers in England
   Ⓒ To discuss the significance of the arts and the lower class
   Ⓓ To support lower taxes for the newly developed middle class

4. According to Adam Smith, what are two qualities necessary for laissez-faire capitalism?
   ① Quality 1: _____
   ② Quality 2: _____

5. Which of the following does NOT support Ruskin's views on free competition?

   Ⓐ He thought it took advantage of the poor.
   Ⓑ He believed it benefited everyone in society.
   Ⓒ He felt it served the interests of the upper class.
   Ⓓ He did not believe it served the greater good of humanity.

6. It is likely that Ruskin felt the closest connection to

   Ⓐ art lovers
   Ⓑ the rich upper class
   Ⓒ the underprivileged
   Ⓓ free market cultures

Organizing & Summarizing

A Complete the following table to arrange the information about John Ruskin.

John Ruskin

Personal Background	19th-Century England	Social Reforms

• (1)_____ & social thinker
  - art = an important pillar of society
• Had many interests
  - literature, architecture & the arts in general
	• Society in flux
	  - growing, educated middle class
	  - division of classes
	• (2)_____
	  - less government control
	• Working class crisis
	  - large numbers living on low wages
	  - (3)_____
	  - overcrowding
		• Opposed ideas of (4)_____
		  - fought against the free market
		  - fought for fixed wages
		• (5)_____ (1862)
		  - opposed standardized labor
		  - production should serve entire society, not privileged few
		• Championed reforms such as:
		  - better housing conditions
		  - free (6)_____
		  - retirement plans

B Based on the information above, complete the following summary.

| the free market | the Industrial Revolution | laissez-fair capitalism |
| fixed wages | overcrowded | an art critic |

John Ruskin was (1)_____ and social reformer of 19th-century Britain. He believed art to be an important pillar of society. During his lifetime, British society was in flux. (2)_____ was creating major changes in the social classes and in working conditions. A larger, educated middle class was emerging. (3)_____ was becoming more popular. Ruskin believed the working class was being forgotten. Wages were low, housing was (4)_____, and children were being put to work. Ruskin fought for social reforms to change these horrid conditions. He opposed (5)_____ and the views of Adam Smith. Ruskin believed such a system only oppressed the poor and made the rich richer. He also believed production should serve humanity, not a select class. Ultimately, he championed (6)_____, better housing, free and universal education, and retirement plans.

UNIT 16: The Theory of Marginal Utility

Thinking about the Topic

1. Look at the above photos. What are some important factors do you consider when you buy things?
2. Look at the title of this unit and the word list below. What do you predict the passage will be about?

Vocabulary Focus

A The following words are from the reading. Check (√) the ones that you already know.

Noun	Verb	Adjective	Adverb
☐ benefit	☐ affect	☐ alternative	☐ inversely
☐ bundle	☐ assume	☐ subsequent	
☐ consumption	☐ attain		
	☐ quantify		

B Write the words next to their matching definitions.

1. _____ different; another
2. _____ an advantage
3. _____ the using up of goods or services
4. _____ to suppose
5. _____ a group
6. _____ to achieve; to reach
7. _____ to state how much there is or how many there are of something
8. _____ in a contrary or opposite manner
9. _____ to influence; to have an impact on
10. _____ coming later or after

The Theory of Marginal Utility

Reading Time: 2 min. 40 sec.

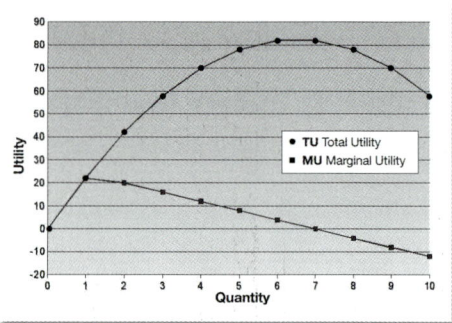

When a hungry person eats at a buffet, which of the first, second, or third helpings would give the person the most satisfaction? Undoubtedly, the first helping would be the most satisfying and the third the least satisfying. In economics, the satisfaction a consumer gains from a good or service is referred to as utility. Also, the additional satisfaction a consumer receives from using one more unit of a good or service is marginal utility.

Marginal utility is an economic concept that was invented to explain the determination of price. The term was first created by Friedrich von Weiser, an Austrian economist, and later made popular by the British economist, Alfred Marshall. Marshall explained that marginal utility is based on benefit. It is the benefit a consumer receives when he or she consumes one more unit of a good or service. This benefit is inversely related to how many units are consumed by a person. The more units of a product that a person purchases, the less satisfaction he or she attains. Thus, consumers alter their consumption until marginal utility and price becomes equal.

For instance, a certain teenage boy loves roller coasters. One day, he goes to the amusement park and rides his favorite roller coaster five times. The first ride is the most exciting and has the highest value of satisfaction for the boy. Each subsequent ride is just a little less exciting or satisfying. Therefore, the marginal utility decreases after the initial ride. The example suggests that the teenager's demand price will be highest at first and then decrease as he acquires more and more rides. In other words, the boy will be willing to pay less money for each subsequent roller-coaster ride after his first ride. Thus, the demand price declines as the quantity purchased increases.

During Marshall's time, the idea of utility in the most basic terms meant usefulness. Also, it was assumed that the quantity of utility of a good or service could be measured. In reality, however, it is very hard to quantify marginal utility of individual goods and services. Thus, today's economics has introduced the concept of qualification. Qualification in this sense means showing preference to various combinations of goods and services called consumption bundles. Currently, marginal utility refers to the quantified change in utility. In other words, a greater amount and variety of goods and services can affect marginal utility in alternative ways.

Your Time: _____ min. _____ sec.

Glossary

demand price: (phr) the highest price a buyer can pay for a certain quantity of good or service

Reading Comprehension

1. What is the purpose of the passage?

   Ⓐ To explain one way in which price can be determined
   Ⓑ To compare marginal utility to consumption costs
   Ⓒ To illustrate the negative aspects of marginal utility
   Ⓓ To discuss different concepts of price modification

2. Which of the following is true about consumer benefit?

   Ⓐ It increases with price.
   Ⓑ It is the same for each consumer.
   Ⓒ It increases as consumption increases.
   Ⓓ It decreases as consumption increases.

3. Why does the author use the roller coaster example?

   Ⓐ To show how amusement parks are overrated
   Ⓑ To explain how marginal utility affects price
   Ⓒ To illustrate the way emotions affect actual cost
   Ⓓ To use a practical example to discredit marginal utility

4. How did economists approach the idea of quantity of utility during Marshall's time as compared to now?

   ① Marshall's era: _____
   ② Today: _____

5. Which of the following has NOT been used to understand the quantity of utility?

   Ⓐ quantification
   Ⓑ qualification
   Ⓒ consumer price
   Ⓓ consumption bundles

6. The author of the passage implies that marginal utility

   Ⓐ is an outdated economic concept
   Ⓑ is an even more complex idea in modern times
   Ⓒ does not explain pricing as well as basic usefulness
   Ⓓ could never accurately identify how prices are calculated

Organizing & Summarizing

A Complete the following table to arrange the information about the theory of marginal utility.

The Theory of Marginal Utility

Origins	Price	Utility

• Created to explain
 (1)_____
 • First developed by Friedrich von Weiser
 • Popularized by
 (2)_____
	• (3)_____
	   - higher with greater demand
	   - lower with less demand
	 • Consumption
	   - consumers adjust until (4)_____ are equal
		• Utility = (5)_____
		   - inverse relationship to consumption
		   → decreases as more units are consumed
		 • Early on
		   - economists thought could be measured
		   - difficult to quantify
		 • Today
		   - mix of quantification & qualification
		   - (6)_____ → combination of goods and services
		   - variety and amount can also affect pricing

B Based on the information above, complete the following summary.

customer satisfaction	marginal utility and price	Alfred Marshall
inversely related	the quantity of utility	consumption bundles

The theory of marginal utility was first thought of by the Austrian economist Friedrich von Weiser. It was later popularized by (1)_____, a British economist. The idea of utility is closely linked to (2)_____. The theory proposes that a consumer's benefit is (3)_____ to how many units of a good or service the customer purchases. The more units consumed, the less benefit is derived. Furthermore, the demand price of a good or service will be higher when consumers need it more and vice versa. Also, consumers will alter their consumption until (4)_____ become equal. In the early days, economists believed (5)_____ could be measured rather easily. Today, however, it is known that quantity is more complicated. Thus, economists have introduced (6)_____. These qualify goods and services in combinations. The variety and amount of these combinations can affect pricing.

Vocabulary Expansion

Part A

A Complete the diagrams with the words from the box.

banknote — MONEY — _____ product — ECONOMICS — _____

| banknote | consumer | currency | check | demand | dime |
| penny | product | quarter | supply | utility | vendor |

B For each group of words, circle the concept that can include the others.

1 aristocracy   democracy   monarchy   government   dictatorship
2 column   architecture   blueprint   roof   floor plan
3 prevent   hinder   stop   block   thwart
4 authority   policeman   principal   judge   parent
5 recession   inflation   downturn   depression   economy

C Complete the sentences using the best words from the above exercises.

1 England has one of the oldest existing _____ in the world.
2 GDP and GNP are both critical measures of a country's _____.
3 The _____ of the new home is open and spacious without many walls.
4 The law of _____ and demand is the base of all market economies.
5 After the _____ spoke to the student body, he gave an award to the top student.
6 In many countries today, banknotes or bills have replaced coin _____ completely.
7 Keynesian theory is central to understanding the Great _____ during the 1930s.
8 Marginal _____ is inversely related to how many units are used by a consumer.
9 The _____ was very lenient to the criminal and sentenced him to just one week in prison.
10 Adam Smith claimed the market would be guided by rational choices of _____ and producers.

Part B

A Complete the diagrams with the words from the box.

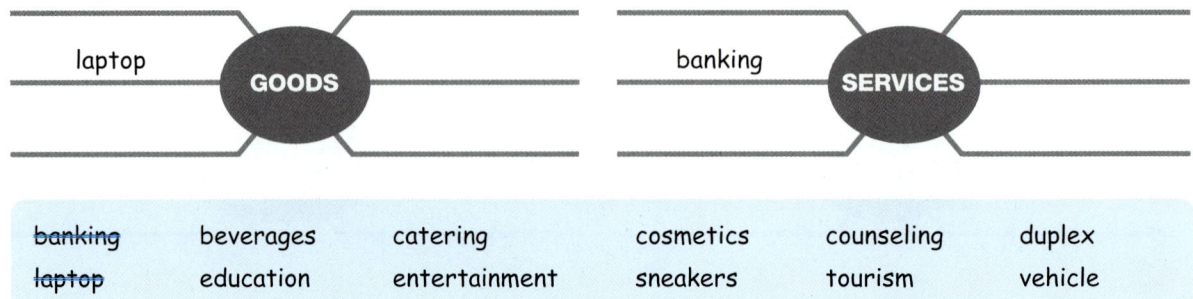

| ~~banking~~ | beverages | catering | cosmetics | counseling | duplex |
| ~~laptop~~ | education | entertainment | sneakers | tourism | vehicle |

B For each group of words, cross out the word that does not belong.

1	dispute	confront	challenge	conform	defy
2	plan	design	recess	strategy	formula
3	cost	income	profits	earnings	revenue
4	decline	rally	lessen	decrease	shrink
5	witness	observe	spy	watch	defend

C Complete the sentences using the best words from the above exercises.

1 _____ is the main source of income for Jamaica.
2 There is no magic _____ for mastering a foreign language easily.
3 Hybrid cars offer significant advantages over conventional _____.
4 He employed one of the country's top lawyers to _____ him in court.
5 I can no longer wear my wool sweater because it _____ when I washed it.
6 It is not healthy to drink too much soft _____ such as sodas and fruit drinks.
7 The stock market _____ sharply after the government announced a stimulus package.
8 The losing team _____ the winners to a rematch the following weekend.
9 Jack started his own _____ business even though he had no formal cooking training.
10 Teenagers tend to _____ to each other by dressing alike rather than picking an individual style.

Law

Overview
Basic Knowledge Building
Unit 17 Major Legal Systems
Unit 18 The Code of Hammurabi
Vocabulary Expansion

Overview

What Is Law?

Law is the study of the rules of conduct in a society. Laws are established and enforced by a government. These rules then become the main mediator between people. However, legal standards can differ greatly from country to country. Ultimately, modern laws are very broad and complex. Courts and judges have been established to help ensure accurate and fair interpretation of the law. Some specific study areas of law are:

- **constitutional law** – the study of the relationship between government and human rights
- **property law** – the study of what people claim ownership of
- **contract law** – the study of promises between parties
- **criminal law** – the study of crimes and their punishment
- **family law** – the study of laws governing marriage, divorce, and the rights of children
- **international law** – the study of law between nations

One of the earliest examples of written law was the Code of Hammurabi in ancient Mesopotamia. The Twelve Tables of early Republican Rome became the first western law code. Roman law would later be a major influence on European and American law. In England during the 18th century, common law became a major milestone in law history as judges made decisions on individual cases. Around the same time, the U.S. drafted its Constitution, the document which set forth the nation's fundamental laws and beliefs in human rights. The Constitution was a landmark document in human history as it restricted the power of government and guaranteed the liberties of citizens.

Law and You

Students of law have a broad range of career choices. They include being a lawyer, politician, judge, lobbyist, arbitrator, consultant, researcher, and professor to name just a few.

Do you want to study law? Ask yourself these questions:

- Do I have excellent oral and written skills?
- Am I a good problem-solver?
- Do I have strong critical thinking abilities?
- Am I good at interpreting complex concepts?
- Do I want to help people overcome difficult situations?

Basic Knowledge Building

Read the following passages and check if the given statements are true (T) or false (F).

❶ The Code of Hammurabi

The Code of Hammurabi is considered by many scholars to be the first set of laws ever written. It was established under the rule of Babylonian King Hammurabi in the mid-1700s B.C. The code is inscribed on a stone slab. It was discovered in 1901 in Iran and is now located in Paris at the Louvre Museum. Included in the set of laws are penalties for crimes, such as theft, highway robbery, and adultery. Some of the earliest forms of monetary values known are also listed in the code. Examples are fines, interest rates for loans, taxation, and even inheritance instructions.

Q. The Code of Hammurabi is useful for the study of ancient systems of economics.   T ☐   F ☐

❷ The Law of the Twelve Tables

The Twelve Tables were an early code of Roman laws dating from around 450 B.C. Some scholars believe they were written to reduce corruption and discrimination against plebeians or commoners. Plebeians could not understand the complexities of Roman law in its practiced oral form. Through the Twelve Tables, however, common people could come to know the law more accurately and avoid being tricked. The Twelve Tables outlined various laws on topics such as marriage, property, civil procedure, debts, and inheritance. Originally, the laws were drawn up on ivory tablets and placed in the Roman Forum for all Romans to see.

Q. The Twelve Tables attempted to create a fair judicial environment for the lower classes.   T ☐   F ☐

❸ Traditional Chinese Law

Traditional Chinese law most likely arose around the 11th century B.C. It was later compiled into six volumes of law by Yue Yi in the early 4th century B.C. Traditional Chinese law was based on two major Chinese philosophies: Confucianism and Legalism. Confucianism emphasized moral conduct and filial piety while Legalism emphasized codified law to support the ruler and counter individual autonomy. Traditional Chinese law helped establish order both within the general populace and nobility. Much of the traditional law was in practice until the late 19th century. However, the revolution of 1911 in China caused a shift from traditional law. From that point on, a more civilian, Western-influenced body of laws appeared.

Q. Traditional Chinese law was first created by Yue Yi in the 4th century B.C.   T ☐   F ☐

❹ The Rule of Law and the Magna Carta

The rule of law is a flexible term as its definition depends on the context in which it is applied. In some cases, it means a government must follow a clear set of established laws. In others, the rule of law could mean no one is ever above the law. The Magna Carta of 1215 is an important historical example of a rule of law. It was reluctantly chartered by King John of England and eventually became the basis of British constitutional law. However, its initial purpose was to thwart King John's continual violations of common law and protect his subjects. The Magna Carta was one of the first rules of law created to limit and constrain potential tyrannical power by a monarch.

Q. King John of England established the Magna Carta to aid his foreign policy.   T ☐   F ☐

❺ Animal Trials

Animal trials were carried out mainly in Europe from the 13th to 18th century. Occasionally, criminal charges were brought against animals for causing harm to human beings. Accused animals were literally brought into a court of law, and charges were heard against them. Documented crimes against animals ranged from murder to property damage. When found guilty, the animals faced the same punishment as a human being in the same situation. Thus, the guilty animals were sometimes exiled or even executed. Domesticated animals like pigs, horses or cows were the most common defendants at animal trials. However, there are also records of house rodents being accused of crimes.

Q. House pets were most often the accused in animal trials.   T ☐   F ☐

❻ The Panopticon

The Panopticon was a revolutionary type of prison designed by the English philosopher Jeremy Bentham in the late 18th century. He wanted prison authorities to have a visual presence over prisoners at all times. Therefore, he designed a prison where guards could view the prisoners. Yet, the prisoners did not know whether they were being watched or not. A central tower was placed in the middle of a circular building. Special lighting techniques to obscure the tower observer were also employed. The administration gained a huge psychological edge over the prison population. Many modern prisons today are based on Bentham's original design.

Q. A Panopticon allows prison guards to secretly watch prisoners' actions.   T ☐   F ☐

❼ Written and Unwritten Constitutions

Today, most nations rely on a written set of laws for people to abide by. More specifically, a written constitution is a document which outlines and explains the basic laws and principles of a given country or nation. It also may establish the specific duties of a nation's government. On the other hand, in some countries' cases, an unwritten constitution may be highly influential. No formal document exists with an unwritten constitution. However, laws and procedures are recognized because they have been practiced repeatedly throughout a nation's history. Thus, they are as essential to a country as if they were written out.

Q. Unwritten constitutions have little influence compared to written ones. T ☐ F ☐

❽ The American Bill of Rights

The United States Bill of Rights is the first ten amendments to the U.S. Constitution. It was ratified by Congress in 1791. The Bill guarantees certain individual rights and freedoms and limits government influence in order to further protect individuals. Some examples of the basic rights the Bill guarantees are freedom of speech, religion, and the right to bear arms. It also protects citizens accused of crimes from "cruel and unusual punishment." Also, concerning criminal procedure, citizens are guaranteed a "speedy and public trial." The Bill of Rights forms the foundation of American law and embodies American values.

Q. The American Bill of Rights is closely connected to the U.S. Constitution. T ☐ F ☐

❾ The Supreme Court of the United States

The Supreme Court is the head of the federal court system and the last court of appeal in the United States. It was established by Article 3 of the U.S. Constitution. The Court itself is made up of one chief justice and eight associate justices. Each member is appointed by the President and then must be approved or confirmed by the Senate. Every year the Court reviews thousands of cases from state and federal level courts, chooses those which most require the interpretation of law, and hears them. Rarely do trials take place in the Supreme Court. Very often, cases which reach the Supreme Court are high-profile. They can be highly controversial because the Court's decision often has lasting impact on the public.

Q. Members of the U.S. Supreme Court are not elected officials. T ☐ F ☐

⑩ The Prohibition of Double Jeopardy

In the field of law, double jeopardy is the concept that a person cannot be tried for the same crime twice using the same charges and under the same circumstances. In the United States, it is embedded in the Fifth Amendment to the Constitution. Double jeopardy attempts to limit a government's continued abuse of power against an individual after a court has made its ruling. In America, a defendant cannot be retried after either an acquittal or conviction, nor may a person be punished more than once for the same crime.

Q. Double jeopardy states that one can stand trial for the same crime multiple times.　T ☐　F ☐

⑪ Civil Law and Criminal Law

Criminal law defines crime and punishment. It involves prosecution by the government of an individual or group of individuals for a crime. At a trial, the prosecutor must prove that the defendant is guilty beyond a reasonable doubt. If convicted, the defendant might face probation, jail time, or in the most extreme cases, capital punishment. In contrast, civil law usually involves a legal procedure between two individuals or groups often in the form of a law suit. The loser will not face jail time but instead is usually forced to pay monetary damages. Typically, sufficient evidence is enough to win a civil law suit.

Q. Persons convicted under civil law will not spend time behind bars.　T ☐　F ☐

⑫ Subpoenas and Arrest Warrants

A subpoena is issued by a court and requires a person to appear in court in order to testify. Refusal to appear brings punishment. The subpoena is an official document detailing what is required of the person and the time and date he or she is to be present. Failure to comply with a subpoena could place the person in contempt of court. This violation could merit criminal charges being brought against that person. On the other hand, an arrest warrant is issued by a judge or other judicial body for the immediate arrest of an individual. Usually, probable cause of a crime must be produced in order for an arrest warrant to be issued.

Q. A subpoena is an official document allowing the police to arrest a criminal.　T ☐　F ☐

UNIT 17 Major Legal Systems

Thinking about the Topic

1 Look at the above pictures. What do you know about the legal procedures in your country?
2 Look at the title of this unit and the word list below. What do you predict the passage will be about?

Vocabulary Focus

A The following words are from the reading. Check (√) the ones that you already know.

Noun	Verb	Adjective
☐ chaos	☐ enforce	☐ neutral
☐ jury	☐ reconcile	☐ rigid
☐ precedent	☐ render	☐ prevalent
		☐ valid

B Write the words next to their matching definitions.

1 _____ something that serves as justification for future action
2 _____ strong; immovable
3 _____ to make; to give; to do
4 _____ a legal panel of one's peers
5 _____ to carry out; to administer; to execute
6 _____ confusion; turmoil
7 _____ solid; authentic; real
8 _____ to make peace; to settle
9 _____ frequent; common
10 _____ unbiased; impartial

Major Legal Systems

A legal system is a set of laws governing a country and the way they are interpreted and enforced. These laws lay the social, political, and economic foundation of a nation. Typically, legal systems define the rights of citizens and the rules and principles they should follow. Of course, the interpretation of certain laws can vary from country to country. Still, without a defined legal system, a country would not be able to function properly. It would simply fall into chaos. A country's legal system is usually based on historical factors and relations with other countries. In the modern world, three major legal systems are most prevalent: civil, common, and religious law.

Civil law is the most popular legal system in the world, and it predates the other two types. It originated with the Roman code of laws. Thus, the system revolves around written legal principles and rules. During a trial, judges simply administer the laws already established. Fundamental to civil law is the notion that there is one valid solution for each legal matter. In a civil law system, open trials are not common practice. Judges review evidence and hear testimony in a closed court of law. Then they make their ruling based on the information and the law. This type of legal procedure is in direct contrast to a common law system.

Common law is a more modern type of legal system that originated in England in the 18th century. It also became the basis for law in the United States. Unlike civil law, common law is based on precedent rather than statutes or rigid codes. A precedent is a previous decision by a court based on its own interpretation of a law. In a common law system, disputes are reconciled by argument before a neutral judge or jury. Ultimately, the judge or jury will render a judgment based on the facts and evidence of the case. Final judgment then essentially becomes a new precedent, or law, and weighs in on future legal matters.

The final major legal system in the world today is religious law. In its basic form, the laws that govern people's lives are believed to come from a divine being. They often are set forth in a sacred text. Usually, religious law includes moral codes supposedly handed down by the divinity. Examples include Islamic, Christian, and Hindu law. Sometimes, the religious beliefs are used simply for guidance. In other cases, they are the basis for a country's entire legal system. In some countries, however, religious codes are combined with another type of legal system such as civil law.

Your Time: _____ min. _____ sec.

Glossary

weigh in on: (phr) to influence

Reading Comprehension

1. Why is this passage written?

   A To reveal the origins of trials and juries
   B To illustrate three systems of law
   C To contrast common law and civil law
   D To suggest common law is impractical

2. Which of the following is true about civil law?

   A It began in England in the 18th century.
   B It was devised by the ancient Greeks.
   C It is the oldest type of legal system.
   D It relies heavily on a jury system.

3. What is the major difference between civil and common law?

   A Civil law is not practiced as much as common law in modern society.
   B Common law is based on precedent while civil law is based on written codes.
   C Unlike civil law, open trials are not frequently conducted in a common law system.
   D The common law system has been in existence longer than the civil law system.

4. According to the passage, what is a precedent?

   _____

5. Which of the following is NOT true about religious law?

   A It only serves as moral guidance for a country.
   B It is practiced in various Islamic and Hindu countries.
   C A supreme being weighs heavily in this legal system.
   D It is often mixed with other types of legal systems.

6. Which of the following can be inferred about legal systems?

   A There are no appeals in civil law.
   B Evidence is not very important in civil law.
   C Civil laws are probably based on religious views.
   D Laws are always evolving in common law.

145

Organizing & Summarizing

A Complete the following table to arrange the information about major legal systems.

Major Legal Systems

Civil law	Common law	Religious law

• Originated with
 (1)_____
 • Clearly defined written code
 • What judges do
   - review evidence &
   (2)_____
   - apply law to cases & make decisions
   - few open trials
 • Little room for interpretation
	• Originated in 18th-century England
	 • Basis for (3)_____
	 • Relies on precedent
	   - affects future cases
	 • What judges do
	   - reconcile disputes by argument
	   - interpret laws & render a judgment
	   → set (4)_____
	 • Laws evolve
		• Claimed to have divine origin
		   - based on religious text
		   - Islamic, Christian, & Hindu law
		 • (5)_____ from a divine being
		   - guide people on how to live a moral life
		   - provide the basis for entire legal system
		 • Often combined with (6)_____

B Based on the information above, complete the following summary.

on precedent	the U.S. legal system	another legal system
early Roman codes	moral guidance	open trials or juries

In the world today, there are three major legal systems. Civil law is the most popular legal system and comes from (1)_____. It is based on clearly defined written laws. Judges typically apply these laws to make a decision. The decision is clear-cut, and there is little need for (2)_____. Common law was established in England in the 18th century and later became the basis of (3)_____. This legal system builds (4)_____. Laws continually evolve and affect future ones as courts interpret present laws. Trial by jury is commonplace. With the religious legal system, laws are given to humans by a divine entity. Sometimes, these laws are simply used for (5)_____. Other times, they serve as the foundation for a country's entire legal system. However, they are typically combined with (6)_____ to serve citizens best.

UNIT 18 The Code of Hammurabi

Thinking about the Topic

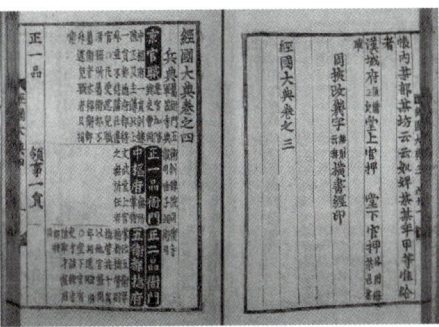

1. Look at the above pictures. What kinds of laws did ancient people have?
2. Look at the title of this unit and the word list below. What do you predict the passage will be about?

Vocabulary Focus

A The following words are from the reading. Check (√) the ones that you already know.

Noun	Verb	Adjective
☐ malpractice	☐ encompass	☐ optimistic
☐ righteousness	☐ carve	☐ primitive
☐ epilogue	☐ engrave	☐ civil
☐ inheritance		

B Write the words next to their matching definitions.

1. _____ to carve designs into; chisel
2. _____ goodness; justice
3. _____ hopeful; positive thinking or outlook
4. _____ carelessness; abuse
5. _____ to surround
6. _____ early; old; one of the first
7. _____ possessions gained from someone's death
8. _____ of citizens in general
9. _____ an ending; a conclusion
10. _____ to cut with a sharp instrument;

The Code of Hammurabi

Time Limit: 2 min. 50 sec.

In 1901, a team of French archeologists discovered a basalt stele in the ruined Mesopotamian city of Susa in western Iran. The black stone slab was about seven feet in height and was engraved with a code of ancient laws. The code was named the Code of Hammurabi after the Babylonian king who enacted it. Today, it is housed in the Louvre Museum in Paris. It is one of the most well-preserved, original set of laws ever found.

The Code of Hammurabi is carved on the face and rear of the stele in cuneiform script, an early writing system of wedge shapes. The entries are on both the front and back of the slab. In the preface of the code, Hammurabi introduces himself as "protector of the weak and oppressed". He then relates how the gods presented him with the code to preserve "righteousness in the land". The legal part of the code describes 282 laws governing Babylonian daily life. The laws are written in plain language so as to be understood by all. The code closes with a lyrical epilogue of Hammurabi's orders to hand down his laws from generation to generation.

Scholars consider Hammurabi's code of laws a primitive type of constitution. It creates basic laws for governing the country and guarantees some civil liberties for citizens. Because even the king is not allowed to change certain fundamental laws, it can protect people from tyrannical rule. Also, the code is concerned with fair trials and monetary issues as well as the rights of the family. It even encompasses penalties for various injustices like malpractice by physicians. Moreover, the code establishes clear economic standards in the form of interest rates and guidelines for inheritance and taxation. These formulas are believed to be the earliest recorded economic system in human history. In the context of criminal law, the code generally follows an "eye-for-an-eye" mentality. In other words, the punishment is equal to the crime committed. This principle is in part intended to prevent excessive punishment relative to the crime.

The most fascinating aspect of the Code of Hammurabi is its humanity. It neither bolsters the king nor grants him omnipotence. Nor does it intend to protect the rich and their property. Instead, it is occupied with lifting up and protecting the poor, the weak, women, and children. Furthermore, its tone is optimistic. It speaks to the hope for a higher quality of life and general peace for the future. Clearly, the Code of Hammurabi is an excellent model of laws exemplifying the rule of law in ancient form.

Your Time: _____ min. _____ sec.

Glossary

cuneiform: (adj) having the form of a wedge; wedge-shaped
omnipotence: (n) the state of having total authority or power

Reading Comprehension

1. What is the main purpose of the passage?

   Ⓐ To show the flaws in Hammurabi's Code
   Ⓑ To discuss the intention of Hammurabi's Code
   Ⓒ To contrast Hammurabi's Code with modern constitutions
   Ⓓ To argue Hammurabi's Code is more complete than many modern systems

2. Which of the following is true of the Code of Hammurabi?

   Ⓐ It does not try to exclude anyone from understanding it.
   Ⓑ It does little to support the rights of minorities and children.
   Ⓒ It ignores money issues of Babylonian society.
   Ⓓ It consists of two hundred and eighty laws.

3. How does the Code of Hammurabi deal with criminal matters?

   Ⓐ Usually wrongdoers only had to pay a fine.
   Ⓑ The lower class citizen was always punished.
   Ⓒ Punishments mirrored the crime committed.
   Ⓓ Hammurabi served as supreme judge of all crimes.

4. What do scholars equate the Code of Hammurabi with, and what does it protect?
   ① Equated: _____
   ② Protection: _____

5. Which of the following is NOT true about Hammurabi's Code?

   Ⓐ It can still be viewed today.
   Ⓑ It makes the king all-powerful.
   Ⓒ It covers a wide range of economic matters.
   Ⓓ It does not address the needs of the lower class.

6. What can be inferred from the passage?

   Ⓐ Babylonian kings were tyrants.
   Ⓑ Only the educated could understand the code.
   Ⓒ Babylonians enjoyed a relatively free society.
   Ⓓ The laws were dissolved after Hammurabi's death.

Organizing & Summarizing

A Complete the following table to arrange the information about the Code of Hammurabi.

The Code of Hammurabi

Physical Traits	Intention & Scope	Humanitarianism

• Black stone slab
  - 7 ft. high
  - engraved with code in cuneiform
    → a total of ⁽¹⁾_____
  - earliest set of written laws ever discovered
• Still survives today
  - ⁽²⁾_____, Paris
	• To protect the weak and to protect the land
	• Primitive constitution
	  - limits king's power
	  - guarantees laws & ⁽³⁾_____
	• Scope
	  - interest rates, inheritance, taxation, & family matters
	  - crime
	    → ⁽⁴⁾"_____"
		• Prevents ⁽⁵⁾_____
		• Protects against tyranny
		• Supports general peace
		• ⁽⁶⁾_____ for the rich
		• Protects the weak & the poor, women & children

B Based on the information above, complete the following summary.

eye-for-an-eye measures	maintain righteousness	taxation and inheritance
excessive punishment	the power of the king	282 codes in cuneiform

The Code of Hammurabi is the earliest set of laws ever discovered. It is a seven-foot-high stone slab with ⁽¹⁾_____ engraved on it. It still survives today and can be seen at the Louvre Museum in Paris. King Hammurabi intended to protect the weak and ⁽²⁾_____ in the land through the codes. In many ways, it is a primitive constitution as it restricts ⁽³⁾_____ and establishes fundamental laws and civil liberties for all citizens. Its codes on ⁽⁴⁾_____ are the earliest known examples of economic law. With crime, Hammurabi's Code implements ⁽⁵⁾_____. In that it prevents ⁽⁶⁾_____, it mirrors more modern law models. Also, it protects against tyranny and tries to instill general peace. It does not give privileges to the rich. On the contrary, it serves the weak and the poor, and women and children.

Vocabulary Expansion

Part A

A Complete the diagrams with the words from the box.

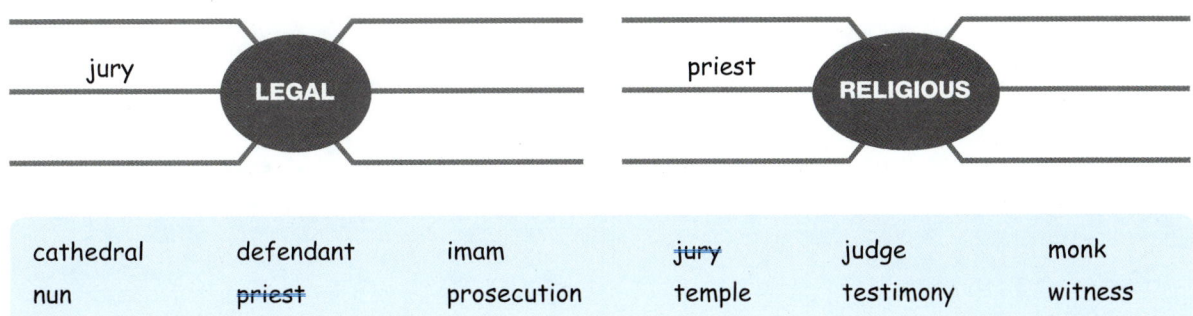

| cathedral | defendant | imam | ~~jury~~ | judge | monk |
| nun | ~~priest~~ | prosecution | temple | testimony | witness |

B For each group of words, circle the concept that can include the others.

1 monarch   ruler   tyrant   president   despot
2 theft   adultery   crime   arson   robbery
3 jailer   prisoner   guard   cell   prison
4 constitution signature   amendment   referendum   legislature
5 filial   maternal   fraternal   familial   paternal

C Complete the sentences using the best words from the above exercises.

1 Confucianism emphasizes moral conduct and _____ piety.
2 The woman's _____ could clearly be seen at the bottom of the receipt.
3 After the teenagers set fire to the barn, they were arrested for _____.
4 Jeremy Bentham designed a prison where _____ could view the prisoners.
5 During a trial, a judge reviews evidence and hears _____ from witnesses.
6 In many countries, jobs of mothers who are on _____ leave are protected by law.
7 Changes in the constitution were implemented in the form of _____.
8 The _____ testified that she saw the man break into the car and drive off.
9 The Chinese government warned Tibetan Buddhist _____ against political activity.
10 The _____ of a country defines its citizens' basic rights and duties.

151

Part B

A Complete the diagrams with the words from the box.

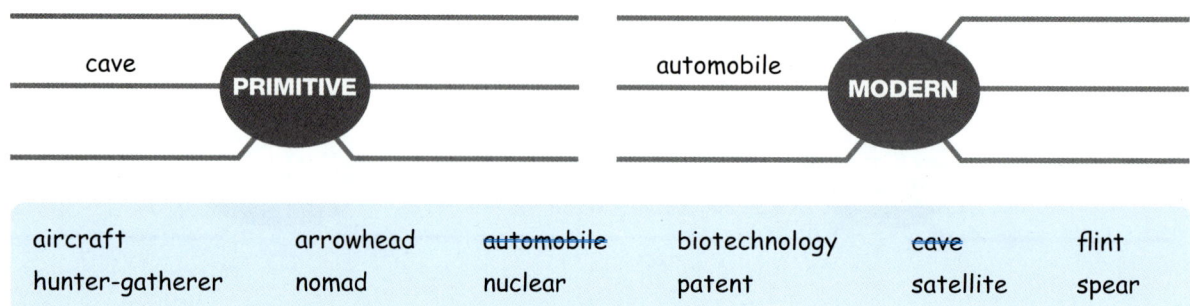

| aircraft | arrowhead | ~~automobile~~ | biotechnology | ~~cave~~ | flint |
| hunter-gatherer | nomad | nuclear | patent | satellite | spear |

B For each group of words, cross out the word that does not belong.

1 liberty   autonomy   freedom   violation   independence
2 approve   permit   sanction   ratify   amend
3 guarantee   promise   deceive   pledge   vow
4 liable   exempt   cleared   excused   spared
5 blame   vacate   criticize   accuse   charge

C Complete the sentences using the best words from the above exercises.

1 Most non-profit organizations are _____ from paying taxes.
2 _____ did not usually permanently settle in one place.
3 Some experts believe that _____ power is the best alternative to coal.
4 Alcoholics tend to _____ themselves about the seriousness of their problem.
5 The ruling and opposition parties agreed to _____ the constitution.
6 Without _____, weather forecasting would be an even more difficult task.
7 The company provides a written _____ that its products will never break.
8 The judge found the defendant _____ for damages, and she had to pay $1,000.
9 The family had to _____ their house after they could no longer pay their mortgage.
10 The Magna Carta was intended to thwart King John's continual _____ of common law.

Ecology

| Overview
| **Basic Knowledge Building**
| **Unit 19** Keystone Species
| **Unit 20** Mutualism *vs.* Commensalism
| **Vocabulary Expansion**

Overview

What Is Ecology?

Ecology is the study of life and the interactions between organisms and their environments. Ecology can be studied at different levels. Some ecologists will study molecules while others study the entire earth. Even though ecology is a branch of biology, it draws upon many other sciences. Some fields of study are:

- **behavioral ecology** – the study of relationships between animal behavior and the environment
- **population ecology** – the study of the structure and dynamics of species populations
- **community ecology** – the study of interactions among different species in the same area
- **evolutionary ecology** – the study of evolution and the adaptation of organisms to their environment

While people have always been interested in other species, ecology as a separate science is fairly new. The father of modern ecology is considered to be Eugen Warming, a Danish botanist. In the late 1800s, he began to write about the impact of the environment on plants. By the mid-1900s, ecology became more popular as people began to recognize the impact that they were having on the environment. As a result, there was growing interest in understanding the relationships between organisms and their surroundings.

Ecology and You

People who study ecology work in a wide variety of places. These include schools, museums, the government, and alternative energy firms.

Do you want to study ecology? Ask yourself these questions:

- **Do I enjoy working outside?**
- **Am I interested in the environment?**
- **Do I enjoy working with animals and plants?**
- **Am I good at other sciences?**
- **Am I patient and detail-oriented?**

Basic Knowledge Building

Read the following passages and check if the given statements are true (T) or false (F).

❶ The Biosphere

In 1875, the geologist Eduard Suess used the term biosphere to describe the location where all living things dwell. Since this initial formulation, the term has been further developed and is now considered to encompass all the ecosystems of the Earth. It includes every living organism on the planet as well as their interactions with the earth, water, and air. The biosphere is thought to have developed about 3.5 billion years ago when the first living organisms began to appear. Today, some scientists have argued that the biosphere itself is a kind of super organism. Each of the plants, animals, and other organisms serve as just a piece of the whole.

Q. The biosphere only includes living organisms.   T ☐   F ☐

❷ Ecosystems

While the types of plants and animals found in an area are important, the impact of non-living factors such as water and temperature on these organisms can also be significant. The term ecosystem was coined in order to describe the relationship between plant and animal populations and their non-living environment. Rainfall and the amount of sunlight, for example, impact the types and numbers of plants and animals that live in a particular region. Most ecosystems are not static. They show changes over time. As a result, different species of plants and animals will be seen in an area at different times.

Q. The plants and animals in an area have the greatest impact on an ecosystem.   T ☐   F ☐

❸ Food Chains

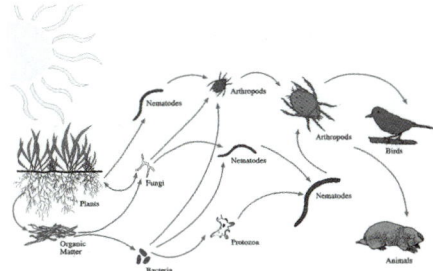

All life gets its energy from the sun. Plants use sunlight directly to create energy in the form of sugar. Animals either eat plants or other animals in order to get their energy. The path of energy is known as a food chain. The base of all food chains starts with plants. The primary consumer is the animal that eats the plants. The secondary consumer is the animal that eats the primary, and so on. At the end of each food chain are decomposers. These are bacteria or fungi that break down organic material and return nutrients back into the soil to be used by plants.

Q. Even animals that do not eat plants rely upon them indirectly.   T ☐   F ☐

❹ Ecological Succession

When new land is formed by the process of plate tectonics, it is unable to support much life. Usually only lichens or other very hardy plant life are able to grow. Over the course of generations, the plants' roots and erosion serve to slowly break the rock down into smaller pieces. This mixture can then support more types of plants. Weeds tend to be the first to move in followed by grasses. As the plants die, their decaying organic matter will serve to increase the thickness of the soil. As more plants move in, small animals then follow. If sufficient rain is present, trees will eventually take root. If not, then the area will stay a grassland. All these environmental changes over time are known as ecological succession.

Q. Weeds are the first type of plant found after new land is created. T ☐ F ☐

❺ Biodiversity

Biodiversity refers to the variety of species found within a particular area. Mostly frequently, it is measured to gauge the health of the area. If the biodiversity within a region decreases, then the health of the region has declined. In general, the most diverse regions on Earth are near the tropics with biodiversity decreasing towards the polar regions. The greatest biodiversity is found in two ecological hotspots. The first is Brazil's tropical rainforests. More than a million species of insects can be found there, and half are only found in Brazil. The second is Madagascar. Since the island separated from Africa more than 65 million years ago, it has been isolated and home to numerous native species.

Q. The tropics would be considered the healthiest regions of Earth due to their biodiversity. T ☐ F ☐

❻ Rainforests

Rainforests are simply forests with high amounts of rainfall. They can be found in both tropical and temperate regions. Generally, rainforests consist of different layers. The very top layer is known as the emergent layer. This is comprised of the tops of the tallest trees. Very few animals can be found here. The canopy is the second layer. It is a nearly continuous layer of foliage made up of treetops. This

layer is the densest area of biodiversity. Below the canopy are the understory and then the forest floor. Contrary to what most people think, the forest floor is actually fairly open as very little sunlight can penetrate its depths.

Q. There are not many plants found at the bottom of rainforests. T ☐ F ☐

❼ Biomass

Biomass is the total weight of living organisms and other biological material within a given region at a given time. While biomass can be used to describe a particular species or natural community, it is most often used to describe a trophic level or an organism's position in a food chain. That is, biomass can be used to describe the weight of all the organisms at a certain stage in a food chain. For example, a cow weighs much more than grass. However, if you add up the weight of all the grass the cow will eat over its lifetime, it will be much greater than the mass of the cow. In this manner, you can estimate the number of cows that any given field will be able to support since you can calculate the biomass of the field.

Q. Biomass is only used to measure the weight of plants.   T ☐   F ☐

❽ Biosphere 2

Biosphere 2 was a large artificial ecological dome built in Arizona in 1991. It contained a rainforest, an ocean, savannah, a desert, and even people. Biosphere 2 was built in the hope that it could become a self-sustaining ecological system. However, very early on, the internal oxygen levels dropped so low that additional air had to be pumped in. Moreover, the people living within the dome were not able to grow enough food to support themselves. Now, many consider Biosphere 2 to be a failure. However, there are some others who consider Biosphere 2 to be a success for its engineering. The structure is the largest closed ecological system to ever have been created.

Q. Biosphere 2 is not widely considered to have significantly advanced science.   T ☐   F ☐

❾ The Hydrologic Cycle

As the sum of the water on the Earth is limited, water is constantly being recycled. Nearly all of the water in the air comes from evaporation from bodies of water such as lakes, rivers, and oceans. It also comes from transpiration from plants. Once the water is in the air, it comes down as precipitation. The precipitation will either make its way to lakes and rivers or it will sink down into the ground. The water under the ground 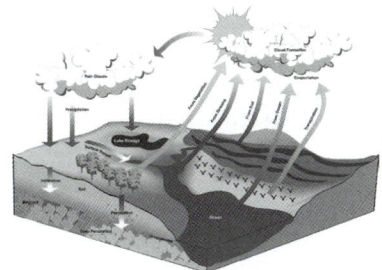 will either be absorbed by plants or flow into rivers and oceans. Then a new hydrologic cycle will start as all the water that is consumed and disposed of will be used again.

Q. The hydrologic cycle is mainly a local phenomenon.   T ☐   F ☐

⑩ The Carbon Cycle

The main element in all living things is carbon. It makes up sugar, proteins, and fats. Since carbon is so important to all organisms, it must be recycled in order to ensure enough nutrients exist for the next generation. This process of carbon recycling is known as the carbon cycle. To illustrate, plants take carbon dioxide from the air and convert it into sugars and starches. Animals eat the plants and use some of the carbon for their own metabolic needs before excreting the remainder in the form of carbon dioxide gas. However, a lot of carbon dioxide is also re-released into the atmosphere through combustion. The burning of wood and oil releases the carbon trapped within, thus raising the level of carbon dioxide in the air.

Q. Plants are responsible for removing carbon dioxide from the air.　T ☐　F ☐

⑪ Biological Magnification

Biological magnification is the tendency of toxic chemicals to become more concentrated as they move up the food chain. The mechanism is fairly simple. If a water supply contains a tiny amount of toxin, a plant which consumes that water will also ingest that toxin. Over a period of time, the toxin levels will increase as the plant constantly requires water. The animal that then eats that plant will add to the level of poison within its body. That is because the animal will eat a number of plants during the course of its life. The toxin concentration will continue to increase as the chemical progresses up the food chain. Thus, animals at the top of the food chain will ultimately have higher amounts of toxins than those at the bottom.

Q. It is safer to eat animals at the base of a food chain than those higher in the food chain.　T ☐　F ☐

⑫ Eutrophication

Eutrophication is the rapid growth of algae in a body of water. This phenomenon is most frequently due to the addition of nutrients as happens, for example, with fertilizer run-off from farms. The effects of eutrophication can be severe. Initially, the nutrients will cause a rapid increase in the amount of algae along the surface of the water. This kills plants living along the bottom by blocking out sunlight. However, the environmental damage does not stop there. Once all the excess nutrients have been used up, the algae begin to die. The decomposition of the algae uses up all the available oxygen in the water. Within a short period of time, all the fish in the water will die, and the area will be nearly devoid of any life.

Q. Eutrophication provides ample nutrients for aquatic plants and animals.　T ☐　F ☐

UNIT 19 Keystone Species

Thinking about the Topic

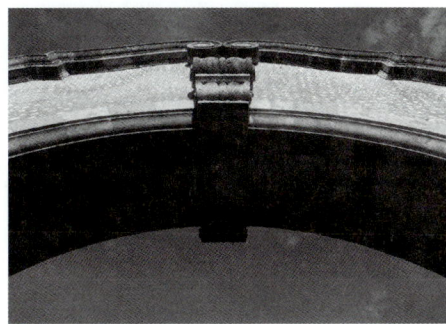 

1 Look at the above pictures. What is a keystone? What do you think its role is?
2 Look at the title of this unit and the word list below. What do you predict the passage will be about?

Vocabulary Focus

A The following words are from the reading. Check (√) the ones that you already know.

Noun	Verb	Adjective
☐ abundance	☐ allocate	☐ subjective
☐ consensus	☐ collapse	☐ unchecked
☐ predator	☐ dub	
☐ reluctance	☐ graze	

B Write the words next to their matching definitions.

1 _____ based on personal feelings and ideas and not on facts
2 _____ to name
3 _____ to distribute; to share out
4 _____ an organism that eats other organisms
5 _____ a large quantity
6 _____ agreement among all the people involved
7 _____ to eat grass or other plants
8 _____ not controlled; unrestrained
9 _____ unwillingness
10 _____ to fall down suddenly; to fail or stop existing suddenly

Keystone Species

In the early 1960s, the ecologist Robert Paine was studying species that lived along the west coast of the U.S. He found that one type of starfish played a major role in the coastal ecosystem. Even though it was a predator, it helped other species in the area by controlling the abundance of grazing animals. When the starfish were removed, two types of mussels grew unchecked. As their numbers increased, they displaced other species. In essence, the starfish were responsible for the diversity of the coastal community. Paine soon published his findings and dubbed the creatures that are paramount to an ecosystem keystone species.

Since his landmark work, keystone species have been more rigidly defined. Most biologists consider them to be species that play critical roles within a community. They also have an impact much greater than would be expected, considering their relative abundance. However, this definition is still fairly subjective. As a result, there can be disagreement among scientists as to whether a group is a keystone species or not.

The failure to reach a consensus has led to some friction. The main reason is that keystone species are major targets for conservation efforts. As they directly influence their community, their absence could cause an ecosystem to collapse. Thus, a significant number of resources are allocated to ensuring that they thrive. Failure to properly identify the correct keystone species, then, would mean that conservation efforts were misspent.

Another source of contention is the choice to broaden the definition of keystone species. Paine's original work cited only predators as being significant. More recently, biologists have named some prey species and plants as keystone species. They argue that the effect on the given ecosystem should be the primary consideration in the designation of a keystone species. The role of the species in question is not essential. However, there is still some reluctance to extend the theory beyond its original scope.

The theory of keystone species is still in its infancy. Until it is further developed, its use to conservationists will remain limited. However, it has had its successes. Most recently, wolves were reintroduced to Yellowstone National Park in the U.S. At first, local residents were worried that the predators would have a negative effect on the numbers of deer and other small mammals. But scientists argued that as the keystone species, they would help improve the health and diversity of local wildlife. In the years since, the wolf population has thrived. Along with the wolves, the number of deer has increased. With further work, the theory of keystone species will be able to play an even greater role in conservation efforts.

Glossary

mussel: (n) any of several marine or freshwater bivalve mollusks that live attached to stationary objects.

Reading Comprehension

1. What is the passage mainly about?

   (A) The various applications of a theory of ecology
   (B) Reasons for the broadening of an indicator species
   (C) Failures of a theory to properly predict the diversity of a species
   (D) Concerns about the use of varying definitions of an ecological term

2. What does the passage say about keystone species?

   (A) They can only be the top predators in an ecosystem.
   (B) They are more important than their numbers would indicate.
   (C) There has been a growing consensus about their proper definition.
   (D) Their influence is primarily due to their abundance within a region.

3. Which of the following is true about conservation efforts?

   (A) Keystone species must be targeted in order for the efforts to be successful.
   (B) Numerous species are targeted to make sure that as many as possible survive.
   (C) There are significant funds available to aid in major conservation efforts.
   (D) The major species are the only ones which benefit from conservation.

4. What does the passage say is the reason for extending the keystone label to non-predators?

   _____

5. Which of the following is NOT an effect of the reintroduction of wolves to Yellowstone National Park?

   (A) It helped increase the population of deer in the park.
   (B) It was a successful application of the keystone species theory.
   (C) It proved the idea that prey animals could be keystone species.
   (D) It raised concerns that the numbers of other animals would decrease.

6. It can be inferred from the passage that the wolves

   (A) failed to positively impact local animals
   (B) had to be controlled to prevent danger to locals
   (C) increased the amount of food available for the deer
   (D) improved the health of other species within the park

Organizing & Summarizing

A Complete the following table to arrange the information about keystone species.

Keystone Species

Identification	Traditional Definition	Alternative Definition	Application
• First identified by (1)_____ in the early 1960s - west coast of the U.S. • (2)_____ - controls the abundance of grazing animals - dubbed keystone species	• Predators that have a more important role in the environment than (3)_____ would suggest - major target for conservation efforts • Problems - (4)_____ - lack of consensus among scientists	• Broadened to include (5)_____ • Effect on the environment more important than role in it • Problem - ongoing reluctance among some scientists	• Used to conserve the environment - successful (6)_____ in Yellowstone

B Based on the information above, complete the following summary.

| non-predators | conservation efforts | the reintroduction of wolves |
| Robert Paine | being targeted for aid | a keystone species |

In the early 1960s, (1)_____ found that a type of starfish played a major role in the ecosystem along the western coast of the United States. As a predator, it balanced the number of grazing animal species in the area. He called the starfish (2)_____. Keystone species are organisms which play a significant role in the local environment. However, there has been disagreement over what a keystone species is. One reason is that keystone species are important for (3)_____. Thus, misidentification would result in the wrong species (4)_____. The second reason is that some scientists want to consider (5)_____ as keystone species. While the keystone species theory has not been completely developed, it has shown its effectiveness. (6)_____ into Yellowstone National Park in America showed the benefits of keystone species on other animals.

UNIT 20 Mutualism *vs.* Commensalism

Thinking about the Topic

1 Look at the above pictures. What are the relationships between the two species in each picture?
2 Look at the title of this unit and the word list below. What do you predict the passage will be about?

Vocabulary Focus

A The following words are from the reading. Check (√) the ones that you already know.

Noun	Verb	Adjective
☐ arrangement	☐ inhabit	☐ immune
☐ symbiosis	☐ benefit	☐ unaffected
☐ leftover	☐ sweep	☐ capable
☐ scavenger		

B Write the words next to their matching definitions.

1 _____ to live in
2 _____ an unused portion
3 _____ an animal that feeds on discarded matter
4 _____ to search thoroughly
5 _____ having the ability to do something
6 _____ not affected by
7 _____ to be helpful
8 _____ an agreement
9 _____ the living together of organisms of different species
10 _____ not changed; not influenced

Mutualism *vs.* Commensalism

Reading Time: 2 min. 40 sec.

Coral reefs are one of the most diverse ecosystems. The species which inhabit these areas are also highly dependent upon each other. They are formed as a result of the symbiotic relationship between coral and algae. The two species partner in a mutually beneficial arrangement. The coral receives food, and the algae are protected. This arrangement is known as mutualism, one of the major types of symbiosis.

In general, symbiosis is a broad term used to describe various relationships between different species within a community. Mutualism is the most positive relationship between species. Within coral reefs, there are a number of mutualistic relationships. The best known is the relationship between the sea anemone and the clownfish. The sea anemone has poisonous stingers capable of stunning a fish. Since the clownfish is immune to its barbs, however, it is protected from its predators as it swims along the tentacles of the sea anemone. In return, the clownfish will often give its host small pieces of fish. In addition, it serves as a lure, attracting much larger prey to the sea anemone.

There is another common type of symbiosis found in the coral reef—commensalism. In this relationship, one species benefits but the other neither benefits nor is harmed. The term commensalism literally means "at the table together". This is because the earliest types of animals observed were those that ate the leftovers of another. In this symbiotic relationship, a predator rarely eats the entire carcass of a kill. Scavengers quickly eat the remains of their free meal. The scavengers benefit while the predator is unaffected.

However, commensalism has been expanded to include benefits beyond food. For instance, porcelain crabs also live with the clownfish among the sea anemones. Since the crabs are filter feeders, they need a place to sweep the water for food. The sea anemones offer the crabs protection as few predators are willing to venture near them. The sea anemones, however, receive nothing from the crabs in return for their service.

In fact, it is not always easy to define the type of symbiotic relationship. Like the porcelain crabs, for example, cleaner shrimps living in the sea anemones are also commensal. But they often have mutualistic relationships with the clownfish living among the sea anemones. For this reason, some scientists believe that the shrimps may not be commensal. By cleaning the clownfish, they may help to keep the ecosystem clean. This indirectly benefits the sea anemones, so the relationship may actually be termed mutualistic.

Your Time: _____ min. _____ sec.

Glossary	mutualistic: (adj) of a relationship between organisms of two different species in which each member benefits
	commensal: (adj) living with, on, or in another organism without causing or receiving injury

Reading Comprehension

1. What is the primary purpose of the passage?

    Ⓐ To discuss two ways in which species become interdependent
    Ⓑ To argue that coral reefs need further protection from scavengers
    Ⓒ To contrast the two different types of species found in the ocean
    Ⓓ To highlight the importance of diversity in the ecosystems

2. According to the passage, mutualism

    Ⓐ benefits one species more than the other
    Ⓑ aids both species in the relationship
    Ⓒ ends up with one species being harmed
    Ⓓ must be agreed upon in advance

3. Which of the following is true about scavengers?

    Ⓐ They only get to eat the food that is given to them.
    Ⓑ They must repay the predators for the meal they receive.
    Ⓒ They are not believed to enter into symbiotic relationships.
    Ⓓ They do not have to expend much energy to get their food.

4. How do porcelain crabs benefit from the sea anemone?

    _____

5. Which of the following would NOT be an example of mutualism?

    Ⓐ A bee pollinating a flower while getting its nectar
    Ⓑ The bacteria living in the gut of a cow helping the cow's digestion
    Ⓒ A hyena eating the remains of a gazelle killed by a lion
    Ⓓ A fungus receiving nutrients from a plant and giving it water in return

6. What can be inferred from the passage about symbiotic relationships?

    Ⓐ They require both species to benefit.
    Ⓑ They benefit prey animals the most.
    Ⓒ They cannot be clearly defined in some cases.
    Ⓓ They are not very common among larger species.

Organizing & Summarizing

A Complete the following table to arrange the information about mutualism and commensalism.

Mutualism vs. Commensalism

Symbiosis	Mutualism	Commensalism
• Various (1)_____ between two different species which inhabit the same place - mutualism & commensalism as major types of symbiotic relationship → not always (2)_____	• (3)_____ - most positive relationship between species • Examples - (4)_____ - sea anemones & clownfish	• One species benefits, but the other is (5)_____ - literally meaning "at the table together" • Examples - predator & scavenger - (6)_____

B Based on the information above, complete the following summary.

the porcelain crab	at the table together	the coral animals and algae
the other is unaffected	sea anemones and clownfish	highly dependent on each other

The animal species which live in coral reefs are (1)_____. The coral reefs themselves are the result of a symbiotic relationship between (2)_____. This is known as mutualism. Other kinds of mutualism found in the coral reefs exist between (3)_____. While the clownfish gets protection from the sea anemone, it also gives the sea anemone food and acts as a lure for larger prey. Commensalism is another type of symbiosis. The term means (4)"_____" because the first type of commensalism observed was when animals would eat the leftovers of predators. Now, the term is used when one species benefits and (5)_____. An example is the relationship between the sea anemone and (6)_____. However, symbiotic relationships can be very complex, so the exact type of relationship may not be clear.

Vocabulary Expansion

Part A

A Complete the diagrams with the words from the box.

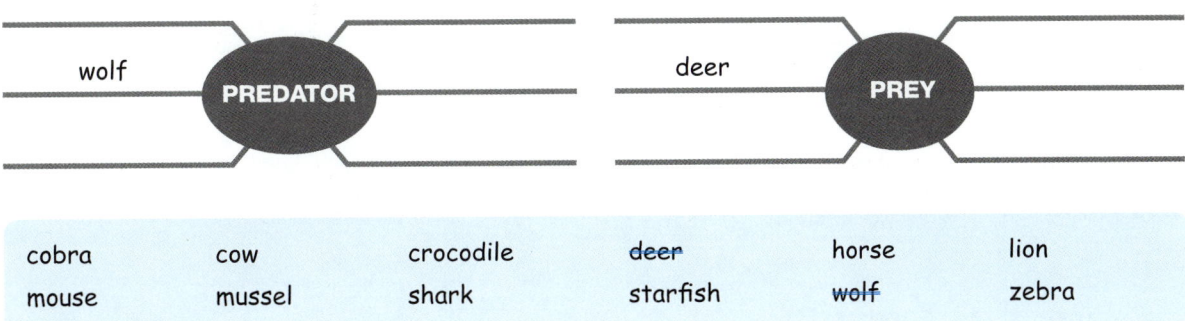

| cobra | cow | crocodile | deer | horse | lion |
| mouse | mussel | shark | starfish | wolf | zebra |

B For each group of words, circle the concept that can include the others.

1 amphibian   crustacean   species   rodent   cetacean
2 desert   tundra   rainforest   savannah   ecosystem
3 time   resource   fund   workforce   effort
4 earthquake   drought   famine   disaster   eutrophication
5 food chain   prey   consumer   decomposer   predator

C Complete the sentences using the best words from the above exercises.

1 _____ are areas that have very little precipitation.
2 _____ are frequently mistaken for alligators since they look similar.
3 The number of _____ found in the wild has been steadily decreasing.
4 _____ is the abnormally rapid growth of algae in a body of water.
5 _____ including frogs and toads can live both on land and in water.
6 The country is suffering from _____ resulting from a long period of drought.
7 At the end of each food chain are _____ such as bacteria and fungi.
8 There are still many unknown species to be found in the Amazon _____.
9 The clownfish serves as a lure, attracting much larger _____ to the sea anemone.
10 Lynette has saved money to open her own shop but still lacks the _____ to start it.

Part B

A Complete the diagrams with the words from the box.

```
    useful ─┐                          dangerous ─┐
           ├─ HELPFUL ─┤                         ├─ HARMFUL ─┤
           │           │                         │           │
```

| advantageous | beneficial | damaging | ~~dangerous~~ | destructive | detrimental |
| gainful | hazardous | injurious | ~~useful~~ | profitable | valuable |

B For each group of words, cross out the word that does not belong.

1. diverse — similar — various — mixed — assorted
2. divergent — mutual — shared — common — communal
3. symbiosis — mutualism — consumerism — parasitism — commensalism
4. secure — protect — defend — endanger — guard
5. evaporation — transpiration — precipitation — distillation — magnification

C Complete the sentences using the best words from the above exercises.

1. The police officer was warned about _____ others.
2. The doctor warned you that smoking is _____ to your health.
3. Despite being twins, Mary and Sarah have _____ interests.
4. Rain, snow, sleet, and hail are the main types of _____.
5. If I had known how _____ the painting was, I would have kept it.
6. The soldiers had to _____ the perimeter once they invaded the building.
7. When two species are _____ to each other, their relationship is mutualistic.
8. The enormous _____ power of the hurricane swept the entire area of Lousiana.
9. In _____, one species benefits but the other neither benefits nor is harmed.
10. Water in the air comes from _____ from bodies of water such as rivers and oceans.

Academic Reading Builder

3

Answer Book

Contents

Anthropology
Basic Knowledge Building — 4
Unit 01 The Hohokam — 6
Unit 02 Clovis Culture — 7
Vocabulary Expansion — 8

Business
Basic Knowledge Building — 8
Unit 03 Types of Advertising Appeals — 10
Unit 04 Product Pricing Policies — 11
Vocabulary Expansion — 12

Genetics
Basic Knowledge Building — 12
Unit 05 Gregor Johann Mendel — 14
Unit 06 Stem Cell Research — 15
Vocabulary Expansion — 16

Political Science
Basic Knowledge Building — 17
Unit 07 Tyranny in Ancient Greece — 19
Unit 08 The Patricians and the Plebeians of Republican Rome — 20
Vocabulary Expansion — 21

Geography
Basic Knowledge Building — 21
Unit 09 Greenland — 23
Unit 10 The Mississippi River and Its Dams — 24
Vocabulary Expansion — 25

Mass Communication	Basic Knowledge Building	26
	Unit 11 Joseph Pulitzer	28
	Unit 12 The History of Magazines	29
	Vocabulary Expansion	30

Psychology	Basic Knowledge Building	30
	Unit 13 Howard Gardner and Multiple Intelligences	32
	Unit 14 Behaviorism, Cognitivism, and Constructivism	33
	Vocabulary Expansion	34

Economics	Basic Knowledge Building	35
	Unit 15 John Ruskin	37
	Unit 16 The Theory of Marginal Utility	38
	Vocabulary Expansion	39

Law	Basic Knowledge Building	39
	Unit 17 Major Legal Systems	41
	Unit 18 The Code of Hammurabi	42
	Vocabulary Expansion	43

Ecology	Basic Knowledge Building	43
	Unit 19 Keystone Species	45
	Unit 20 Mutualism *vs.* Commensalism	46
	Vocabulary Expansion	47

Anthropology 인류학

Basic Knowledge Building

1. 네안데르탈인

네안데르탈인은 멸종한 초기 인류 종이라고 생각된다. 하지만 일부 전문가들은 이 의견에 동의하지 않고 그들을 전부 별개의 종으로 간주한다. 네안데르탈인은 20만 년에서 2만8천 년 전 사이에 유럽 지역에서 살았고 지금은 멸종 상태다. 그들은 몸집이 다부지고 튼튼했고 현대 인류와 마찬가지로 직립보행을 했다. 뇌의 용량은 오늘날의 호모 사피엔스 사피엔스와 비슷하다. 화석에서 나온 증거들을 볼 때 네안데르탈인은 원시적인 석기를 사용했다. 대개 동굴에 살았으며 요리와 난방에 불을 이용했다. 또한 사냥에 능했다. 일부 전문가들은 그들이 원시적인 언어를 사용했을 가능성이 있다고 주장한다.

Q. T☐ F☑

> extinct 멸종한 disagree 동의하지 않다 stumpy 땅딸막한
> fossil 화석   primitive 원시적인

2. 신석기 혁명

신석기 혁명은 인류 역사상 최초의 농업혁명이었다. 그것은 초기 인류의 생활방식에 변화를 초래했다. 이 시기 동안 사람들은 사냥과 채집 생활을 버리고 정착 생활을 하며 영구적인 생활방식을 택했다. 신석기 혁명은 점진적인 사건이었다. 그것은 아시아, 유럽, 아프리카의 여러 지역에서 발생했다. 첫 발생 시기는 기원전 약 8천 년에서 3천 년 사이였다. 농업과 동물 사육이 두 가지 새로운 유행이 되었다. 마을과 도시들이 생겨나기 시작하고 인구가 급증했다. 고대 사회는 보다 복잡해지기 시작했다. 신석기 시대의 다른 중요한 특징으로는 석기의 사용, 직조, 도기 등이 있다.

Q. T☑ F☐

> agricultural 농업의   domestication 사육, 길들이기
> permanent 영구적인   gradual 점진적인   surge 급등하다

3. 고대 이집트의 달력

고대 이집트의 달력은 여러 모로 현대의 달력과 비슷하다. 우선, 1년이 365일로 되어 있었다. 이 날들은 열두 달로 나뉘어졌다. 각 달은 열흘씩 세 시기로 구분되었다. 연말이면 5일을 더했다. 처음에는 달에 그냥 숫자를 매겼다. 나중에 중왕국 무렵에는 농사철에 따라 여러 달을 묶어서 이름을 붙였다. 이집트의 1년은 침수기, 성장기, 수확기의 세 계절로 나뉘어졌다. 초기 이집트인들은 농사를 지었기 때문에 나일강이 생활의 중심이었다. 자연히 달력은 나일강의 주기를 반영했다. 이 역법은 기원전 238년까지 사용되었다.

Q. T☑ F☐

> divide 나누다 span (짧은) 기간 inundation 침수 harvest 수확
> reflect 반영하다

4. 수메르 문명

수메르인들은 인류 역사상 최초의 문명을 이룬 것으로 여겨진다. 그들은 남부 메소포타미아 즉 지금의 이라크 남부지역과 이란 남서부 지역에 해당되는 지역에 살았다. 전문가들은 이 문명이 기원전 5천 년과 4천 년 사이에 시작되었다고 믿는다. 체계가 잘 잡힌 그들 사회의 기반은 도시국가였다. 도시국가들은 어떤 때는 연합했다가 다른 때는 별개로 움직였다. 수메르인들은 주로 농사를 지어 생계를 이어갔다. 그래서 그들은 최초의 수로와 관개시설을 만들었다. 또한 금속세공에도 능했다. 수메르인들의 또 다른 중요한 발명품으로는 설형문자가 있다. 그것은 초기 형태의 문자였다. 기호를 점토판에 찍어 정보를 기록하고 전달했다. 수메르인들은 기원전 18세기경에 바빌로니아인들에게 흡수되었다.

Q. T☐ F☑

> civilization 문명 rely on ~에 의존하다 irrigation 관개
> thrive 번성하다 absorb 흡수하다

5. 클로비스 문화

고고학자들은 약 1만3천 년 전에 북아메리카 지역에 클로비스인들이 살았다고 생각한다. 그들은 아마도 대륙에 정착한 최초의 인류였을 것이다. 그들의 문화는 1930년대에 뉴멕시코에서 클로비스 공예품이 발견되면서 알려졌다. 클로비스 유적지에서 발견된 흔한 공예품은 클로비스 촉이다. 이것은 창에 쓰이는 뾰족한 부싯돌 상단부이다. 클로비스 촉을 보면 클로비스인들이 들소와 매머드 같은 덩치 큰 동물들을 사냥했다는 것을 알 수 있다. 그래서 전문가들은 클로비스인들 때문에 매머드가 멸종했다고 생각한다. 클로비스 문화는 약 500년 남짓 번성했던 것으로 추정된다. 그 후에는 아마도 다른 지역 민족들이 클로비스인들을 대체했을 것이다.

Q. T☐ F☑

> artifact 공예품 flint 부싯돌 spear 창 extinction 멸종
> estimate 추정하다

6. 스톤헨지

스톤헨지는 잉글랜드 남부에 있는 고대의 돌덩이들이다. 이 선사시대 거석은 아마도 오랜 기간을 두고 여러 단계에 걸쳐 세워졌을 것이다. 고고학자들은 첫 단계가 기원전 약 3,000년경 시작하여 기원전 1,600년경 끝이 났을 것으로 추정한다. 그 돌들은 동심원 모양으로 배열되어 있다. 스톤헨지는 현대 인류가 지닌 커다란 수수께끼 가운데 하나다. 누가 스톤헨지를 세웠는지 아무도 모른다. 더욱이, 정확한 건설 사유도 여전히 논란거리이다. 하지만 숭배 장소였다는 것이 일반적인 이론이다. 현대에 이루어진 발굴에 따르면 그것은 분명히 한때 매장지로 사용되었다. 또 다른 생각은 고대에 태양과 달을 관찰하는 관측소로 사용되었다는 것이다.

Q. T☐ F☑

> prehistoric 선사시대의 megalith 거석 archeologist 고고학자
> concentric 동심원의 excavation 발굴 observatory 관측소

7. 올멕인

올멕인은 고대 멕시코인이다. 그들은 중앙아메리카 남부에 살았다. 고고학자들은 그들이 기원전 1300년과 400년 사이에 존재했다고 믿는다. 현대의 유적지를 보면 그들은 강을 따라 살거나 거대한 평원에 살았다. 올멕인이 뛰어난 어부들이었다는 증거가 존재한다. 그들은 또한 조각에도 능했다. 애용했던 두 가지 재료는 옥과 현무암이었다. 거대한 의식용 두상들이 오늘날까지 남아 있다. 그들 중 일부는 무게가 수십 톤이나 나간다. 올멕인은 또한 거대한 의식용 고분과 피라미드도 주거지에 건설했다. 그들은 미래의 중앙아메리카 문명을 위한 광범위한 문화적 기반을 마련했다.

Q. T ☑ F ☐

> archaeologist 고고학자 adept 숙련된 ceremonial 의식의
> mound 고분 civilization 문명

8. 아나사지 문화

아나사지는 현대 푸에블로 인디언들의 초기 조상이다. 그들은 미국의 포 코너스 지역에 살았는데, 이곳은 콜로라도, 유타, 뉴멕시코, 애리조나 주가 만나는 건조한 지역이다. 아나사지라는 말은 나바호어로 "고대인"이라는 뜻이다. 아나사지 문화는 일반적으로 2천년 전에 시작된 것으로 추정된다. 일부 전문가들은 그보다 훨씬 일찍 시작되었을 것으로 추정한다. 최초의 아나사지인은 진흙과 벽돌로 지어진 움집에 살았다. 문화가 발달하면서 절벽과 협곡의 벽을 파서 정교한 주거지를 만들기 시작했다. 처음에 아나사지인은 수렵 채집 생활을 했다. 하지만 나중에는 옥수수, 호박, 콩 등을 키우기 시작했다. 정교한 바구니와 도자기, 장신구, 도구도 만들었다. 그런 건조한 사막 지역에서 그들이 생존했다는 것은 놀랍다. 그것을 볼 때 그들은 결연하고 창조적인 초기의 아메리카 민족이었다.

Q. T ☐ F ☑

> ancestor 조상 elaborate 정교한 initially 처음에
> ornament 장신구 remarkable 놀라운

9. 스키타이인

스키타이인은 흩어져 사는 유목민족이었다. 그들은 러시아 남부에 살았다. 그들은 기원이 확실하지 않지만 아마도 기원전 7세기부터 기원전 1세기까지 존재했을 것이다. 그들의 사회는 말을 중심으로 이루어졌던 것으로 보인다. 그들은 말을 다루는 데 능숙했고 말을 사용해 적을 정복하고 위협했다. 스키타이 여성들 역시 남성과 마찬가지로 말을 타고 전사로서 싸움에 임했다고 한다. 일부 전문가들은 심지어 스키타이인들이 말을 탄 최초의 민족이었다고 믿는다. 말이 있었기에 그리스인을 비롯한 다른 문화와 민족을 개척하고 조우할 수 있었다. 오늘날 우리가 스키타이인에 관해 알고 있는 많은 것이 그리스 역사가인 헤로도토스 덕분이다.

Q. T ☑ F ☐

> disorganized 조직화되지 않은 nomadic 유목의
> intimidate 위협하다 explore 개척하다, 탐험하다
> attribute ~의 덕분으로 돌리다

10. 프레몬트 문화

프레몬트인들은 오늘날 미국 땅에 해당되는 유타, 콜로라도, 아이다호 지역에 살았다. 그들의 문화는 700년에서 1250년 사이에 절정을 이뤘다. 그들은 아나사지인들과 비슷한 점이 많았다. 예를 들어, 처음에는 수렵 채취 생활을 하고 움집에 살며 옥수수를 주식으로 삼았다. 가혹한 동절기를 버틸 식량을 저장하기 위해 곡물창고를 만드는 지혜도 있었다. 또한 공예품도 만들었다. 흔한 공예품으로는 도자기와 그림문자가 있다. 프레몬트 그림문자는 주로 바위나 동굴 벽에 사람 형상으로 전해진다. 프레몬트 문화는 1250년과 1500년 사이에 자취를 감추었다. 기후가 원인이었을 수도 있다. 아니면 다른 종족이 프레몬트인을 내몰았을 수도 있다.

Q. T ☑ F ☐

> similarity 유사성 granary 곡물 창고 pictograph 상형문자
> vanish 자취를 감추다 displace 쫓아내다

11. 잉카 문명

잉카인은 남아메리카에 살았던 고대 민족이다. 그들은 12세기에서 16세기까지 번성했다. 그들의 위대한 제국은 에콰도르에서 칠레 북부까지 산악지대에 걸쳐 있었다. 잉카제국은 서로 연계해 있는 독자적인 부족들로 이루어져 있었다. 각 부족에는 부족장을 정점으로 한 엄격한 위계질서가 있었다. 따라서 잉카제국은 통합적인 단일 민족으로 이루어진 부족 연합국 이상이었다. 잉카인들은 타고난 농부이자 기술자였다. 그들은 도로를 건설하고 산지 농업을 위한 독창적인 테라스식 경작지를 만들었다. 또한 안데스 산맥에 터널과 다리를 건설했다. 고대 잉카 도시인 마추픽추의 유적은 페루의 8천 피트 고도에 여전히 존재하고 있다. 안타깝게도, 잉카문명은 1531년 프란시스코 피사로가 이끄는 스페인 정복자들에게 짓밟혔다.

Q. T ☑ F ☐

> independent 독자적인 hierarchy 위계 confederation 연합국
> ingenious 독창적인 elevation 고도

12. 문화 전파

문화 전파란 사람들 사이에 문화적 특징의 이동이나 교류가 이루어지는 것을 일컫는 용어다. 교류는 개인 간에 일어날 수도 있고 문화 간에 일어날 수도 있다. 하지만 문화 전파는 사상에만 한정되지 않는다. 미술이나 음악처럼 새로운 모든 것이 대상이 될 수 있다. 흔히 문화 전파는 직간접적으로 이루어질 수 있다. 직접 전파는 두 문화가 서로 가까이 있을 때 일어난다. 무역과 같은 직접적인 접촉으로 두 문화가 융합된다. 간접 전파는 매개자나 매개국가가 새로운 특징들을 두 문화에 소개해서 일어난다. 오늘날은 인터넷이 간접적인 문화 전파를 촉진하는 주요 매개체이다.

Q. T ☐ F ☑

> diffusion 전파 transfer 이동하다 novel 새로운
> qualify 자격이 되다 blend 융합

Unit 01 The Hohokam

Thinking about the Topic
Answers can vary. It is best to elicit as many answers from students as possible.

Vocabulary Focus

B
1. sparse 드문, 희박한
2. decline 감소, 약화
3. ingenious 독창적인, 영리한
4. flourish 번창하다
5. drought 가뭄
6. irrigation 관개, 물 대기
7. vanish 사라지다
8. ample 풍부한
9. magnificent 웅장한, 화려한, 격조 높은
10. expansion 확장, 확대

호호캄인

호호캄인은 미국의 애리조나 남부의 강 유역에 살았던 고대 민족이다. 대다수 학자들은 그들이 기원전 300년경부터 기원후 1400년대까지 살았다는 데 의견이 일치한다. 그들은 아메리카 남서부에서 최초로 완전한 농경문화를 이루었다. 호호캄인들은 또한 건축과 공예에도 능했다. 그들은 독창적인 건축 기술을 사용해 거대한 다층 거주지를 만들었다. 약 800년경 호호캄 문명은 중앙아메리카 남쪽의 마야 문명이나 아즈텍 문명과 같은 보다 잘 알려진 문명에 대적할 만큼 발전했다. 호호캄인들이 그렇게 오랜 기간 번성할 수 있었던 주요 이유 중의 하나는 훌륭한 관개시설이 있었기 때문이다.

단언, 호호캄인들이 이룬 가장 위대한 성과는 발달한 관개수로 시스템이었다. 대부분은 솔트 앤드 힐라강 유역에 건설되었다. 그들 중 일부는 대단히 커서 고대 중국과 이집트의 수로에 필적할 만했다. 가장 큰 수로 중 하나는 길이가 24킬로미터, 폭이 10미터 이상이었다. 이러한 관개수로 덕분에 호호캄인들은 메마른 사막 지역에서도 번성할 수 있었다. 지속적인 물 공급과 풍부한 식량 덕분에 호호캄인들은 지역의 공동체를 거대한 도심지로 바꾸어 놓았다. 더 발전했을 때에는 옥수수, 콩, 호박, 면, 담배와 같은 다양한 작물들을 키웠다.

호호캄 문화의 또 다른 특징으로는 구기 경기장이 있다. 그것은 다른 호호캄 공동체들이 서로 화합하고 의식을 치르는 중요한 장소였다. 일부 공동체에는 대규모 구기 경기장이 있어서 의식적 경기를 치르는 데 사용되었다. 서로 다른 지역에서 온 두 팀이 경기를 해 거대한 돌이나 고무로 된 공을 목표 지점까지 굴렸다. 안타깝게도, 경기의 정확한 규칙은 오늘날 알려져 있지 않다. 구기 경기장은 거래와 모임 장소로도 이용되었다. 호호캄인들은 구기 경기장에 모여 농사 계획을 짜고 미래의 확장 계획도 짰다. 또한 그들은 아나사지인이나 모골론인들과 같은 인근 부족들뿐만 아니라 멕시코 중부의 인디언과 무역을 하기도 했다.

호호캄 문화는 1150년경에 몰락의 길로 들어서기 시작했다. 여러 해에 걸쳐 보다 많은 유적지가 건설되는 대신 버려졌다. 1300년경 대부분의 관개 시설들은 환경적인 한계에 다다랐다. 어쩌면 이것이 다음 100년 동안 이 문화가 완전히 자취를 감춘 원인이었을지 모르지만, 확실한 이유는 여전히 의문으로 남아 있다. 하지만 어떤 문명의 생존이 수자원에 완전히 의존할 경우 가뭄이나 지나친 관개는 문명이 급속하게 몰락하는 원인이 될 수 있다.

canal 운하, 수로

Reading Comprehension

1 (B) 2 (A) 3 (C) 4 ① Two teams competed with each other by moving a stone or rubber ball to a goal. ② The rules and procedure of the game are not known. 5 (D) 6 (C)

Organizing & Summarizing

A
1. Aztecs & Mayans
2. water supply issues
3. long, large canals
4. maize, beans, squash, cotton & tobacco
5. ball games
6. Anasazi & Mogollon

B
1. 300 B.C. to about 1400 A.D.
2. the Mayans and Aztecs
3. irrigation systems and ball courts
4. team competitions
5. rituals and trade
6. water supply issues

호호캄인들은 기원전 300년부터 기원후 약 1400년까지 아메리카 남서부의 사막 지역에 살았다. 그들은 건축과 기술 분야에 능한 것으로 잘 알려져 있다. 문명이 전성기를 맞았을 때 그들은 마야 문명이나 아즈텍 문명과 같은 당시의 다른 발달한 문명에 필적했다. 호호캄인들의 가장 위대한 업적 가운데 두 가지는 관개시설과 구기 경기장이다. 그들은 길고 거대한 관개시설을 건설하여 모진 사막 기후에서도 살아남아 번성할 수 있었다. 아마도 관개시설은 중국이나 이집트인의 관개시설과 어깨를 견주었을 것이다. 구기 경기장은 팀 경기에 사용되었다. 또한 다른 마을끼리 모여서 의식을 치르거나 무역을 하기도 했다. 미래의 합동 농사 계획이나 확장을 위한 계획을 짜기도 했을 것이다. 호호캄인들은 또한 아나사지인과 같은 다른 인디언 부족들과 구기 경기장에서 무역을 하기도 했다. 하지만 호호캄인들은 갑자기 자취를 감추었다. 일부 학자들은 그것이 물 공급 문제 때문이라고 보고 있다.

Unit 02 Clovis Culture

Thinking about the Topic
Answers can vary. It is best to elicit as many answers from students as possible.

Vocabulary Focus

B
1 monstrous 거대한
2 seal 끝내다, 마감하다
3 terrain 땅; 토양
4 well-preserved 잘 보존된
5 utensil 용기, 그릇
6 migrate 이동하다, 이주하다
7 marshy 습지의, 늪의, 질퍽한
8 hypothesis 가설, 가정
9 pursuit 추적, 추구
10 collapse 무너지다, 붕괴하다

클로비스 문화

클로비스인은 마지막 빙하기 말기인 약 13,500년 전에 북아메리카에 최초로 등장한 선사시대 팔레오인디언이었다. 그들의 문화는 1932년 일부 공예품이 뉴멕시코 주의 클로비스 근처에서 발견되면서 고고학자들에게 처음으로 알려지게 되었다. 이 때문에 그들은 지금 클로비스인이라고 불린다. 오늘날에는, 그들이 북아메리카뿐만 아니라 중앙아메리카에서도 살았다고 알려져 있다. 처음에 클로비스인들은 북아메리카에 살았던 최초의 민족으로 여겨졌다. 그러나 최근 들어 클로비스인보다 더 오래된 민족들이 있었던 것으로 밝혀졌다.

클로비스인이 어떻게 북아메리카에 도달하고 그들이 어디에서 왔는지는 아직까지도 논란이 많다. 한 가지 이론에 따르면 그들은 알래스카 지역에 살다가 식량을 찾아 남쪽으로 이동했다. 또 다른 가설에 따르면 클로비스인의 조상이 남아메리카에서 왔다고 한다. 학자들은 클로비스 문화와 특징이 비슷한 클로비스 시대 이전의 유적지가 브라질과 칠레에 있다고 지적한다. 보다 최근에는 클로비스인이 유럽에서 배를 타고 그린란드에서 뉴욕까지 펼쳐졌던 빙판의 가장자리를 따라 북아메리카로 왔다는 주장도 등장했다. 하지만 이 가운데 어떤 이론도 고고학자들이 전폭적으로 받아들이지는 않는다.

보존 상태가 양호한 다양한 공예품들을 보면 클로비스인의 생활을 알 수 있다. 여러 유적지에서 발굴된 증거 중에는 클로비스촉이라는 이름이 붙은, 홈이 파인 돌촉도 있다. 아마도 창 끝에 붙여서 큰 동물을 사냥하는 데 썼을 것이다. 유적지에서 발굴된 클로비스촉의 대다수는 길이가 1인치에서 5인치 사이이다. 비교적 큰 촉들은 엄청나게 큰 마스토돈과 매머드 같은 큰 짐승을 사냥하는 데 필요했다. 이 거대한 짐승들은 한 마리만 잡아도 큰 부족 전체가 한 달 동안 먹을 식량이 해결되었기 때문에 선호되었다. 고기뿐만 아니라 클로비스인은 뼈와 엄니, 가죽을 이용해 집을 짓고 조리기구와 다른 무기를 만들었다. 클로비스인은 사냥감이 물을 먹을 수 있는 늪지대에 모여 있을 때 매복 사냥을 했을 것이다. 토양이 물러서 동물들이 움직이기가 쉽지 않았을 것이다.

대체적으로 클로비스 문화는 약 5백 년 동안 지속되었으리라고 추정된다. 그들은 매머드와 마찬가지로 흔적도 없이 갑자기 사라진 것 같다. 수많은 이론들이 그들이 갑자기 사라진 이유를 설명하고자 했다. 한 가지는 매머드와 직접 관련이 있다. 클로비스인이 매머드와 다른 큰 사냥감들을 과도하게 사냥한 나머지 주요 식량원을 사라지게 만들어서 자신의 운명마저도 끝장내 버렸다는 것이다. 하지만, 보다 그럴듯한 이론은 빙하기 이후의 기후 변화로 인해 환경의 전체적인 붕괴가 일어났다는 것이다.

> vanish without a trace 흔적도 없이 사라지다

Reading Comprehension

1 (A)   2 (C)   3 (D)   4 ① They hunted the mastodon and the mammoth. ② They ate the meat from the big game and used the bones, tusks, and skin for tools and shelters.   5 (A)   6 (B)

Organizing & Summarizing

A
1 around 13,500 years ago
2 over-hunting
3 sudden climate change
4 from Alaska
5 from Europe   6 stone spear tips
7 ambush hunting   8 bones & tusks

B
1 about 13,500 years ago
2 from Europe to Greenland
3 the bones and ivory
4 mastodons and mammoths
5 Clovis points
6 due to over-hunting

클로비스인은 약 13,500년 전에 북아메리카에 살았던 고대 팔레오인디언이다. 하지만 기원은 분명치 않다. 일부 전문가들은 그들이 알래스카 지방에서 남쪽으로 이동했을 것으로 본다. 다른 이들은 그들이 유럽에서 배를 타고 빙하를 따라 그린란드를 거쳐 마침내 대륙으로 이동했을 것이라고 생각한다. 클로비스인의 생활은 큰 사냥감을 사냥하는 것이 주를 이루었다. 한 마리만 사냥해도 그 고기로 전체 부족이 거의 한 달간 먹을 수 있었다. 가죽으로는 집을 만들고 뼈와 엄니를 이용해 도구를 만들었다. 그들은 돌촉으로 된 창과 매복 사냥 기술로 마스토돈과 매머드를 잡았다. 클로비스촉이라고 불리는 이 창촉들은 가

장 잘 보존된 클로비스 문화 공예품이다. 클로비스인은 약 5백 년간 존재하다가 갑자기 자취를 감추었다. 확실한 이유는 알려지지 않았다. 하지만 일부 전문가들은 과도한 사냥 때문이었을 것으로 본다. 다른 이들은 환경에 끔찍한 영향을 미친 급격한 기후 변화가 원인이라고 본다.

Vocabulary Expansion

Part A

Ⓐ **AGRICULTURAL:** crop, irrigation, livestock, maize, pesticide, soil
INDUSTRIAL: banking, coal, commerce, railroad, steam, steel

Ⓑ
1 tool   2 disappearance
3 bone   4 pottery   5 dry

Ⓓ
1 needle   2 commerce   3 steel
4 banking   5 crops   6 ankle
7 extinction   8 dehydrated   9 vase
10 irrigation

Part B

Ⓐ **SOUTH AMERICA:** Argentina, Chile, Columbia, Paraguay, Peru, Venezuela
CENTRAL AMERICA: Costa Rica, El Salvador, Guatemala, Honduras, Nicaragua, Panama

Ⓑ
1 concentric   2 appearance   3 surrender
4 temporary   5 clumsy

Ⓓ
1 Chile   2 experienced   3 expert
4 temporary   5 Panama   6 surrendered
7 concentric   8 clumsy   9 quality
10 elaborate

Business 비즈니스

Basic Knowledge Building

1. 새뮤얼 슬레이터

새뮤얼 슬레이터는 미국 직물업계의 아버지이다. 그는 1768년 잉글랜드에서 출생했다. 그곳에서 직물 제조 기술을 배웠다. 그 후 직물과 직물 기술에 대한 지식을 갖춘 채 미국으로 불법 이주했다. 오래지 않아 그는 1793년에 로드 아일랜드에서 최초의 면직물 방적공장을 만들었다. 이것은 미국 산업혁명의 시작으로 간주된다. 일단 사업에 발을 들여놓자 그는 수많은 방적공장을 세우고 부를 얻었다. 마침내는 뉴잉글랜드에 있는 모든 중소도시의 생활이 그가 지은 방적공장을 중심으로 돌아갔다. 슬레이터는 1835년에 숨을 거두었다.
Q. T☐ F☑

> textile 직물   illegally 불법으로   immigrate 이주하다
> establish 설립하다   revolve around ~을 중심으로 돌아가다

2. 미국 대륙횡단 철도

1869년 미국 최초의 대륙횡단 철도가 완공되어 동서를 연결했다. 그것은 미 서부의 인구 증가와 발전에 결정적 역할을 했다. 간선을 따라 급속한 경제 성장이 이루어졌다. 주들 간에 통상 교류가 늘면서 인구가 급증했다. 대륙횡단 철도는 서부의 천연자원과 동부 도시의 시장을 연결하는 중요한 구실을 했다. 서부에서 광물을 채굴해 동부의 공장으로 쉽게 운송했다. 철도 덕분에 미국은 거의 모든 면에서 재빨리 하나의 국가로 성장할 수 있었다.
Q. T☑ F☐

> transcontinental 대륙을 가로지르는   spawn ~을 생기게 하다
> witness 목격하다   commerce 통상, 상업   transport 운송하다

3. 지퍼

지퍼는 1890년 미국의 발명가이자 외판원이었던 위트콤 저드슨이 발명했다. 초기의 지퍼는 미끄럼식 여밈 장치 이상이었다. 저드슨은 1893년에 특허를 냈다. 투자자들이 그의 발명품에 주목하고 지원을 했기 때문에 그는 계속 수정과 개선 작업을 할 수 있었다. 지퍼는 1차 대전 때 병사들에게 처음 소개되었다. 덕분에 재킷과 조끼를 더 빨리 여밀 수 있었다. 하지만 대중에게는 1920년대가 되어서야 소개되었다. 지퍼의 모양은 여러 해에 걸쳐 계속 바뀌었다. 판매량도 증가했다. 오늘날 지퍼는 필통에서부터 청바지에 이르기까지 모든 분야에 사용된다.
Q. T☑ F☐

> slide 미끄럼   fastener 잠그는 기구, 여밈 장치   revise 수정하다
> improve 개선하다   tweak 미세 조정하다

4. 크레스 파이브 앤 다임즈

S.H. 크레스 공사는 1896년 새뮤얼 크레스가 설립했다. 그 회사는 미국 전역에 걸쳐 싸구려 잡화점 체인을 만들었다. 상점들은 저렴한 물건을 팔아 인기를 얻었다. 하지만 크레스 파이브 앤 다임즈 건물은 아름다운 미학적 요소도 지니고 있었다. 건물들은 멋지게 설계되고 꾸며졌다. 또한 종종 도심 상업 지구에 위치해 있었다. 미학적 요소와 쇼핑 공간이라는 두 가

지 요소가 고객들을 끌어들였다. 크레스의 주요 경쟁업체 가운데 한 곳이 울워스였는데, 이 회사 역시 성공적인 구멍가게 체인이다. 오늘날에는 쇼핑몰이 싸구려 잡화점이 누렸던 인기를 누리게 되었다. 하지만 많은 크레스 건물들이 여전히 새로운 점포나 사무실이 있는 도심 지역을 빛내 주고 있다.

Q. T☐ F☑

> found 설립하다 five-and-dime store 싸구려 잡화점
> exhibit 전시하다 aesthetics 미학 grace 빛나게 만들다

5. 미국의 초기 노동운동

미국에서 최초의 노동운동이 시작된 것은 19세기 말과 20세기 초였다. 최초의 노조 가운데 하나가 노동기사단이었다. 그것은 1869년에 조직되어 미국 전체 노동자의 복지를 위해 싸웠다. 하지만 구성원이 너무 다양해서 내부 갈등이 생긴 탓에 응집력이 부족했다. 오래지 않아 노동기사단의 인기는 시들해졌다. 또 다른 초기 노조로는 미국 노동총연맹이 있는데, 1886년에 창설되었다. 그것은 다양한 분야의 시간제 노동자들로 구성되었다. 그 조직은 더 나은 근로조건과 높은 임금을 얻고자 했다. 하지만 경영진은 대개 노동자들을 개인 단위로 다루는 쪽을 좋아했다. 파업과 시위가 자주 일어났다. 정부는 질서 유지를 위해 자주 군대를 동원해야 했다.

Q. T☐ F☑

> cohesion 응집력 diversity 다양성 conflict 갈등
> favor 편들다, 호의를 보이다 strike 파업

6. 과학적 관리법

과학적 관리법 즉 "테일러리즘"은 19세기 후반 강철 공장의 십장이었던 프레드 테일러가 개발했다. 테일러는 노동자의 생산성을 최대화하기 위해 이 시스템을 고안했다. 그는 공장의 작업을 가장 간단한 업무들로 나누고 그 업무를 최대의 효과를 얻을 수 있는 방법으로 배열했다. 그런 다음 숙련된 관리자들로 하여금 반숙련공과 미숙련공을 감독하게 했다. 이 방법 덕분에 시간은 절약되고 생산성이 향상되었다. 테일러리즘이 확산되면서 노동 현장은 대단히 엄격하게 관리되었다. 노동자들은 더 큰 압박을 받았다. 하지만 과학적 경영은 성공을 거두었다. 노동자들은 생산성이 늘어날 경우 포상금을 받았다. 테일러리즘은 전 세계적으로 많은 관리 체계에서 오늘날까지도 영향을 미치고 있다.

Q. T☑ F☐

> maximize 최대화하다 sequence 일정한 순서로 배열하다
> efficiency 효율성 regiment 엄격히 관리하다 incentive 포상

7. 순회관리

순회관리(MBWA)란 1940년대에 휴렛 팩커드사의 창업자가 처음 고안해낸 개념이다. 그것은 관리자의 현장 중심 관리법을 강조한다. 관리자는 노동자들의 눈에 띄어야 하고 노동자들이 다가갈 수 있어야 한다. 의견뿐 아니라 질문도 받을 수 있어야 한다. 또한 순회관리는 실제로 개별 노동자가 하는 일을 실제로 수행할 줄 아는 관리자를 선호한다. 직접 대면을 통한 대화가 메모나 팩스, 이메일, 심지어 회의보다도 중요하다. 결국, 이러한 일대일 대응법이 노동자들로부터 흔히 더 많은 기여를 유도해낼 수 있다. 순회관리는 경영진과 직원 사이의 종종 위협적이기까지 한 관계를 해소하려는 시도이다.

Q. T☑ F☐

> emphasize 강조하다 accessible 접근 가능한 perform 수행하다
> dissolve 해소하다 intimidating 위협적인

8. 버즈 마케팅

버즈 마케팅은 판매를 촉진하거나 제품 인지도를 높이기 위해 사용되는 마케팅 기법이다. 그것은 기존의 사회적 조건에 기초를 둔다. 다시 말해, 고객들로 하여금 특정 제품에 대한 긍정적 반응을 퍼뜨리도록 하는 것이다. 이러한 의미에서, 그것은 입소문과 아주 비슷하다. 하지만 인터넷과 포드캐스트 같은 오늘날의 기술을 이용해서도 긍정적인 반응을 바이러스처럼 퍼뜨릴 수 있다. 이런 경우에는 바이러스 마케팅이라고 부른다. 예를 들어, 마케팅 전문가들은 특정한 사람들이나 집단을 대상으로 삼아 유혹적인 광고로 그들을 "감염"시키고자 한다. 일단 소수 목표 고객이 감염되면 그 무리 내에서 광고가 퍼져나갈 수 있다. 오늘날 버즈 마케팅 또는 바이러스 마케팅 기법은 여전히 영화에서부터 음악에 이르기까지 다양한 회사들이 사용하고 있다.

Q. T☐ F☑

> boost 촉진하다, 끌어올리다 awareness 인식, 인지도
> positive 긍정적인 infect 감염시키다 enticing 유혹적인

9. 시장 세분화

시장 세분화란 일종의 비즈니스 전략이다. 대규모 시장을 보다 작은 규모로 쪼갠다. 각각의 소규모 집단에 있는 소비자들은 인구통계학적 공통점이 있다. 예를 들어, 비슷한 또래이거나 성별이 같다. 교육과 소득 수준도 마케팅 전문가들이 고려하는 다른 특징들이다. 시장 세분화는 고객의 필요를 이해하는 데 도움이 되는 도구이다. 이 방법의 이점으로는 신상품 아이디어를 들 수 있다. 또 다른 이점은 세분화되고 더 폭넓은 인구 집단에서 시장점유율이 늘어난다는 것이다. 회사들은 심지어 소비자를 대상으로 여론조사를 하기도 한다. 이를 통해 소비자들의 구체적인 필요를 파악할 수 있다. 또한 궁극적으로 소비자의 충실도를 끌어올릴 수 있다.

Q. T☑ F☐

> segmentation 세분화 split 쪼개다 demographic 인구통계학적인
> poll 여론 조사를 하다 loyalty 충실도

10. 프랜차이징

프랜차이즈는 일종의 비즈니스이다. 모회사 또는 프랜차이저가 개인이나 가맹점에게 제품을 판매할 수 있는 권리를 준

다. 프랜차이즈 가맹점은 흔히 해당 사업 및 브랜드를 위한 특수교육을 받는다. 또한 가맹점은 시장에서 브랜드 인지도를 얻는다. 광고 역시 가맹점에게 주어지는 또 다른 혜택이다. 일반적으로 프랜차이저가 광고 비용을 댄다. 프랜차이징은 미국에서 인기 있는 사업 모델이 되었다. 코카콜라와 버거킹 같은 회사들이 크게 성공한 예이다. 오늘날 많은 프랜차이즈들이 전세계적으로 인정받고 있다. 패스트푸드와 음료 회사를 넘어 의류산업 등에 이르기까지 영역이 크게 확장되었다.

Q. T ☐ F ☑

> grant 주다 license 허가 recognition 인지도 benefit 혜택
> fund 자금을 대다

11. 회사 소유 형태

회사 소유권에는 협동조합, 주식회사, 합자회사, 개인회사의 네 가지 유형이 일반적이다. 협동조합은 개인들이 모인 집단이다. 그들은 한데 모여 회사를 차린다. 그 이유는 혼자서 사업을 시작하는 것보다 성공할 확률이 크기 때문이다. 오늘날에는 농업 분야에서 가장 일반적이다. 주식회사는 주주들이 구성하는 법인체이다. 그들은 주식회사에서 이익을 얻을 수 있다. 하지만 손실에 대해서는 책임지지 않는다. 사업을 관리하기 위해 경영진을 뽑는다. 동업회사는 두 사람 이상이 맺는 계약이다. 그들은 한 사업을 공동 소유한다. 마지막으로, 개인회사는 한 사람이 회사를 소유하고 이익을 내기 위해 회사를 경영하는 경우이다. 이것은 비즈니스에서 가장 흔한 경우이다.

Q. T ☐ F ☑

> agricultural 농업의 sector 분야, 부문 legal entity 법인체
> oversee 감독하다 contract 계약

12. 전자출판

전자출판은 글을 디지털로 발행하는 것을 말한다. 기사나 전자책, 심지어는 도서관 전체를 이 방식으로 발행할 수 있다. 인터넷과 함께 DVD, CD 등이 흔한 전자출판 수단이다. 전자출판의 한 가지 이점은 신문에 비해 보다 빨리 독자에게 다가갈 수 있다는 것이다. 하지만 일부 전자출판물은 결국 지면으로 인쇄된다. 또 다른 이점은 보다 환경친화적이라는 점이다. 종이를 덜 쓸수록 펄프를 덜 사용하게 되고 숲 전체를 구할 수도 있다. 마지막으로, 전자출판은 아주 작은 공간에 엄청난 양의 정보를 저장할 수 있다. 그래서, 판매자는 서점이나 도서관보다 한결 더 많은 읽을 거리를 제공할 수 있다. 이것은 절판본이나 희귀본에 없어서는 안 될 소중한 존재다.

Q. T ☑ F ☐

> electronic 전자의 publish 발행하다, 출판하다 vendor 판매자
> invaluable 매우 귀중한 out-of-print 절판된, 인쇄되지 않는

Unit 03 Types of Advertising Appeals

Thinking about the Topic
Answers can vary. It is best to elicit as many answers from students as possible.

Vocabulary Focus

B 1 covert 감추어진, 비밀의
2 annoyance 골칫거리, 성가신 것
3 dictate 영향을 주다; 명령하다
4 standby 대역
5 associate 연관 짓다, 관련시키다
6 coincidence 우연
7 subtle 미묘한
8 encompass 둘러싸다; 포함하다
9 intrusion 침범, 침해
10 unwarranted 부당한, 불필요한

광고 소구의 종류

광고는 비즈니스에서 중요한 요소이다. 광고가 성공하면 회사는 기록적인 생산과 이익을 기대할 수 있다. 하지만 지루한 광고는 제품이나 회사를 망칠 수도 있다. 지난 15년간 인터넷은 브랜드 마케팅과 인지도에서 완전히 새로운 가능성을 열었다. 하지만 그렇다고 해서 이전의 광고 대체물들이 더 이상 소용이 없다는 것은 아니다. 미디어는 많은 대기업들에게 여전히 중요한 역할을 하는 광고 소구의 유형이다. 그것이 모든 광고의 대부분을 차지한다. 다른 광고 소구로는 간접광고와 옥외광고를 들 수 있다.

미디어 광고는 마케팅에서 크고 다양한 영역을 포괄한다. 방송광고에는 텔레비전과 라디오가 있다. 인쇄광고는 대개 신문이나 잡지에 실린다. 방송매체에는 기업들이 특정 텔레비전이나 라디오 방송에 광고를 내기 돈을 지불한다. 방송 시간의 길이뿐만 아니라 방송사와 프로그램의 인기도가 광고비를 결정한다. 마찬가지로, 기업은 잡지의 광고 지면을 살 수도 있다. 역시, 광고의 크기와 인쇄 매체의 판매부수가 광고비를 결정한다. 텔레비전 프로그램과 인쇄 매체는 특정 부류의 시청자와 독자를 끌어들이기 때문에 기업은 신속하게 특정 고객층을 겨냥해서 제품을 마케팅 할 수 있다.

간접광고와 옥외광고도 여전히 소비자의 소비에 영향을 미친다. 우선, 간접광고는 영화에서 가장 흔히 쓰인다. 그것은 보다 미묘한 광고 형태이다. 예를 들어, 영화의 어떤 장면에서 유명한 배우가 코카콜라를 마신다. 이것은 결코 우연이 아니다. 코카콜라 회사는 이 장면에서 제품이 나오도록 돈을 지불했다. 그리하여 잘하면 잠재고객이 그 음료를 배우와 연관 짓게 되고 코카콜라를 더 많이 구매하게 된다. 두 번째로, 옥외광고 역시 성공적인 광고기법이다. 전광판이 좋은 예이다. 하지만 기업들

은 버스나 택시의 옆면, 공원 벤치, 지하철, 운동장처럼 대중의 눈에 쉽게 띄는 다른 장소에도 회사 이름이나 제품을 광고한다.

인터넷은 보다 최근의 또 다른 광고 형태이다. 스팸메일과 웹사이트의 팝업창이 일반적인 방법이다. 하지만 일부가 성공적이고 믿을 수 있는 회사의 광고인 반면 대부분은 검증되지 않은 회사나 서비스여서 많은 인터넷 사용자들이 귀찮아 한다. 심지어 허락도 없이 뜨는 광고들을 차단해 주는 특수한 인터넷 도구까지 등장했다. 원치 않는 광고를 차단하는 것은 인쇄매체와 방송매체 같은 전통적인 광고에서는 어려운 일이다. 그래서 광고주는 수익의 많은 부분을 가장 인기 있는 오락과 정보를 제공하는 데에다 쓴다.

lackluster 지루한 billboard 대형 광고판

Reading Comprehension
1 (D)   2 (B)   3 (A)   4 Billboards are an example of outdoor advertisng.   5 (D)   6 (C)

Organizing & Summarizing
A
1 popularity, airtime & size
2 specific audiences
3 indirect marketing
4 star quality
5 consumer control
6 on billboards, on taxis, or in train stations

B
1 ad space or time
2 circulation size
3 social demographic
4 indirect marketing
5 their brand with superstars
6 often unavoidable

광고 소구에는 여러 종류가 있다. 미디어가 가장 큰 광고 형태이다. 미디어 광고를 하는 전형적인 매체로는 텔레비전과 신문, 잡지가 있다. 회사들은 인쇄 광고나 텔레비전 광고의 형태로 광고 지면이나 시간대를 산다. 광고비는 프로그램의 인기도와 판매부수에 따라 결정된다. 미디어 덕분에 회사는 특수한 사회 계층을 목표로 삼을 수 있다. 간접 광고 소구는 영화에서 흔히 볼 수 있는 일종의 우회적인 마케팅 형태이다. 기업은 제품을 영화 장면에 삽입한다. 이런 식으로 관객은 브랜드와 인기 배우를 연결 짓게 된다. 옥외광고는 대부분 전광판, 택시, 다른 공공 장소에서 볼 수 있다. 보다 최근에는 광고가 인터넷을 이용하게 되었다. 팝업 창이나 스팸메일도 유용한 방법이다. 이러한 광고를 차단하도록 설계된 도구까지 나왔다. 이것은 종종 피할 수 없었던 텔레비전이나 라디오 광고에 비해 소비자들이 누릴 수 있는 한 가지 이점이다.

Unit 04 Product Pricing Policies

Thinking about the Topic
Answers can vary. It is best to elicit as many answers from students as possible.

Vocabulary Focus
B
1 illegal 불법의
2 pitfall 위험, 함정
3 entice 유혹하다
4 monopoly 독점
5 bargain 헐값의, 매우 저렴한
6 react 반응하다, 응답하다
7 subside 줄어들다, 감소하다
8 assumption 가정, 추정
9 switch 바꾸다, 바뀌다
10 clientele 고객층

제품 가격 정책

가격 책정은 마케팅의 중요한 요소이며, 재화나 용역의 최종 가격은 흔히 심사숙고 끝에 결정된다. 경쟁업체와 이윤 목표치가 일반적인 고려사항이다. 하지만 가격 책정 전략의 종류 역시 성공적인 마케팅에 중요하다. 오늘날 사용되는 두 가지 가장 일반적인 전략은 스키밍 가격과 침투 가격이다.

가격 스키밍이란 시간을 두고 나중에 가격을 인하할 생각으로 초기에 가격을 높게 책정하는 것이다. 기업은 소비자가 수요와 관련해 지불하려고 하는 가장 높은 액수에 근거하여 가격을 매긴다. 다시 말해, 기업은 먼저 특정 재화나 용역에 대해 프리미엄을 지불하려는 소비자 집단을 목표로 삼는다. 일단 그 수요가 충족되어 사그러들면 다음 소비자 층에 맞춰 가격을 조정한다. 각 집단의 수요가 충족될 때까지 스키밍은 계속된다. 가격 스키밍은 특정한 상황에서 성공을 거둘 수 있다. 먼저, 높은 가격을 치르는 소비자의 수가 충분해야 한다. 둘째로, 높은 가격이 좋은 품질에 부응해야 한다. 가격 스키밍의 가장 큰 위험 가운데 하나는 경쟁이다. 종종 가격 스키밍은 시간이 걸리기 때문에 경쟁업체가 더 저렴한 가격에 해당 제품을 모방하거나 대체품을 내놓는다. 이러한 경쟁은 제품의 이윤 구조에 상당한 영향을 미친다.

대조적으로, 침투 가격은 스키밍 가격의 정반대이다. 이 전략을 쓰는 회사는 재화나 용역의 가격을 처음에 낮게 책정한다. 새로운 고객을 끌어들이려는 의도이다. 침투 가격은 경쟁력 있는 가격 때문에 소비자들이 브랜드를 바꿀 것이라는 가정에 기초하고 있다. 처음에는, 이윤을 희생해서 새로운 고객 확보한다. 이로 인해 기업은 경쟁업체가 대응을 하기 전에 시장에서 우위를 점할 수 있다. 처음부터 비용 관리를 하기 때문에 침투 가격은 대단히 효율적이다. 하지만 이 전략은 약점도 있다. 가장 위험한 점 가운데 하나가 이미지이다. 소비자들은 그

기업을 저가와 연결시킨다. 이러한 이미지 때문에 나중에 시장에서 더 경쟁력 있는 수준으로 가격을 올리기가 어렵다.

어떤 시장 환경에서는, 침투 가격과 스키밍 가격 둘 다 성공할 수 있다. 하지만 둘 다 법을 잘 지켜야 한다. 스키밍의 경우 기업은 '가격 차별화'를 하지 않도록 주의해야 한다. 일부 국가에서는 그것이 불법이다. 마찬가지로, 극단적인 침투 가격도 '약탈적 가격'이 될 수 있으며, 이것 역시 많은 국가에서 불법으로 간주된다. 약탈적 가격은 다른 경쟁업체들이 시장에 진출하지 못하도록 막기 때문에 해당 기업의 독점이 생길 수 있다.

price discrimination 가격 차별   predatory pricing 약탈적 가격 책정

Reading Comprehension

1 (C)   2 (B)   3 (D)   4 ① Extreme penetration pricing is called predatory pricing. ② It can create a monopoly.
5 (C)   6 (A)

Organizing & Summarizing

Ⓐ 1 pay the most
    2 maximizes profit
    3 new customers
    4 price discrimination
    5 cheap prices & low quality
    6 predatory pricing

Ⓑ 1 on the high end
    2 maximize profits
    3 time-consuming
    4 on the bargain end
    5 low prices
    6 a monopoly

기업들이 사용하는 두 가지 주요 제품 가격 정책은 스키밍 가격과 침투 가격이다. 가격 스키밍에서는 그 가격을 지불할 의사가 있는 기존 소비자에 맞추어 가격을 높이 책정한다. 가격이 높다는 것은 일반적으로 재화나 용역의 품질이 좋다는 것을 의미한다. 그런 다음, 시간을 두고 가격을 단계적으로 내린다. 이상적으로는, 기업이 스키밍을 통해 이윤을 극대화할 수 있다. 하지만 몇 가지 약점이 있다. 한 가지는 시간이 많이 걸린다는 것이다. 이로 인해 경쟁업체가 시장에 진출해 전략을 약화시킨다. 또 다른 약점은 흔히 불법으로 간주되는 가격 차별화를 들 수 있다. 가격 침투는 스키밍과는 정반대의 심리를 이용한다. 처음에 가격을 아주 낮게 책정해서 새로운 고객을 끌어들인다. 처음에는 이윤이 중요하지 않다. 그러나 시간이 지나면 가격이 인상된다. 하지만 기업의 이미지에 문제가 생길 수 있다. 소비자들은 항상 기업을 싸구려와 동일시한다. 더욱이, 침투 가격은 독점으로 이어지는 약탈적 가격이 될 수도 있다. 이것은 또 다른 불법 행위이다.

Vocabulary Expansion

Part A

Ⓐ **SHOPPING:** clerk, consumer, customer, good, mall, vendor
   CLOTHING: blouse, jacket, shirt, skirt, trousers, vest

Ⓑ 1 company   2 media   3 location
   4 subway   5 textile

Ⓒ 1 corporation 2 subway   3 vendor
   4 turnstile   5 radio   6 trousers
   7 exterior   8 outdoor   9 consumer
   10 textile

Part B

Ⓐ **ADVERTISING:** audience, billboard, commercial, direct mail, flier, handbill
   COMPANY: employee, investor, labor, management, salespeople, shareholder

Ⓑ 1 decipher   2 demographic 3 vivid
   4 obvious   5 fair

Ⓒ 1 labor   2 goals   3 vivid
   4 ambiguous   5 criminal   6 demographic
   7 decipher   8 investors   9 glanced
   10 aimed

Genetics 유전학

Basic Knowledge Building

1. 세포 분열

세포 분열은 생물에서 두 가지 중요한 역할을 한다. 첫 번째로 유사분열은 생물의 전반적인 성장에 필요하다. 세포가 분열되면 생물 내의 세포 수가 증가한다. 이 과정이 없으면 생물은 성장할 수도 없고 손실되거나 죽은 세포를 대체할 수도 없다. 그런가 하면 감수분열은 성세포를 만드는 분열 과정이다. 번식에 쓰이는 난자와 정자가 감수분열로 만들어진다. 두 과정은 유사하지만 감수분열에서는 정상세포보다 염색체의 수가 반인 세포가 만들어진다. 난자와 정자가 결합해 새로운 생명체가 만

들어지면 전체 염색체 수는 원래대로 된다.

Q. T ☑ F ☐

> organism 유기체, 생물   replace 대체하다   reproduction 번식
> chromosome 염색체   fuse 융합하다

2. 염색체

세포의 핵 속에는 DNA(디옥시리보핵산)가 있다. 하지만 DNA는 세포 분열 과정에서 제대로 복제, 분열되어 새로운 세포로 분리되기 위해 응축되어야 한다. 먼저, DNA가 히스톤이라고 하는 공 모양의 단백질 주위를 감는다. 그런 다음 DNA-히스톤 복합체가 염색질에 들어가고, 이어서 염색질은 염색체 속에 또아리를 튼다. 인간의 세포에는 46개의 염색체가 있다. 반은 어머니에게서, 반은 아버지에게서 받는다. 이 염색체 가운데 두 개가 성염색체이다. 태아가 두 개의 X염색체를 받으면 여자가 된다. X염색체 한 개와 Y염색체 한 개를 받으면 남자가 된다.

Q. T ☐ F ☑

> chromosome 염색체   nucleus 핵   condense 응축되다
> separate 분리하다   inherit 물려받다

3. DNA의 구조

일단 DNA가 유전자 정보를 가진 물질로 확인이 되자 과학자들은 그 구조를 알아내려고 경쟁을 벌였다. 제임스 왓슨과 프랜시스 크릭이 DNA 분자의 독특한 이중나선 구조를 최초로 밝혀냈다. 본질적으로, DNA는 뒤틀린 사다리 모양이다. 옆쪽은 인산염과 당으로 되어 있고, 가로장은 질소성 염기로 되어 있다. 구조의 핵심은 염기가 쌍을 이루어 배열되어 있다는 것이다. DNA 구조를 풀면 두 개의 동일한 가닥이 양쪽으로 분리된다. 이것 때문에 DNA가 스스로를 복제하여 다음 세대로 전달될 수 있다.

Q. T ☑ F ☐

> identify 확인하다   be composed of ~로 구성되어 있다
> unzip 풀다   identical 동일한   strand 가닥

4. RNA

RNA(리보핵산)는 DNA와 매우 비슷하지만 세포 내에서의 기능은 아주 다르다. RNA는 크게 두 종류로 mRNA(전령 RNA)와 tRNA(운반 RNA)가 있다. 둘 다 세포내 단백질 합성에 이용된다. mRNA는 핵 속에 있는 RNA의 한 부분을 복제한다. 핵을 떠나기 전에 DNA의 남은 부분이 잘려 나간다. 그런 다음 mRNA는 단백질 합성이 일어나는 리보솜으로 간다. 리보솜은 tRNA를 mRNA에 붙이는 중개자 구실을 한다. tRNA는 단백질을 구성하는 물질인 아미노산을 운반한다. tRNA는 정해진 순서대로 mRNA에 부착되고 그 후 아미노산이 서로 연결된다. 이런 식으로 DNA는 핵을 벗어나지 않고도 단백질 생산을 통제한다.

Q. T ☐ F ☑

> protein 단백질   synthesis 합성   mediate 중재하다
> attachment 부착   sequence 순서

5. 인간의 배아

여성의 난자는 나팔관 중 하나에서 수정이 된다. 수정된 접합체는 자궁으로 가는 동안 여러 차례 분열한다. 일단 자궁에 도달하면 자궁 내벽에 착상해 자라게 된다. 이 시점의 접합체를 배아라고 부른다. 인간의 배아기는 약 두 달 동안 지속된다. 뇌와 척수가 가장 먼저 발달되는 장기에 속한다. 첫 달 말경이 되면 심장이 생기고 뛰기 시작한다. 그뿐만 아니라, 팔과 다리가 자랄 곳에 조그마한 싹이 보인다. 나머지 기관들도 자라기 시작하고 배아는 곧 움직일 수 있게 된다. 8주가 되면 모든 주요 장기가 형성되고 배아는 이제 태아라고 불린다.

Q. T ☑ F ☐

> fertilize 수정시키다   implant 착상하다   embryo 배아   bud 싹
> fetus 태아

6. 인간 게놈 프로젝트

인간 게놈 프로젝트는 인간의 전체 DNA를 해독하려는 국제적인 시도였다. 사람마다 DNA가 다르긴 하지만 많은 유전자가 사람들 간에 동일하다. 그 프로젝트는 유전자 연구가 갓 시작되었던 1990년에 시작되었다. 소요된 비용과 시간이 엄청났으며 완성되기까지 13년의 시간이 걸렸다. 과학자들은 인간 게놈 혹은 인간 DNA의 전체 내용물을 더 잘 이해하게 되면 의학과 생물공학 분야에 발전이 이루어질 것으로 보았다. 이미 이 프로젝트에서 실질적인 이익을 거두었다. 과학자들은 유방암과 같은 질병을 유발하는 여러 유전자를 밝혀낼 수 있었다. 그 결과, 지금은 유방암의 경우처럼 사람이 자신에게 그 질병을 일으키는 유전자가 있는지 확인할 수 있게 되었다.

Q. T ☐ F ☑

> decode 해독하다   time-consuming 시간이 많이 걸리는
> biotechnology 생물공학   tangible 실질적인   benefit 이익

7. 유전자 요법

많은 질병이 유전자 결함 때문에 발병한다. 유전자 요법의 목표는 환자의 세포에 정상적인 유전자를 삽입하여 질병을 치료하는 것이다. 일부 초기 치료는 성공을 거두었다. 하지만 유전자 요법에는 실제로 몇 가지 단점이 있다. 우선, 치료가 반복적으로 이루어져야 한다. 게다가, 신체의 면역체계가 치료에 거부반응을 일으켜서 환자가 사망할 수도 있다. 이러한 장애에도 불구하고, 과학자들은 유전자 요법으로 개별 환자를 맞춤 치료하는 게 가능할 것으로 믿고 있다. 보다 최근에는 망막 질환이 있는 환자들의 시력을 회복시키는 데 성공하기도 했다.

Q. T ☑ F ☐

> faulty 결함이 있는   remedy 치료하다   drawback 단점
> immune 면역의   restore 회복하다

8. 유전자 조작 생물체

GMO란 유전자 조작 생물체를 말한다. 그것은 새로운 유전자가 주입된 동식물이다. 그런 동식물을 가리킬 때 흔히 유전자 변형이라는 말을 쓴다. 최초의 GMO는 약물을 만들어내도록 유전자를 주입한 박테리아였다. 하지만 더 흔하게는 식물을 유전적으로 조작해 열악한 조건을 이겨내거나 더 많은 수확을 올린다. GMO로 만든 식품을 먹었을 때의 안전성이 아직 입증되지 않았기 때문에 GMO 사용을 금지하는 나라들이 많다. 금지에 반대하는 사람들은 유전자 변형 식물이 일반 식물과 다를 바 없으며 다양한 조건에서 자랄 수 있기 때문에 전세계 기아 문제 해결에도 도움이 된다고 주장한다. 과학자들은 심지어 GMO 기술을 이용해 유전자 변형 동물까지 만들었다. 하지만 그들의 일차 목표는 연구에 응용하는 것이지 상업적으로 이용하려는 게 아니다.

Q. T ☑ F ☐

> modify 변형하다   withstand 견디다   yield 수확량
> transgenic 유전자 변형의   commercial 상업의

9. 재조합 DNA

재조합 DNA, 즉 rDNA는 새로운 유전자를 추가해 변형한 DNA이다. 방법은 꽤 간단하다. 효소를 사용해 DNA의 원형 고리를 쪼갠다. 그런 다음 새로운 유전자를 제자리에 붙이고 고리를 숙주에 넣는데, 일반적으로 박테리아가 숙주로 사용된다. 숙주인 박테리아는 그 DNA 고리를 자신의 DNA로 여긴다. 현재 rDNA의 용도로는 호르몬 생산이 있다. 좋은 예가 인슐린인데, 인슐린은 당뇨 치료에 사용되는 고가의 호르몬이다. 과학자들은 rDNA를 사용해 인슐린 유전자를 박테리아에 넣는다. 박테리아를 조심스럽게 배양해서 많은 양의 호르몬을 생산하게 한다. 과학자들은 생산된 인슐린을 퍼내서 이전 가격보다 훨씬 저렴한 가격에 당뇨병 환자에게 판매할 수 있다.

Q. T ☐ F ☑

> recombinant 재조합의   glue 붙이다   diabetes 당뇨병
> scoop 퍼내다   previous 이전의

10. 돌연변이

돌연변이는 DNA 유전 암호의 변화를 말한다. 그것은 여러 가지 방식으로 일어날 수 있다. 가장 흔하게는, DNA가 잘못 복제되어 변화가 생긴다. 하지만 일부 화학물질과 방사선, 심지어 바이러스도 유전자 돌연변이를 일으킬 수 있다. 일반적으로, 돌연변이는 비정상인 단백질을 만들기 때문에 위험하다. 하지만 간혹 가다 돌연변이가 숙주에게 도움이 되기도 한다. 그렇게 되면 숙주에게는 더 번성하게 된다. 이로 인해 개체군 전체에 돌연변이 유전자가 퍼진다. 이런 식으로 돌연변이는 개체군에 새로운 특성이 도입되는 방법이 되기도 한다. 돌연변이는 모든 진화 과정의 원천이다.

Q. T ☑ F ☐

> mutation 돌연변이   radiation 방사선   abnormal 비정상적인
> confer 주다   evolutionary 진화의

11. DNA 지문감식법

일란성 쌍둥이는 예외지만 모든 사람은 저마다 DNA가 다르다. 각자 아데닌, 구아닌, 시스신, 티민으로 된 염기 배열이 다르다. 그리하여 모든 사람은 정밀한 염기 배열 순서를 통해 정확하게 식별될 수 있다. DNA 지문 감식은 DNA 배열이 서로 일치하는지를 보기 위해 두 가지 DNA 샘플을 비교하는 것이다. DNA는 제한 효소를 추가하면 길이가 다른 조각들로 끊어진다. 과학자들은 DNA 조각들을 젤에 넣고 여기에 전류를 흘러 보낸다. 조각의 길이가 짧을수록 젤에서 더 멀리 이동한다. 두 가지 DNA 샘플이 동일하면 젤에 나타나는 선이 동일하다.

Q. T ☑ F ☐

> fingerprint 지문을 감식하다   exception 예외   sequence 순서
> restriction 제한   fragment 조각

12. 우생학

다윈이 진화론을 발표한 뒤로 사람들은 어떤 사람들이 자녀를 갖지 못하게 해서 인류를 개량할 수 있는지 궁금해하기 시작했다. 1900년대 초반에는 부적합하거나 열등하다고 여겨지는 사람들에게 강제로 불임 시술을 하는 수많은 법이 통과되었다. 기본적인 생각은 그들이 자녀를 갖지 못하도록 해서 전체 인구의 평균 지능을 높이자는 것이었다. 하지만 히틀러가 나치 정권 하에서 유대인을 집단 학살하는 구실로 우생학을 이용하는 바람에 우생학의 인기는 시들해졌다. 지금은 의사들이 장애를 지닌 태아를 찾아내기 위해 유전자 감별을 이용한다. 부모들이 장애가 심각한 태아를 낳을지 말지 선택해야 하는 경우도 있기 때문에 유전자 감별은 매우 논란이 많은 기술이다.

Q. T ☐ F ☑

> eugenics 우생학   unfit 부적합한   undergo 겪다   sterile 불임의
> genocide 집단 학살   debilitate 쇠약하게 하다

Unit 05 Gregor Johann Mendel

Thinking about the Topic

Answers can vary. It is best to elicit as many answers from students as possible.

Vocabulary Focus

B 1 estimate 추정하다, 어림잡다

2 inheritance 유전, 유전적 성질

3 contradict 모순되다, 반박하다

4 independently 독립적으로, 별도로

5 resemble 닮다

6 trait 형질, 특성

7 intact 온전한, 손상되지 않은

8 offspring 자손, 후손

9 deduce 연역하다, 추론하다
10 disastrous 파괴적인, 비참한

그레고르 요한 멘델

오래 전부터 형질은 부모에게서 자식한테 유전된다고 알려져 왔다. 사람들은 자녀가 그들을 닮는다는 것을 알고 있었다. 농부들도 새끼 짐승이 어미를 닮은 것을 보았다. 하지만 19세기 중반까지 정확한 이유와 기전은 베일에 싸여 있었다. 오스트리아 수사였던 그레고르 요한 멘델은 부모의 어떤 형질이 자손에게 유전될지 수학적으로 예측할 수 있다는 사실을 발견했다. 이 발견은 농업에 혁신을 가져왔을 뿐만 아니라 유전의 기전을 이해하는 데 새로운 빛을 비춰 주었다.

멘델은 아마도 완두콩을 이용한 연구로 가장 잘 알려져 있을 것이다. 완두콩은 값이 싸고 공간도 거의 차지하지 않는데다 번식 속도도 빨랐다. 그는 여러 해 동안 이 식물을 기르며 각 세대의 자손을 자세히 기록했다. 그는 매년 약 5천 그루의 완두콩을 심었던 것으로 추정된다. 꽃 색깔이나 완두콩 색깔과 같은 특징을 살펴보고 멘델은 형질이 부모에게서 자식한테 그대로 전해진다는 것을 알아냈다. 그는 일부 형질이 한 세대 동안은 가려져 있다가 그 다음 세대가 되어서야 나타난다고 추론했다. 또한 다양한 형질이 독립적으로 유전될 수 있다는 것도 알아냈다. 그의 연구는 널리 퍼져 있던 융합에 대한 믿음과는 반대되는 것이었다. 그 당시 대다수 과학자들은 자손은 부모의 특징을 융합해서 생긴다고 믿었다. 멘델의 연구는 형질이 부모에게서 유전되기는 하지만 형질 그 자체는 변하지 않는다는 것을 확실히 보여주었다.

1866년, 멘델은 조그만 지역 학술지에 연구 결과를 발표하고 여러 과학자들에게 복사본을 보냈다. 대다수는 멘델의 연구를 무시했다. 단 한 명의 과학자, 칼 폰 네겔리가 관심을 보였다. 하지만 그는 멘델에게 조팝나물을 연구해 보라고 권했고 이것은 끔찍한 결말을 낳았다. 조팝나물은 아주 특이한 무성생식으로 번식한다. 그래서 멘델이 이 새로운 식물로 자신의 연구 결과를 다시 증명하려 애썼지만 이전의 결과를 얻을 수가 없었다. 그러자 그는 자신의 이론에 대한 자신감을 잃고 연구를 중단했다.

멘델의 연구 목표는 그 지역 농부들의 수확량을 늘려주는 것이었다. 그들이 더 유용한 작물을 경작하도록 도울 방법을 개발하고 싶어했던 것이다. 그는 자신이 거의 모든 종을 설명하는 데 사용할 수 있는 유전 이론을 발견했다고 생각하지 않았다. 자신의 연구 성과가 나중에 미칠 영향을 미처 알지 못한 채 그는 세상을 떠났다. 멘델의 연구는 거의 한 세대 동안 묻혀 있었다. 20세기가 되어서야 비로소 그의 연구 성과는 재발견되었고, 멘델은 마침내 응당 받아야 할 명예를 누리게 되었다.

> shed new light on ~을 더 쉽게 이해할 수 있게 하다
> stumble upon ~을 우연히 발견하다

Reading Comprehension

1 (C)　2 (B)　3 (A)　4 Mendel could not duplicate his research as hawkweed reproduces in a very unusual manner.　5 (C)　6 (D)

Organizing & Summarizing

A　1 blending theory
2 fast reproduction
3 inherited independently
4 in 1866
5 unusual reproduction manner
6 theory of inheritance

B　1 inheritance
2 pea plants
3 blended together
4 independently of each other
5 receive much recognition
6 modern genetics

사람들은 오랫동안 유전에 관해 알고 있었고 부모가 그들의 형질을 자녀에게 전한다는 사실도 알고 있었다. 하지만 그레고르 요한 멘델이 완두콩 실험을 시작하고 나서야 유전의 기본적인 기전이 규명되었다. 완두콩의 특징과 형질이 한 세대에서 다음 세대로 유전되는 방식을 연구함으로써 멘델은 다음 세대들이 어떠할지 예견할 수 있는 방법을 고안했다. 게다가, 그의 연구는 형질이 융합되지 않는다는 것을 입증했다. 그것들은 온전하게 서로 독립적으로 유전된다. 그는 놀라운 연구 결과를 발표했지만 과학계의 인정을 그다지 받지 못했다. 사실 그가 들은 충고 때문에 추가적인 연구를 하지 않게 되었다. 그는 자신의 연구 성과가 미칠 영향을 알지 못한 채 숨을 거두었다. 수십 년이 지나 그의 연구 성과는 재발견되었고, 그는 현대 유전학의 아버지가 되는 영예를 누렸다.

Unit 06 Stem Cell Research

Thinking about the Topic

Answers can vary. It is best to elicit as many answers from students as possible.

Vocabulary Focus

B　1 advocate 옹호론자, 지지자
2 ban 금지
3 illegal 불법의
4 culture 배양하다
5 embryo 배아
6 halt 멈추다, 중단하다

7 constitute 구성하다
8 stalemate 곤경, 진퇴양난
9 ethical 윤리적인
10 hinder 방해하다

on the rocks 어려움에 처한 stopgap measure 미봉책, 임시방편
lag behind 뒤처지다

줄기세포 연구

줄기세포는 체내에서 어떠한 세포로도 자랄 수 있다. 그것은 초기 단계의 배아의 내세포괴에서 얻거나 성인 조직에서 채취한다. 이 두 가지 중에 배아줄기세포가 질병 치료에 더 큰 잠재력이 있다. 이미 많은 배아 세포주가 존재한다. 이러한 세포주에 관한 현재의 연구를 통해 이미 여러 가지 의학적 이점이 밝혀졌다. 하지만 줄기세포 연구는 논란의 소지가 있다. 지지자들과 반대자들이 계속해서 논쟁을 벌이는 중이다.

줄기세포 연구에 반대하는 일차적인 이유는 인간의 배아를 사용해야 한다는 것이다. 줄기세포 연구에 반대하는 사람들은 임신할 때부터 생명이 시작된다고 믿는다. 그래서 인간의 배아에서 줄기세포를 얻는 것을 낙태로 보고 비윤리적이라고 여긴다. 그들은 도덕적이고 종교적인 이유에서 그것에 반대한다. 하지만 지지자들은 배아는 인간의 형태를 갖추고 태어나기까지는 생명체가 아니라고 본다. 그들은 생명을 위협하는 질병을 고칠 치료제를 발견할 수 있다는 가능성이 연구를 반대하는 것보다 더 중요하다고 생각한다. 결국 무엇이 생명인지를 둘러싼 첨예한 논쟁으로 인해 줄기세포 연구는 진퇴양난의 상태에 처해 있다.

사실, 많은 국가에서는 더 이상의 배아줄기세포 연구를 엄격히 규제하지만 중단하지는 않기로 결정했다. 그 나라들은 실험 목적으로 배아를 만드는 것을 불법으로 간주한다. 그 결과, 현재는 오직 기증 받은 배아만 사용할 수 있다. 이러한 배아들은 어떻게든 파괴될 것이기 때문에 금지 조치는 비판자들의 우려를 일부분 해결한다. 반면에, 연구자들은 이 금지 조치를 문제에 제대로 대처하지 않는 미봉책으로 본다.

복제는 줄기세포 연구에서 나머지 중요한 문제이다. 복제는 과학자들이 아픈 환자의 쇠약해가는 기관을 대체할 새로운 기관을 만들고자 할 때 필요하다. 값진 과학기술인 복제는 새로운 장기가 환자의 낡은 장기와 정확히 들어맞고 신체의 면역체계에 나타나는 거부반응을 최소화할 수 있게 해준다. 하지만 복제는 똑같은 우려를 불러 일으킨다. 환자에게 이식할 조직을 배양한 다음에는 배아를 파괴하게 된다. 게다가, 만약 이 기술이 현실화되면 복제인간을 만들 가능성도 있다.

현재로서는, 여러 국가에서 인간 배아의 복제와 줄기세포 연구를 위한 배아 생성을 둘 다 금지하고 있다. 해당 국가들의 정부는 현재 그러한 연구의 윤리성을 놓고 논쟁을 벌이고 있다. 하지만 모든 국가가 배아줄기세포 연구를 금지하고 있는 것은 아니다. 그 결과, 많은 일류 연구가들이 연구에 방해를 받지 않는 연구소로 옮겨가는 것을 고려하고 있다. 그들은 윤리적인 문제가 생명을 구할 치료제 개발만큼 중요하지는 않다고 주장한다. 따라서 인간 배아줄기세포 연구에 참여하지 않기로 한 국가들은 다른 국가에 뒤처질 것을 각오해야 한다. 이러한 우려 때문에 해당 국가들은 되도록 빨리 논란을 해결하라는 더 많은 압력을 받고 있다.

Reading Comprehension

1 (B)   2 (C)   3 (A)   4 Cloned organs are more likely to produce an exact match of the patient's tissues, decreasing the chances the patient's body will reject the organ.   5 (B)   6 (D)

Organizing & Summarizing

Ⓐ 1 adult tissues   2 early-stage embryos
    3 new organs   4 abortions
    5 human clones   6 brain drain

Ⓑ 1 any type of cell
    2 embryonic stem cells
    3 abortion
    4 a ban on the creation
    5 clone organs
    6 human cloning

줄기세포는 어떠한 종류의 세포도 될 수 있는 잠재력이 있다. 특히, 배아줄기세포에 관한 초기 연구는 수많은 질병을 치료할 수 있다는 가능성을 보여 주었다. 하지만 많은 사람들은 그런 연구를 허용해야 하는지를 놓고 윤리적이고 실제적인 이유로 논쟁을 벌이고 있다. 반대자들이 내놓는 주요 이유는 배아줄기세포를 채취하는 것은 낙태와 같다는 것이다. 지지자들은 그 기술의 잠재적인 이익이 부정적인 면보다 더 크다고 주장한다. 이러한 의견 대립 때문에 많은 국가에서는 새로운 배아줄기세포주 생성을 금지하게 되었다. 이것은 또한 복제 연구에도 영향을 미쳤다. 과학자들은 아픈 사람들에게 이식할 장기를 복제하고 싶어한다. 하지만 반대자들은 이것 때문에 생명이 파괴되고 인간 복제가 일어날 수 있다고 주장한다. 현재 여러 국가에서 금지 조치가 논란이 되고 있으며 아직 해결되지 않은 채 남아 있다.

Vocabulary Expansion

Part A

Ⓐ **COVER:** cloak, conceal, hide, mask, obscure, shroud
   FIND: discover, expose, locate, spot, unearth, unmask

B
| 1 offspring | 2 tree | 3 cell |
| 4 crop | 5 time | |

C
1 cubs	2 ginkgo	3 wheat
4 decade	5 discovering	6 hide / conceal
7 generations	8 shrouded	9 chromosomes
10 foals		

Part B

A FOR: advocate, champion, defend, favor, promote, support
AGAINST: block, check, counter, defy, oppose, resist

B
| 1 toxin | 2 compromise | 3 permission |
| 4 aid | 5 necessary | |

C
1 defended	2 antidote	3 resisting
4 prohibition	5 aiding	6 necessary
7 draw	8 temporary	9 permission
10 promote		

Political Science 정치학

Basic Knowledge Building

1. 국가의 발전

인간 사회는 여러 단계로 진화해왔다. 처음에는 수렵채집 집단으로 구성된 사회였다. 집단은 전임 지도자가 없었다는 점에서 평등했다. 약간 더 복잡한 것이 부족이다. 부족은 어느 정도 사회적 계급이 존재하지만 여전히 가족과 혈연에 기초를 두고 있다. 어떤 경우에는 부족장이나 연장자가 부족의 지도자가 되기도 한다. 족장 사회에서는 한 개인이 확실한 지도자 역할을 하며 계급의 구별이 더 두드러진다. 왕, 전사, 장인, 노예는 족장 사회의 전형적 위계 구조이다. 마지막으로, 근대 국가가 등장한다. 그것은 정해진 지역 내의 사람들을 지배하는 정치 제도이다. 국가는 흔히 지역, 지방, 연방 단위로 구분된다.
Q. T □   F ☑

evolve 진화하다   lineage 가계, 혈통   chiefdom 족장 사회
distinction 구별   population 인구

2. 도편추방

도편추방은 고대 아테네에서 시작되었다. 그것은 저명하거나 정치적으로 위협이 될 만한 시민을 도시국가에서 축출하는 정치적 수단이었다. 해마다 집회를 열어 그 해에 도편추방을 실시할지 투표를 했다. 만약 과반이 도편추방에 찬성하면 날짜가 정해졌다. 그 날 각 투표자는 추방 또는 축출하고 싶은 사람의 이름을 도기 조각에 적었다. 그리고는 표를 가장 많이 얻은 사람을 유배시켰다. 몇몇 사람들의 경우 아테네로 더 일찍 소환되기도 했지만 대개는 10년을 떠나 있어야 했다. 흥미로운 점은 추방당한 사람이 재산이나 시민권을 잃지는 않았다는 점이다.
Q. T ☑   F □

ostracism (도편)추방   banish 추방하다   prominent 눈에 띄는
majority 다수   exile 유배

3. 독재정치, 과두정치, 민주정치

인류 역사에는 여러 형태의 지배 체제가 있었다. 독재정치는 스스로 올라선 지도자가 통치를 한다. 이런 형태의 지도자는 독재자 또는 전제군주라고 부른다. 보통 그들은 권력을 유지하기 위해 군대에 많이 의존한다. 과두정치에서는 최상류 집단이 국가의 최고 권력을 쥐고 있는데, 이 집단은 대개 가문이나 부에 따라 결정된다. 흔히 자녀를 미래의 과두정치 지도자로 키우지만 여전히 가문의 연장자들이 조종을 한다. 민주정치는 시민이 권력을 쥐고 자유롭게 지도자를 선출하는 통치 형태이다. 민주주의 국가의 시민은 보편적 자유를 누릴 권리가 있다.
Q. T ☑   F □

despot 독재자, 독재군주   tyrant 전제군주, 폭군, 참주
supreme 최고의   oligarch 과두 정치의 지도자
manipulate 조종하다

4. 니콜로 마키아벨리

니콜로 마키아벨리는 15세기와 16세기를 살았던 이탈리아의 정치철학자였다. 젊을 때는 외교관이었다. 그는 전쟁을 목격했고, 프랑스와 독일, 이탈리아의 저명한 지도자들과 두루 정치를 논했으며, 고전 정치 이론을 연구했다. 10년을 봉직한 후 마키아벨리는 직위를 잃고 투옥되었다. 그때 저명한 정치 논문인 〈군주론〉(1532)을 썼다. 마키아벨리의 경험에서 우러난 그 문서는 지도자가 어떻게 권력과 영향력을 얻고 행사해야 하는지 설명한다. 또한 지도자의 성공과 도덕성에 대한 내용도 있다. 마키아벨리는 지도자가 정치 권력을 유지하기 위해서는 당근과 채찍을 적절히 활용할 줄 알아야 한다고 주장했다. 마키아벨리의 견해는 훗날 여러 정치지도자들과 사상가들에게 영향을 끼쳤다.
Q. T □   F ☑

diplomat 외교관   prominent 저명한   imprison 투옥시키다
treatise 논문   retain 유지하다

5. 군주제의 종류

역사적으로, 군주제에는 절대군주제와 입헌군주제라는 두 가지 기본적인 종류가 있다. 절대군주는 국토와 국민을 소유한

다. 그들은 자기 마음대로 통치한다. 흔히 그들은 왕권신수설 즉 군주가 신과 평민을 직접 연결하는 존재라는 사상으로 자신의 권위를 정당화한다. 역사적으로는 프랑스의 루이 14세가 좋은 예이다. 입헌군주제는 그 반대이다. 이 통치 형태에서는 왕이나 여왕이 국가의 수장이기는 하지만 그들의 행동은 의회에서 정한 헌법이나 법률의 구속을 받는다. 더욱이, 수상이 정부의 수장 노릇을 한다. 절대군주제와는 달리 입헌군주제에서는 대개 확실한 힘의 균형이 존재한다.

Q. T☐ F☑

monarchy 군주제 constitutional 입헌의 justify 정당화하다
characterize 특징짓다 parliament 의회

6. 정부의 형태

정부는 여러 형태로 나눌 수 있다. 왕국은 왕이나 여왕이 우두머리가 되는 조직사회이다. 연방은 원래 특정 계층이 아니라 모든 국민의 복지를 위해 통치되는 국가를 의미했다. 오늘날에는 국가연합을 뜻하기도 한다. 이 국가들은 종종 역사적, 정치적 유대관계가 있다. 다음으로 합중국이 있다. 이 중앙집권 형태의 정부는 몇 개의 주로 구성되어 있다. 하지만 이 주들은 연방헌법에 따라 나름의 내부 문제를 다스린다. 마지막으로, 공화국은 군주가 없는 국가이다. 권력은 시민에게 있으며 시민들은 대표자를 선출해 법을 집행한다.

Q. T☑ F☐

commonwealth 연방 denote 뜻하다 federation 합중국
representative 대표자 administer 집행하다

7. 권력 분립

권력 분립의 개념과 시행은 절대권력과 정반대이다. 권력 분립 제도 안에서는 어떠한 정부 부문도 다른 부문보다 더 큰 영향력을 행사할 수 없다. 그래서 국가를 독재로부터 보호할 수 있다. 오늘날, 미국은 권력 분립의 훌륭한 예를 보여 준다. 사법, 입법, 행정이라는 정부의 세 부문이 각기 다른 역할을 한다. 그들은 서로에 대해 견제와 균형이라는 체제를 유지한다. 이 때문에 어떠한 정부 기관도 다른 기관보다 더 큰 권력을 갖지 못하게 되어 있다. 하지만 이것은 연방 수준에만 해당된다. 미국의 경우 연방 정부와 주 정부 사이에 권력이 더 나누어진다. 그래도 실제로 어떤 경우에는 여러 권력이 부문들 간에 중첩된다.

Q. T☐ F☑

separation 분리 tyrannical 전제적인, 폭압적인 judicial 사법의
legislative 입법의 executive 행정부의

8. 투표제도

선거와 관련해 주요한 세 가지 투표제도가 있다. 첫째는 과반수 지배의 원칙이다. 두 후보 중에 과반을 득표한 쪽이 승자가 된다. 오늘날, 이것은 일반선거에서는 거의 사용되지 않고 찬반을 결정해야 하는 의회의 입법안 투표에 더 많이 사용된다. 또 다른 일반적인 투표제도는 비례대표제이다. 정당이 얻는 의석 수가 대중의 지지를 얼마나 많이 받느냐에 비례하는 일반선거에서 흔히 볼 수 있다. 지지도가 높을수록 더 많은 의석을 차지하고 그렇지 않는 경우는 그 반대이다. 이 투표제도에서는 승리가 가장 중요하다. 마지막 제도는 다수결 투표이다. 이 제도에서는 표를 가장 많이 받은 사람이 승자가 되는데, 일반적으로 과반을 넘길 필요가 없고 가능하지도 않다.

Q. T☑ F☐

majority 과반수 proportional 비례의 representation 대표
candidate 후보자 plurality 상대적 다수

9. 미국의 여성 참정권

미국 헌법이 처음 제정되었을 당시에는 여성의 투표권이 구체적으로 명기되어 있지 않았다. 1800년대 중반 남북전쟁 말기에 여성의 투표권 또는 참정권을 지지하는 운동이 힘을 얻었다. 그 운동을 이끈 사람은 여성 권리 옹호자였던 수잔 B. 앤소니였다. 1900년대 초반에는 헌법 수정을 요구하면서 워싱턴 D.C.와 다른 도시들에서 많은 시위가 일어났다. 서부의 몇몇 주들이 마침내 주 선거에서 여성에게 투표권을 주었다. 하지만 1920년이 되어서야 비로소 주와 연방 단위에서 모든 여성에게 투표권을 주기로 한 수정헌법 제 9조가 의회에서 마침내 통과되었다.

Q. T☐ F☑

suffrage 참정권 advocate 옹호자 demonstration 시위
amendment 수정 조항 ultimately 궁극적으로

10. 편승효과

편승효과란 다른 사람들이 이미 했다는 이유로 사람들이 어떤 결정을 내리거나 어떤 식으로 행동하도록 만드는 사회적 현상을 말한다. 본질적으로, 편승효과는 사람들이 무리를 따르는 경향이 있음을 보여준다. 그것은 특히 정치 선거에서 두드러진다. 사실상 그 용어는 1848년 미국의 대통령 선거 기간에 탄생했다. 다른 경우에는 때때로 투표자들이 이기는 쪽에 있고 싶어하기 때문에 앞서 가는 후보에게 투표하는 경향을 보이기도 한다. 초기의 텔레비전 여론조사가 투표자의 결정에 영향을 미쳐 몇몇 연구에서 밝혀진 대로 편승효과를 높이기도 한다.

Q. T☐ F☑

phenomenon 현상 tendency 경향 recognizable 인지할 수 있는 originate 시작되다 presidential 대통령의

11. 미국의 대통령 선거 절차

미국의 대통령 선거는 4년마다 실시되는데, 절차가 길고 복잡하다. 일찌감치 후보자가 지명되면 지지자를 모으고 선거 기금을 마련한다. 다음 단계는 당원들의 투표로 결정되는 대의원 선출 당원대회와 대통령 후보 예비선거가 있다. 선거가 있는 해의 6월에는 주요 정당들이 백악관 입성에 가장 적합하다

고 생각하는 사람을 지명하는 전당대회가 열린다. 11월에는 대통령 선거가 열리고 시민들이 투표를 한다. 인구 수에 따라 각 주마다 선거인단에서 정한 선거인 수가 있다. 만약 어떤 후보가 한 주에서 승리를 거두면 그 주의 선거인단 표를 다 차지한다. 그렇게 해서 적어도 270개의 선거인단 표를 획득하는 사람이 미국의 대통령이 된다.

Q. T □ F ☑

complex 복잡한   nominate 지명하다   election 선거
convention 집회   capture 획득하다

12. 지방자치제

일반적으로 자치제는 스스로 통치한다는 개념이다. 지방자치제는 이러한 개념의 연장이라고 볼 수 있다. 그 용어는 보다 작은 지역에 보다 많은 권력을 주는 것을 의미한다. 대개 더 큰 중앙 당국이 더 작은 지방 운영을 위한 규칙을 정하게 된다. 하지만 지방은 스스로 통치할 여지가 얻는다. 어떤 점에서 지방자치는 더 수준 높은 민주주의를 의미한다. 연방 통제가 분산되어 세력이 약화되는 반면 지방의 관리는 증가한다. 지방 자치의 이점으로는 지방 자치가 시민들의 필요를 더 잘 충족시킬 수 있다는 점이다.

Q. T ☑ F □

extension 연장   authority 당국   decentralize 분산시키다
prevalent 우세한   supervision 관리

Unit 07 Tyranny in Ancient Greece

Thinking about the Topic
Answers can vary. It is best to elicit as many answers from students as possible.

Vocabulary Focus

B   1 subdue 진정시키다, 가라앉히다
    2 prosperity 번영, 번성
    3 void 공간, 공석
    4 commonplace 평범한, 흔한
    5 bolster 강화하다, 부양하다
    6 despot 독재군주, 독재자
    7 desperately 필사적으로
    8 oppression 억압, 압박
    9 redistribute 재분배하다
    10 restrict 제한하다, 억제하다

고대 그리스의 독재정치

기원전 7세기 동안에 그리스는 큰 사회 불안을 겪기 시작했다. 귀족과 일반 평민 사이에 커다란 구별이 생겼다. 경제, 정치, 사회적 갈등이 일상사가 되었다. 점점 더 많은 일반 시민들이 부유한 지도층에게 불신을 품었다. 귀족 계층은 심지어 자기들끼리 싸움을 벌이기 시작했다. 그래서 가난한 시민들은 대안적인 지도자를 찾기 시작했다. 그들의 요구를 들어주고 귀족 계층에 맞설 수 있는 새로운 지도자를 절실히 원했다. 오래지 않아 참주라고 알려진 새로운 지도자가 고대 그리스의 다양한 도시국가에 등장해 참주정치라고 하는 새로운 정부 형태를 만들었다.

참주들은 비전통적인 방법으로 권력을 잡았다. 그들은 대개 법이나 상속 같은 수단을 빌어 통치할 수 있는 공식적인 권한이 없었다. 흔히 무력과 폭력을 써서 통치권을 얻는 데 성공했다. 또한 참주들은 대개 중산층 출신이었다. 그들은 하층계급에게 희망과 번영을 약속해서 빠른 시간 내에 지지를 얻었다. 하지만 고대 그리스의 참주가 폭군은 아니었다는 사실을 기억해야 한다. 오히려, 그들은 피에 굶주린 노예 주인이 아니라 "덕망 있는" 지도자로 널리 받아들여졌다.

그리스의 참주정치는 기원전 650년부터 500년까지 지속되었다. 일반적으로 참주는 그리스 사회에 많은 긍정적 영향을 미쳤다. 무엇보다도, 귀족의 권력이 크게 제한되었다. 이로 인해 당시의 계층간 갈등을 잠재우는 데 도움이 되었다. 게다가, 하층계급의 생활도 향상되었다. 농업 생산이 늘어났고 억압이 줄어들었다. 많은 경우 조세가 감면되었고 토지도 귀족에게서 빈곤층에게로 재분배되었다. 참주는 제조업과 무역도 장려했는데, 이로 인해 일자리가 더 많이 생겼고 생산성도 향상되었다. 마지막으로, 그리스 문화도 참주의 혜택을 보았다. 참주는 흔히 예술의 확실한 후원자였다. 그래서 참주정치 하에서 종교, 예술, 문학, 건축 분야에서 보다 큰 발전과 향상이 있었다.

참주정치는 고대 그리스에서 정치적인 공백을 메우고 중간 계급과 하층계급을 지원한 것만은 아니다. 더욱 발전된 정부의 형태로 나아가는 디딤돌 노릇도 했다. 법의 성문화는 참주 정치의 또 다른 중요한 산물이 되었다. 더 많은 법이 기록되면서 사람들 사이에 새로운 평등 개념이 실현되었다. 아테네에서는 이것이 결국 민주주의 정신으로 발전하여 참주정치에 뒤이어 나타날 정부 형태에 영향을 끼쳤다. 기원전 510년경 아테네는 민주 정부가 다스리는 최초의 정치적 실체가 되었다.

codification 성문화, 법전화

Reading Comprehension

1 (B)   2 (C)   3 (D)   4 ① They promised hope and prosperity. ② They were viewed as "good" rulers.   5 (D)
6 (A)

Organizing & Summarizing

A
1 650 to 500 B.C.
2 the middle class
3 peace and prosperity
4 class conflict
5 farm production & jobs
6 redistributed land
7 codification of laws
8 Athenian democracy

B
1 600 to about 500 B.C.
2 the middle class
3 good and fair rulers
4 manufacturing and agriculture
5 The codification of laws
6 the earliest form of democracy

고대 그리스 시대의 참주정치는 기원전 약 600년부터 500년까지 지속되었다. 참주는 스스로 옹립된 지배자였다. 그들은 중산층 출신인 경우가 많았다. 때로 무력을 사용해 권력을 얻기도 했고 인정받지 못했던 하층민들에게 평화와 번영을 약속했다. 이것이 오랫동안 부유한 귀족층 지배자를 갈아치우고 싶어했던 하층민들의 마음에 들었다. 참주는 하층민들의 문제에 대한 완벽한 해결책이었다. 참주는 독재자가 아니었다. 대신에, 그들은 덕망 있고 공평한 지배자로 여겨졌다. 고대 그리스는 여러 모로 참주 지배의 혜택을 누렸다. 우선, 귀족의 권력이 줄어들었다. 일시적이긴 했지만 계급 갈등이 줄어들면서 사회가 안정되었다. 또한 일자리가 증가되고 제조업과 농업의 생산성이 향상되었다. 조세도 감면되고 토지는 재분배되었다. 게다가, 참주들은 흔히 예술을 통해 문화를 장려했다. 마지막으로, 이러한 통치 시기를 거친 후 더 나은 정부 형태가 등장했다. 법의 성문화가 더 보편화되었다. 아테네에서는 이로 인해 최초의 민주주의가 발달했다. 참주 통치 후에 평등과 사회적 균형이 더욱 가능해졌다.

Unit 08 The Patricians and the Plebeians of Republican Rome

Thinking about the Topic
Answers can vary. It is best to elicit as many answers from students as possible.

Vocabulary Focus

B
1 privileged 특권을 지닌
2 govern 다스리다, 통치하다
3 illiterate 문맹의
4 blend 섞다
5 mobility 이동성, 유동성
6 peasant 농민
7 extravagance 사치
8 exclude 배제하다, 제외하다
9 eligible 자격이 있는; 적합한
10 conflict 갈등을 일으키다, 충돌하다

로마 공화정의 귀족과 평민

고대 로마에는 귀족과 평민의 두 가지 시민 계급이 있었다. 그들의 가치는 대조를 이루며 종종 서로 충돌하곤 했다. 귀족은 특권을 지닌 지배층인 반면 권리가 거의 없는 일반 로마 시민들이 평민층을 이루었다. 이러한 구별은 기원전 6세기 초 로마 공화정 초기에 생겨났다. 두 계층 간의 이동은 거의 없었다. 하지만 기원전 3세기경 평민들이 더 많은 권리와 영향력을 얻고 귀족은 권력을 많이 잃게 되면서 두 계층이 섞이기 시작했다.

절정기에 귀족계급은 여러 가지 특권을 누렸다. 원래 귀족들은 가장 영향력 있는 로마 가문의 후손들이었다. 그들의 조상은 로마를 건국한 사람들이었다. 그래서 그들은 로마 의회에서 의석을 차지하고 막강한 정치적 영향력을 행사했다. 이 덕분에 그들은 수백 년 동안 로마를 독점적으로 통치할 수 있었다. 또한 귀족들은 모든 공직과 종교직을 차지했다. 그들은 집정관과 정권의 임시 수장, 사제가 될 수 있었다. 흥미롭게도, 그들만이 사제가 될 수 있었는데, 이는 그들이 신들과 더 잘 소통할 수 있다고 여겨졌기 때문이다. 더욱이, 귀족들은 부유한 지주로서 호화롭고 사치스러운 생활을 영위했다. 그들 중 다수가 로마에는 주택을, 시골에는 별장을 가지고 있었다. 하지만 귀족이 누린 가장 독특한 특권은 그들만이 로마의 황제가 될 수 있다는 것이었다.

대조적으로, 평민들은 로마 시민의 과반을 차지하고 있으면서도 많은 권리에서 배제되었다. 일반적으로, 그들은 여러 곳에서 귀족을 위해 일하는 장인이거나 농부였다. 그들은 정규교육을 받을 수 없어서 대개 문맹이었다. 또한 귀족 정부를 위해 세금을 내면서도 정치적 권리는 없었다. 군단사령관직을 제외하고는 관직을 가질 수 없었고, 귀족 지배자가 내린 결정에 이의를 제기할 수도 없었다. 더욱이, 귀족과의 결혼도 금지되었다. 평민은 사회적 신분 상승을 상상할 수도 없었다. 하지만 기원전 494년에 있었던 이른바 '신분 투쟁'에서 평민들은 결국 한데 뭉쳤다.

신분 투쟁은 평민이 주도한 변화와 정치적 평등을 위한 운동이었다. 평민들은 전시에 로마를 돕지 않음으로써 점차 더 많은 정치 권력을 얻었고 마침내 자유를 획득했다. 의회에서 의원으로 선출될 권리를 획득함으로써 역사적 이정표가 마련되었다. 호민관직도 생겨났다. 호민관은 평민들을 귀족 집정관들로부터 보호해 줄 힘이 있었다. 기원전 287년 신분 투쟁이 끝날 무렵에는 공식적으로 귀족과 평민이 평등하게 대우받았다.

interim 임시의, 잠정적인

Reading Comprehension

1 (C)　2 (B)　3 (A)　4 ① The Conflict of Orders gave the plebeians more power. ② The Conflict of Orders commenced in 494 B.C. and ended in 287 B.C.　5 (D)
6 (A)

Organizing & Summarizing

Ⓐ　1 Roman Senators　2 wealthy landowners
　3 peasants & artisans　4 illiterate
　5 military tribune　6 by the 3rd century B.C.
　7 the Conflict of Orders
　8 Plebeian Tribune

Ⓑ　1 the early 6th century B.C.
　2 the Roman founders
　3 senators, magistrates, and priests
　4 outnumbered the patricians
　5 the Conflict of Orders
　6 elected into the Senate

로마의 귀족과 평민은 기원전 6세기 초부터 존재했다. 귀족은 로마 건국자들의 후손으로 이루어진 소수의 특권층이었다. 그들은 부유했고 모든 정치적 권력을 쥐고 영향력을 행사했다. 그들은 의원, 집정관, 사제와 같은 공직을 독점했다. 이 교육받은 지배층은 향후 300년 간 로마 문명을 통치했다. 대조적으로, 평민들은 가난하고 교육도 받지 못한 시민들이었다. 그들은 정치적 영향력도 없었으며 주요한 공직도 차지할 수 없었다. 또한 시민권도 거의 누릴 수 없었다. 하지만 수적으로는 귀족보다 훨씬 많았다. 기원전 494년 그들은 더 많은 권리와 정치 권력을 얻기 위해 신분 투쟁을 전개했다. 오래지 않아 그들은 더 많은 정치 권력을 얻었고 결국 의회에서 의원으로 선출될 권리도 획득했다. 귀족들은 서서히 정치적 우위를 빼앗겼다. 기원전 287년 신분 투쟁이 끝날 무렵에는 계층 간의 평등이 훨씬 더 확연해졌다.

Vocabulary Expansion

Part A

Ⓐ　**DEMOCRACY:** civil rights, election, equality, freedom, majority, president
　DESPOTISM: absolute power, authoritarian, dictator, imbalance, oppression, unchallenged

Ⓑ　1 tool　　　2 career　　　3 election
　4 diplomat　5 government

Ⓒ　1 oligarchy　2 candidates　3 envoy
　4 election　　5 oppression　6 ambassador
　7 civil rights　8 mayor　　　9 saw
　10 ballots

Part B

Ⓐ　**ARTISAN:** baker, blacksmith, carpenter, jeweler, mason, quilter
　MILITARY: colonel, general, lieutenant, soldier, sergeant, tribune

Ⓑ　1 deny　　　2 dependence　3 foundation
　4 aristocrat　5 fake

Ⓒ　1 fake　　　　2 general　　　3 witnessed
　4 foundation　5 blacksmith　　6 denied
　7 aristocrats　8 watching　　　9 tribune
　10 dependence

Geography 지리학

Basic Knowledge Building

1. 자연지리학

자연지리학은 지리학의 한 분야이다. 그것은 지구상의 자연 지형들을 상호적 존재로 파악한다. 그것은 전세계 자연 환경의 과정에 관한 연구와 그것들이 서로 어떻게 관련이 있는지에 대한 연구를 강조한다. 자연지리학의 중요한 하위 분야 가운데 하나가 지형학이다. 그것은 지표면과 지표면의 형성 과정을 연구한다. 또 다른 한 가지는 기후학으로, 기후와 날씨가 지구에 어떻게 영향을 미치는지를 연구한다. 또한 수질학 분야에서는 전문가들이 강이나 바다 같은 여러 형태의 수역이 환경에 어떻게 영향을 미치는지를 탐구한다. 자연지리학에서 가장 중요한 것은 지구의 특징들이 어떻게 그리고 왜 형성되는지를 더 잘 이해하기 위해 여러 가지 개념들을 통합하는 것이다.
Q. T ☑　F ☐

interactive 상호적인　entity 실체　emphasize 강조하다
climatology 기후학　integration 통합

2. 인문지리학

인문지리학은 지리학에서 인기 있는 분야이다. 그것은 인간과 물리적 환경 사이의 관계를 연구한다. 인간 활동이 물리적 세계에 어떤 영향을 미치는가가 이 분야의 특별한 관심사이다. 정치, 사회, 경제, 정부 등이 하나 같이 중요한 작용을 한다. 전문가들은 다른 지역이나 시대를 비교, 대조하는 과정에서 이런 요소들의 패턴을 찾는다. 통계 분석과 모델 수립도 인문지리학 연구의 중요한 일부이다. 더 최근에는 광범위한 도시화와 과밀화, 오염으로 인해 도시지리학이 인문지리학의 중요한 하위 분야가 되었다. 그것은 미래의 삶의 질을 향상시키는 데 도움을 줄 수 있다.

Q. T☐ F☑

> explore 개척하다 analysis 분석 integral 필수의, 절대 필요한
> statistical 통계적인 expansive 확장하는, 팽창하는
> urbanization 도시화 overcrowding 과밀화

3. 지대의 형태

지대란 다른 지역들과 구별되는 어떤 특징을 공유하는 지역을 말한다. 지대에는 공적지대와 기능지대의 두 가지 하위 부류가 있다. 공적지대는 사람들이 언어, 종교, 국적과 같은 공통적인 특징들을 어떻게 공유하느냐에 따라 구분된다. 또한 기후, 지형, 초목과 같은 환경적 특징으로 분류되기도 한다. 국가나 지방뿐만 아니라 기후와 지형 지대 역시 전형적인 공적지대의 예이다. 기능지대는 사업이나 경제 활동을 통해 주변 지역과 연결되어 있는 요지나 중심지에 기초하고 있다. 예를 들어, 대도시 지역은 교통과 통신 시스템에 의해 주변 지역과 연결되어 있다.

Q. T☑ F☐

> separate 구별하다 functional 기능적인 landform 지형
> vegetation 초목 node 중심점

4. 툰드라

툰드라는 대개 춥고 나무도 자라지 않고 평평한 지리학적 지역이다. 보통은 동물이 거의 살지 않는 극단의 환경이다. 먹이 사슬이 거의 없기 때문에 툰드라의 생태계는 대단히 취약하다. 툰드라에는 북극권 툰드라와 고산 툰드라의 두 가지 종류가 있다. 북극권 툰드라는 지구의 극지방에 있으며, 고산 툰드라는 수목의 생장한계선을 지나 고산지대에 존재한다. 북극 툰드라는 고산 툰드라에 비해 강수량이 적다. 또한 북극권 툰드라에는 영하의 기온 때문에 영구동토층이 존재한다. 영구동토층이란 영구히 얼어붙어 있는 토양층을 말한다. 대조적으로, 고산 툰드라는 북극 툰드라만큼 춥지 않기 때문에 영구동토층이 없다.

Q. T☑ F☐

> geographical 지리학적인 extreme 극단적인 minimal 최소한의
> fragile 취약한 permanently 영구적으로

5. 카나리아 제도

카나리아 제도는 아프리카의 북서 해안에 위치해 있다. 고대 화산에 의해 형성된 7개의 섬으로 이루어져 있다. 테네리페 섬의 테이데 화산은 전 세계에서 세 번째로 큰 화산이다. 그 화산은 높이가 해발 3,700미터가 넘는 휴화산이다. 마지막 분출은 20세기 초반에 일어났다. 카나리아 제도는 연중 온화한 기후이다. 게다가, 무역풍이 지나는 경로에 위치해 있어 습윤한 기후와 건조한 기후를 다 누릴 수 있다. 카나리아 제도는 인류의 탐험에서도 중요한 역할을 했다. 15세기에 스페인의 식민지가 된 이후 카나리아 제도는 콜럼버스 원정대를 비롯하여 아메리카 대륙으로 향한 스페인 사람들에게 중요한 단기 체류지가 되었다.

Q. T☐ F☑

> dormant 활동하지 않는 eruption 분출 temperature 기온
> stopover 체류지 expedition 탐험대

6. 도시화

도시화란 점점 더 많은 사람들이 도시나 도시 근교에 살게 되는 과정을 말한다. 이 현상은 주로 시골 지역으로부터 주민이 유입되기 때문에 일어난다. 도시화는 개인과 가족이 경제적인 기회와 더 나은 삶을 찾아 도시로 향하기 때문에 생긴다. 예를 들면, 농촌에서와 같은 제한된 삶을 뒤로 하고 무한한 가능성이 있어 보이는 도시 지역의 잠재성에 희망을 품고 도시로 향한다. 도시의 주된 매력 중 하나는 사회적 유동성에 대한 가능성이다. 사람들은 도시에서 열심히 일하면 누구라도 높은 사회적 지위에 오를 수 있다고 생각한다. 오늘날 점점 더 많은 사람들이 구시대적 삶의 방식을 버리고 도시로 가고 있다. 더 나은 일자리만이 유일한 매력은 아니다. 현대적인 보건의료 서비스와 양질의 교육, 심지어 오락의 기회도 사람들을 도시로 유혹한다.

Q. T☑ F☐

> suburb 근교 influx 유입 resident 거주자 mobility 유동성
> entice 유혹하다

7. 화이트 플라이트

화이트 플라이트는 인구통계학적 용어다. 백인 중산층과 근로자층이 도심에서 교외로 이동 또는 이주하는 것을 말한다. 화이트 플라이트는 1950년대 미국에서 처음 일어났다. 미국 학교들의 인종차별 폐지가 초기의 시발점이 되었다. 하지만 화이트 플라이트의 원인으로 여겨지는 다른 요소들이 존재한다. 범죄와 인구과밀로 도시 지역이 몰락했다는 게 한 가지다. 또 다른 요인으로는 동네의 인종적 긴장을 이용하는 블록버스팅이 있다. 이것은 부동산업자들이 백인 부동산 소유주들에게 흑인들이 마을로 이사해 들어올 것이라는 암시를 주어 집을 팔도록 압력을 주는 것이다. 또한 교통 인프라가 향상되어 더 많은 백인들이 분주한 도시로 출퇴근하면서 교외에서 보다 안락한 생활을 누릴 수 있게 되었다.

Q. T☑ F☐

> demographic 인구통계적인 migration 이주
> desegregation 인종차별 폐지 decay 몰락 overcrowding 과밀
> commute 통근하다

8. 위성도시

위성도시란 더 큰 도시에 바로 인접한 중소도시를 말한다. 일반적으로 위성도시는 인접한 큰 도시가 확장되기 전에는 독립적인 도시였다. 그래서 나름의 지방 정부가 있고 주변 도시에 생존을 전적으로 의존하지는 않는다. 그들은 나름대로 도심과 시청도 있다. 하지만 역사적으로 자급자족 하던 많은 위성도시들이 바뀌고 있다. 인근 대도시가 계속 확장되면서 일부 위성도시는 인접한 주요 도시에 더 많이 의존하게 되었다. 좋은 예가 캘리포니아의 오클랜드이다. 오클랜드는 여전히 주요 항구도시지만 거기에 사는 많은 시민들이 샌프란시스코에 있는 직장으로 출퇴근한다.

Q. T☐ F☑

> expansion 확장 adjoin 인접하다 survival 생존
> self-sufficient 자급자족의 adjacent 인접한

9. 지도제작술

지도 제작 분야는 지도와 도표를 이용해 지리적 영역을 표시하는 것이다. 지도 제작 덕분에 사람들은 지구를 평면으로 볼 수 있다. 최초의 지도는 정확하지도 튼튼하지도 않았다. 설계의 많은 부분이 어림짐작이었다. 하지만 나침반과 같은 항해 도구가 발명되면서 모든 게 바뀌었다. 지도가 개량되면서 세상을 더 정확히 볼 수 있게 되었다. 망원경과 같은 더 발전된 발명품들이 지도 제작에 도움을 주었다. 오늘날에는 컴퓨터 기술과 인공위성 덕분에 즉석에서 지표면의 모양을 알 수 있다.

Q. T☑ F☐

> cartography 지도제작술 depiction 표시 durable 튼튼한
> guesswork 어림짐작 navigational 항해의

10. 알렉산더 폰 훔볼트

알렉산더 폰 훔볼트는 18세기와 19세기의 독일 탐험가이자 생물학자였다. 그는 그 세대에서 가장 유명한 과학자 가운데 한 명이었다. 남아메리카에서 했던 탐험과 발견은 향후 지리학 분야의 기초를 마련하는 데 큰 역할을 했다. 남아메리카를 5년 동안 여행하면서 그는 식물, 화산 활동, 해수의 흐름에 있어 중요한 발견을 했다. 심지어 안데스 산맥의 구성에 대한 초기 기록을 남기기도 했다. 또한 그의 작업은 기상학 분야에도 기여했다. 그는 지구 자기장의 세기가 극지방에서 적도 쪽으로 이동함에 따라 감소한다는 것을 알아냈다.

Q. T☐ F☑

> acclaimed 호평을 받은 framework 체제, 틀, 기반 current 해류
> magnetic 자기의, 자성을 띤 meteorological 기상학적인

11. 파나마 운하

파나마 운하는 중앙아메리카에서 태평양과 대서양을 연결하는 물길이다. 이 거대한 프로젝트는 1881년 프랑스인이 처음으로 시작했다. 하지만 수많은 난관 때문에 8년 동안이나 방치되었다. 다음으로 미국이 그 건설 공사를 맡아 1914년 마침내 운하를 개통했다. 파나마 운하는 갑문 시스템으로 되어 있다. 서로 다른 높이의 수로들이 서로 이음매 없이 연결되었기 때문에 당시로서는 공학의 이정표가 되었다. 이 운하 덕분에 선박들이 더 이상 남아메리카를 빙 돌아가지 않아도 되었기 때문에 해양 무역과 상업이 폭증했다.

Q. T☑ F☐

> immense 거대한 setback 난관, 어려움 undertake 떠맡다
> milestone 이정표 commerce 상업

12. 위성항법장치(GPS)

위성항법장치(GPS)는 지구상에서 정확한 항해와 물체의 위치 파악을 가능하게 하는 위성망을 말한다. 시스템은 삼변측량술에 기초하고 있다. 이것은 삼각형의 기하학을 이용해 위치를 파악하는 방법이다. 기본적인 과정은 수신기가 세 대 이상의 인공위성으로부터 오는 신호의 소요 시간을 측정해 인공위성과 지구 사이의 거리를 결정하는 것이다. 정확성을 기하기 위해 인공위성의 정확한 위치를 계속해 관찰해야 한다. 이렇게 해서 상호교차점 가운데 하나가 항상 지구 위에 표시되어 정확한 위치를 파악한다. GPS는 원래 미 국방부에서 이용할 목적으로 개발되었다. 하지만 1980년대에 전 세계인들에게 개방되었다. 그 이후로 GPS는 지도 제작자부터 히말라야 등반가, 사커맘(자녀 교육에 열성적인 주부) 에 이르기까지 모든 이들에게 중요한 장치가 되었다.

Q. T☑ F☐

> satellite 인공위성 precise 정확한 geometry 기하학
> interaction 교차점 available 사용 가능한

Unit 09 Greenland

Thinking about the Topic

Answers can vary. It is best to elicit as many answers from students as possible.

Vocabulary Focus

B 1 unadulterated 순수한, 오염되지 않은
   2 optimism 낙관주의, 낙관론
   3 aquatic 수중의, 물의
   4 misnomer 잘못된 명칭
   5 estimate 추정치, 추산
   6 illuminate 밝히다
   7 terrain 땅, 지역

8 dominate 우위를 차지하다
9 hover 공중을 날다, 선회하다
10 harsh 가혹한, 혹독한

그린란드

그린란드는 북극해 북쪽에 위치한 섬으로, 세계 최대 규모의 섬이다. 이 섬은 10세기경 바이킹족이 처음 발견했다. 훨씬 뒤인 1700년대에는 덴마크가 이 거대한 지역을 최초로 식민지로 삼았다. 오늘날 그린란드는 덴마크의 연장 영토로 자치가 허용되고 있다. 하지만 그린란드의 인구는 대단히 적다. 5만5천 명이 겨우 넘는 것으로 추정된다. 절반이 넘는 인구가 이누잇족이고 나머지는 스칸디나비아인의 후손이다. 대다수 주민이 해안과 수도인 누크 인근에 산다. 주거 지역이 분산되어 있는 이유는 섬의 80퍼센트 이상이 만년설로 뒤덮여 있기 때문이다.

그린란드의 환경은 매우 열악하다. 여름은 짧고 평균 기온이 섭씨 10도를 약간 웃돈다. 겨울에는 자주 섭씨 영하 50도까지 떨어진다. 섬의 대부분이 빙판으로 덮여 있어 숲도 없다. 그렇지만, 그린란드에서는 독특한 생태계를 찾아볼 수 있다. 이끼, 지의류, 양치류, 작은 관목, 작은 수목 등 다양한 식물 종이 존재한다. 이들은 전형적인 북극권 툰드라 식물들이다. 또한 그린란드는 북극곰, 여우, 순록, 북극여우와 같은 동물들의 보금자리이기도 하다. 그들은 섬의 혹독한 환경에 잘 적응했다. 고래나 물개와 같은 수중 포유류도 그린란드 주변의 해역에 자주 나타난다.

그린란드는 경제와 생계를 전적으로 해양에 의존하고 있기 때문에 다른 섬나라들과 유사성이 있다. 어업이 생활 방식 대부분을 좌우한다. 새우와 연어, 대구가 가장 많이 잡히는 어종이다. 이 어종 가운데 새우가 단연 가장 큰 수입원이다. 어류 가공업이 제조업 분야를 이끌고 있다. 수산물은 대다수가 덴마크와 유럽 연합의 나머지 지역으로 직접 수출된다. 최근 그린란드 정부는 경제를 다변화하려는 시도를 해왔다. 지질학적 조사를 통해 섬의 일부에 풍부한 광물 자원이 있을지도 모른다는 결과가 나왔다. 근해에 매장되어 있는 석유도 경제에 큰 힘이 될 수 있다. 금과 다이아몬드 같은 귀한 광물도 그린란드의 전망을 낙관하게 한다.

그린란드라는 이름은 약간 잘못 붙여진 듯 하지만 그린란드 섬은 오염되지 않은 자연의 아름다움으로 가득 차 있다. 이러한 이유로 그 섬을 인기 관광지로 만들려는 하는 노력이 뒤따랐다. 지금은 여러 항구에서 일부 유람선이 정기적으로 운항하고 있다. 가장 인기 있는 명소 중 하나는 일룰리사트 얼음피요르드로, 그린란드의 서해안에 위치한 거대한 빙하이다. 그것은 2004년에 유네스코 세계 문화유산으로 지정되었다. 또 다른 명소는 오로라라고 하는 북극광이다. 이 대기 현상은 그린란드의 툰드라 상공을 주기적으로 밝게 비춘다.

UNESCO 유네스코, 유엔 교육 과학 문화 기구

Reading Comprehension

1 (D) 2 (B) 3 (A) 4 ① The fishing industry drives the economy of Greenland. ② Its biggest earner is shrimp.
5 (C) 6 (A)

Organizing & Summarizing

Ⓐ 1 80% 2 Denmark
3 Inuit Indians 4 55,000
5 below −50℃ 6 moss, lichen, ferns
7 shrimp 8 minerals & oil

Ⓑ 1 Denmark in the 1700s
2 Inuit decent
3 Arctic tundra plant life
4 the fishing industry
5 oil and precious minerals
6 the aurora borealis

바이킹족에 의해 처음 발견된 그린란드는 세계 최대 규모의 섬이다. 그 섬은 1700년대에 덴마크의 식민지가 되었다. 그린란드는 북극해 북쪽에 위치해 있다. 섬의 80퍼센트 이상이 얼음으로 덮여 있기 때문에 인구의 대다수가 해안 지역 부근에 살고 있다. 대부분은 이누잇족의 후손이다. 기후는 매우 추워서 여름 평균 기온이 섭씨 10도, 겨울에는 영하 50도까지 내려간다. 그린란드에는 이끼와 지의류, 양치류, 작은 관목, 작은 수목과 같은 북극권 툰드라 식물들이 자란다. 또한 북극곰, 늑대, 순록, 고래, 물개와 같은 다양한 야생동물이 그린란드와 그 주변에 살고 있다. 경제는 거의 전적으로 어업 활동을 통한 해양에 의존하고 있으며 새우가 주수입원이다. 하지만 경제가 다변화하고 있다. 석유와 귀금속에 대한 탐사가 진행 중이다. 또한 장관을 이루는 빙하와 북극 밤하늘의 오로라를 보기 위해 관광객이 유람선을 타고 몰려 들면서 관광업도 각광을 받고 있다.

Unit 10 The Mississippi River and Its Dams

Thinking about the Topic

Answers can vary. It is best to elicit as many answers from students as possible.

Vocabulary Focus

Ⓑ 1 utilize 이용하다, 사용하다
2 modernization 현대화, 근대화
3 crucial 매우 중요한
4 migratory 이주성의, 이동성의
5 commercial 상업적인
6 precious 값진, 귀한
7 oppose 반대하다

8 habitat 서식지, 서식처
9 artery 동맥; 간선
10 navigate 항해하다

미시시피강과 댐

미시시피강은 미국에서 가장 큰 강이며 대단히 중요한 물길이다. 강은 북쪽의 미네소타 주 이타스카호에서 남쪽의 멕시코만으로 흐르며 길이는 2,340마일 정도이다. 이 강은 미국의 발달과 성장에 핵심적 역할을 했다. 미국 역사의 초창기에는 순식간에 통상과 무역의 주된 동맥이 되었다. 오늘날, 그 강은 미시시피 상류와 하류의 두 부분으로 나누어진다. 상류는 미네소타의 수원에서 시작되어 남쪽으로 오하이오강까지 뻗어 있다. 하류는 오하이오강에서부터 루이지애나주 뉴올리언스 근처의 하구까지 이어져 있다. 강의 상부에는 일련의 갑문과 댐이 설치되었다. 이것은 선적을 위해 강의 수심을 깊게 만들기 위해 필요했다.

1930년대에 미국 정부는 미시시피강 상류 지역을 운항로로 더 잘 활용해야 할 필요가 있음을 깨닫고 일련의 댐 건설 계획을 세웠다. 1940년대 초에 총 29개의 수문과 댐이 지어졌다. 이를 건설한 일차적인 의도는 미시시피강 상류의 수위를 조절하는 것이었다. 댐으로 인해 여러 개의 웅덩이가 만들어져 바지선 운항이 더 용이해졌다. 수심이 깊어져 강의 상업적 운항이 가능해졌다. 갑문과 댐 시설이 없었다면 강이 너무 얕아 선적을 운항할 수 없었을 것이다. 이 프로젝트가 완공되자 미시시피강 상류의 수심은 균일하게 9피트 깊이가 되었다.

하지만 미시시피강이 선적과 상업에만 중요한 역할을 하는 것은 아니다. 수백 종의 동물들이 미시시피강 유역의 서식지에서 사는데, 이것은 미국 전체 면적의 40퍼센트에 달한다. 이 동물들은 거의 300여 종에 달하는 어류와 약 50여종의 포유류를 포함한다. 전문가들은 또한 전문가들은 미국 철새의 절반가량이 연중 특정 시기 동안 미시시피강 근처에서 서식한다고 믿고 있다. 따라서, 미시시피강은 미국의 전체 생태계에 중요한 역할을 한다.

오늘날에는 미육군공병단이 미시시피강에 있는 댐들의 관리를 맡고 있다. 또한 강과 소중한 환경을 보호하는 책임도 맡고 있다. 현재 수문과 댐 시설이 노후화되는 조짐을 보이고 있다. 많은 단체들이 홍수 조절을 위해 시설을 보다 효율적으로 바꾸는 현대화 작업을 요구해왔다. 하지만 다양한 환경단체들은 그렇게 될 경우 미시시피강의 자연 습지가 파괴될 것이라고 주장하면서 그러한 프로젝트에 반대한다.

commerce 통상, 상업   barge 거룻배

Reading Comprehension

1 (B)　2 (D)　3 (C)　4 ① There are about 300 different species of fish. ② There are over 50 different kinds of mammals.　5 (B)　6 (A)

Organizing & Summarizing

Ⓐ　1 commercial river　2 2,340 miles
　3 9 ft. depth　4 flood control
　5 river basin　6 50 types
　7 migratory birds
　8 U.S. Army Corps of Engineers

Ⓑ　1 about 2,340 miles
　2 by the 1940s
　3 barge navigation
　4 better flood control
　5 40 percent of the U.S.
　6 migratory birds

미시시피강은 미국을 북에서 남으로 거의 2,500마일 정도의 길이로 흐른다. 그 강은 미국의 발달에 중요한 역할을 했다. 1940년경 일련의 수문과 댐이 미시시피강 상류에 건설되었다. 이 시설로 인해 수심이 균일하게 9피트가 되어서 바지선 운항에 이상적인 깊이가 되었다. 이 덕분에 미시시피강의 상업과 무역이 최대화되었다. 하지만 오늘날 이 시설은 낡아서 홍수를 더 잘 조절하기 위해 개선할 필요가 있다. 그러나 환경론자들은 이로 인해 강 유역의 야생동물 서식지에 피해가 갈 것을 우려한다. 미시시피강 유역은 미국 국토의 40퍼센트 이상을 차지하기 때문에 수백 종의 어류와 약 50종의 포유류가 이곳에 서식하고 있다. 또한 미국 철새의 절반이 이 지역에 머무르기도 한다. 현재는 미육군공병단이 주변환경 보호뿐만 아니라 수문과 댐의 유지보수도 책임지고 있다.

Vocabulary Expansion

Part A

Ⓐ　**TERRAIN:** desert, dune, glacier, gorge, mountain, valley
　WATERWAY: channel, lake, ocean, river, sea, strait

Ⓑ　1 mouth　2 ecosystem　3 weather
　4 commute　5 milestone

Ⓒ　1 milestones　2 typhoon　3 commute
　4 glacier　5 gums　6 subway
　7 ecosystem　8 radio　9 tornadoes
　10 scavengers

Part B

Ⓐ　**RAILROAD:** conductor, locomotive, station,

spike, track, train
RIVER: barge, captain, current, dock, port, steamboat

B
1 separating 2 limp 3 ceiling
4 forest 5 coarse

C
1 conductor 2 spikes 3 adjacent
4 currents 5 dock 6 concrete
7 limp 8 port 9 skyscrapers
10 coarse

Mass Communication
매스 커뮤니케이션

Basic Knowledge Building

1. 요하네스 구텐베르크

요하네스 구텐베르크는 15세기 독일의 인쇄공이자 금세공사였다. 그는 일반적으로 서양에서 금속활자를 발명한 사람으로 잘 알려져 있다. 금속활자로는 고품질 인쇄가 가능했기 때문에 혁신이 삽시간에 유럽 전역으로 퍼져나갔다. 또한 금속활자로 인쇄를 더 빠르고 효과적으로 할 수 있었다. 예를 들어, 금속활자 이전에는 책을 손으로 베끼거나 손으로 판 목판으로 찍어내야 했다. 이러한 책들은 인쇄기로 인쇄한 것만큼 내구성이 있지도 않았다. 구텐베르크의 발명품은 책을 더 저렴하고 구하기 쉽게 해주었고 일반인의 문자 습득을 향상시켰다. 금속활자 덕분에 서적 산업은 영원히 바뀌었다.

Q. T ☑ F ☐

goldsmith 금세공사 press 인쇄기 efficiently 효과적으로
carve 새기다 durable 내구성이 있는, 질긴 literacy 읽고 쓰는 능력

2. 대중 사회

대중 사회란 산업혁명 이후의 산업화된 사회 분위기를 설명하기 위해 사용하는 용어다. 일반적으로 말해, 그것은 산업화된 사회에 사는 사람들을 개성을 잃은 사람들로 묘사한다. 자본주의와 소비주의가 대중 사회를 지배한다. 이런 식으로 대중 사회는 개성을 잃어버린 것으로 여겨진다. 소비자들은 상품의 생산자와 만나는 일이 드물다. 사람들은 비슷한 일을 하며 비슷하게 행동하는 가족으로 채워진 비슷해 보이는 가정에서 생활한다. 대중 사회는 또한 수준 높은 문화의 몰락이 특징으로 나타나기도 한다. 사람들은 흔히 문학이나 그림 같은 예술보다는 텔레비전과 같은 대중매체를 더 선호한다.

Q. T ☐ F ☑

industrialize 산업화하다 individuality 개성 dominate 지배하다
faceless 개성이 없는 decline 몰락

3. 페니 신문

페니 신문은 19세기 미국에서 인기를 누렸다. 그것은 길거리에서 1센트에 팔려 신문의 독자층을 확대하는 데 기여했다. 페니 신문이 나오기 전에는 신문을 정기 구독해야만 했고 페니 신문에 비해 가격도 상대적으로 비쌌다. 페니 신문은 직접적이고 이해하기 쉬운 문체로 일반인들에게 다가갔다. 언어는 보다 다채로웠고 사람 사는 얘기들이 대중 인쇄물에 처음으로 등장하기 시작했다. 뉴욕과 시카고 같은 도시 지역의 인구가 급증하면서 페니 신문의 인기에 불을 붙였다.

Q. T ☑ F ☐

broaden 확대하다 readership 독자층 publication 출판물
cater 제공하다 fuel 연료를 공급하다 popularity 인기

4. 윌리엄 랜돌프 허스트 1세

윌리엄 랜돌프 허스트 1세는 19세기와 20세기 미국의 영향력 있는 미디어 거물이었다. 그는 상류층 백만장자 가정에서 출생했다. 하버드대학에 다녔으며, 그 후 부친은 그에게 〈샌프란시스코 이그재미너〉지를 경영하게 했다. 허스트는 상당한 재산과 노력을 투자해 그 신문을 성공시켰다. 그 후 뉴욕시의 신문인 〈모닝 저널〉을 인수했다. 허스트는 종자가 다른 신문인이었다. 노동계층을 독자층으로 삼고 신문의 가격을 대폭 인하했다. 다른 신문사들도 이런 흐름을 따르지 않을 수 없었다. 허스트는 보다 많은 신문, 잡지, 영화사를 매입해 자신의 제국을 계속 확장해 나갔다. 하지만 1950년대 초 인생 말년에는 이러한 모험이 대부분 실패로 끝난 상태였다.

Q. T ☐ F ☑

mogul 거물 breed 종 slash 삭감하다 publication 출판물
purchase 구매하다

5. 짤막한 전신의 역사

원시적인 형태의 전신은 북이나 심지어 불의 형태로 고대부터 존재했다. 하지만 현대의 전신이 가능해진 것은 전기가 발명되고 나서였다. 19세기에 유럽의 과학자들은 전선을 통해 메시지를 보낼 수 있다는 것을 깨달았다. 1820년대 미국에서는 사무엘 모스가 전자석을 사용해 먼 거리로 메시지를 보냈다. 그는 점과 선으로 된 모스 부호를 개발해 알파벳을 전기신호로 바꾸었다. 곧 도시와 국가, 대륙을 연결하는 장거리 전신 케이블이 가설되었다. 1860년대 후반에는 수중 전선으로 유럽과 미국이 연결되었다. 전신은 1세기 정도 사용되다가 더 현대적인 컴퓨터 기술로 대체되었다.

Q. T ☐ F ☑

primitive 원시적인 telegraphy 전신 advent 도래
electricity 전기 render 바꾸다, 표현하다 replace 교체하다

6. 통신사

통신사는 정보를 수집해 신문, 라디오, 텔레비전과 같은 미디어 대리점에 정보를 제공하는 기관이다. 세계에서 가장 큰 두 통신사는 로이터통신과 연합통신(AP)이다. 로이터통신은 1851년 런던에서 설립되었다. 금융과 경제 정보를 독자들에게 전문적으로 제공하는 세계적인 통신사이다. 하지만 기자들은 전 세계에서 다양한 뉴스를 취재한다. 대서양을 건너편에서는 연합통신이 1846년 미국에서 창설되었다. 200개가 넘는 뉴스 사무소를 전 세계 약 120개국에서 운영하며 기사를 제공하는 세계 최고의 통신사이다. 오늘날 연합통신은 다른 미국 미디어 회사들이 소유하고 있다.

Q. T ☑ F ☐

collect 수집하다   outlet 대리점   specialize in ~을 전문으로 하다
financial 금융의   subscribe 구독하다

7. 라디오와 니콜라 테슬라

라디오는 여러 발명가들과 기술자들이 중요한 발견을 하는 과정을 통해 발명되었다. 그들의 기여로 마침내 정보의 무선전송이 가능해졌다. 논란의 여지가 있지만, 굴리에모 마르코니가 "라디오의 아버지"로 여겨져 왔다. 하지만 덜 알려진 발명가인 니콜라 테슬라는 더 이전에 궁극적으로 현대식 라디오의 개발에 도움을 준 여러 가지 중요한 발견을 했다. 테슬라는 1800년대 후반에 전파를 생성하는 과정에 대한 특허를 최초로 받았다. 하지만 라디오 탄생의 길을 연 건을 그의 교류 연구였다. 더욱이, 테슬라는 다중 주파수 전송, 4파장 회로, 진보된 전파 수신기 등을 개발했다. 또한 오늘날에도 여전히 여러 가지 현대 전자제품에 사용되는 에너지 변환기인 테슬라 코일을 설계하여 특허를 받기도 했다.

Q. T ☐ F ☑

transmission 정보   arguably 논란의 여지가 있지만
obscure 잘 알려지지 않은   alternate 번갈아 일어나다
patent 특허를 내다

8. 르포르타주

저널리즘에서 르포르타주란 일반적으로 특별한 주제나 사건에 관한 전체 뉴스 보도의 전반적인 스타일이나 관점을 가리킨다. 르포르타주의 중요한 요소 가운데 하나는 미디어가 어떤 사건을 어떻게 서술하느냐에 대한 비판이다. 또 다른 요소로는 뉴스기사를 작성하고 찍는 데 사용하는 기술이다. 하지만 르포르타주는 또 다른 의미를 띨 수도 있다. 그것은 어떤 사건에 대한 신문기자의 목격담을 가리킬 수도 있다. 흔히 신문기자는 주제에 몰입해서 현장 취재를 통해 특정 사건에 대한 전문적인 목격자가 되기도 한다. 그들은 나중에 다양한 미디어 통로를 통해 자신들의 인상과 견해를 표현한다.

Q. T ☐ F ☑

portray 묘사하다   facet 국면, 양상   eyewitness 목격자
account 설명   immerse 몰두케 하다   slant 왜곡시키다

9. 종군기자

종군기자는 분쟁의 한가운데서 활동하는 기자를 말한다. 최초의 종군기자는 아마도 고대 전쟁 중에 생겨났을 것이다. 이런 식의 저널리즘은 현장에서 가장 위험하지만 흔히 가장 성공적이기도 하다. 기자가 현장 속으로 깊이 파고들수록 신문 판매량과 텔레비전 시청률이 높아진다. 최근에는 베트남전, 코스보전, 이라크전에서 군인들을 따라 전쟁터를 돌아다니는 기자들이 더 많아졌다. 역사상 많은 종군기자들이 전쟁기사를 취재하려다가 죽음을 맞았다.

Q. T ☑ F ☐

conflict 분쟁   antiquity 고대   rating 시청률   roam 돌아다니다
pay the ultimate price 최후의 대가를 치르다, 죽음을 맞다

10. 보도사진

보도사진은 사진을 통해 기사를 보여주는 일종의 저널리즘이다. 부분적으로 비디오가 사용되기도 하지만 일반적으로 스틸 사진이 들어간다. 이 분야의 독특한 점은 대단히 객관적이고 정확하다는 것이다. 다시 말해, 사진 자체가 기사를 들려준다. 일반적으로, 사진은 논쟁의 여지가 있을 수 없다. 최근에는 하이테크 디지털 카메라와 인터넷이 생기면서 보도사진이 전성기를 맞았다. 사진기자들은 더 이상 사진을 현상하거나 통신사로 영상을 보내느라 소중한 시간을 허비할 필요가 없다. 이미지는 즉시 전송할 수 있다. 그리하여 실제 사건이 발생하자마자 사진을 웹이 올릴 수 있다. 흔히, 글이나 실제 기사는 약간 나중에 나온다.

Q. T ☐ F ☑

objective 객관적인   dispute 논쟁하다   develop 현상하다
upload 전송하다   instantaneously 즉시

11. 디지털 통신

디지털 통신은 정보를 주고 받는 빠르고 대중적인 수단이다. 자료는 이메일, 핸드폰, 웹을 통해 전자식으로 교환된다. 이러한 통신 형태가 사람들 간의 통신 방식을 급격하게 변화시켰다. 개인들은 시간과 공간의 제약을 거의 받지 않고 디지털 미디어를 통해 연락을 주고 받을 수 있다. 인터넷 덕분에 거의 모든 종류의 자료를 언제 어디서나 얻을 수 있다. 즉각적인 접속과 연결로 최근 들어 디지털 통신 분야의 수요가 많이 늘었다. 또 다른 이점은 저장이 쉽다는 것이다. 정보를 저장해서 필요하면 언제나 다시 볼 수 있다. 그리하여 편리성은 디지털 시대의 또 다른 교의가 되었다.

Q. T ☐ F ☑

electronically 전자기적으로   drastically 급격히   constraint 제약
access 접근(하다), 이용(하다)   tenet 교의

12. 시민 저널리즘

시민 저널리즘은 비전문가들도 뉴스의 내용을 만들고 비평할 수 있다는 개념이다. 언론사 경험이 없는 일반인도 오늘날

에는 뉴스거리를 생산할 수 있게 해주는 기술을 이용할 수 있다. 보도 가치가 있는 사건을 찍은 비디오나 사진을 블로그에 올리는 것은 한 가지 예에 불과하다. 또는 다른 언론 정보를 통해 잡지 기사의 타당성을 확인하는 것이 또 다른 예이다. 시민 저널리즘의 핵심은 누구라도 할 수 있다는 것이다. 세계 전역에서 일어나는 일에 적극 참여하기 위해 전문 언론인이 되어야 할 필요는 없다. 더욱이, 시민 저널리즘은 정보의 범위와 깊이를 더 넓고 깊게 만든다. 그것은 독자적이며 흔히 주류 언론에 비해 편견이 없다.

Q. T ☑ F ☐

> newsworthy 보도 가치가 있는 validity 타당성 crux 핵심
> independent 독자적인 unbiased 편견이 없는

Unit 11 Joseph Pulitzer

Thinking about the Topic
Answers can vary. It is best to elicit as many answers from students as possible.

Vocabulary Focus
B 1 acquisition 인수, 습득
2 emigrate 이민 가다
3 monetary 재정의, 돈의
4 viable 성장[성공]할 수 있는
5 prosperity 번영, 번창
6 prestigious 명망 있는, 명문의
7 revive 되살리다, 소생시키다
8 immortality 불후의 명성
9 legacy 유산
10 overhaul 개편, 정비

조셉 퓰리처

조셉 퓰리처는 미국의 정치가이자 출판업자였다. 그는 처음에 헝가리에서 출생해 남북전쟁에 참여하기 위해 미국으로 건너갔다. 종전 후에는 기자가 되었다. 오래지 않아 그는 비전과 야망 덕분에 미국 대중매체 분야에서 초기 개척자가 되었다. 일생 동안 여러 신문사를 사들여 부유하면서도 강력한 존재가 되었다. 그가 죽고 나서 그의 이름을 딴 퓰리처상이 제정되었다. 퓰리처상은 미국에서 언론인, 작가, 음악가에게 수여하는 가장 권위 있는 상 가운데 하나이다.

퓰리처는 망해가는 신문사를 사서 정비한 뒤 이윤을 남기고 팔았다. 1883년 그는 〈뉴욕 월드〉지를 사서 공격적 저널리즘으로 이를 소생시켰다. 퓰리처는 독자들의 흥미를 끄는 기사와 선정주의로 신문의 방향을 돌렸다. 그런 다음 신문의 부수를 늘릴 목적으로 황색저널리즘을 사용했다. 이 기법은 공감 전술, 오해의 소지가 다분한 헤드라인, 연재만화, 틀린 사실 등을 사용해 판매부수를 늘렸다. 폭로성 기사 역시 황색저널리즘의 중요한 요소가 되었다. 퓰리처의 전략은 엄청난 성공을 거두었다. 1895년 무렵 〈뉴욕 월드〉는 미국 전체에서 가장 큰 신문이 되었다. 더 중요한 것은, 퓰리처가 미국 내 신문업의 미래를 바꿔 놓았다는 것이다.

하지만 조셉 퓰리처는 자신의 재산이나 명성만 추구하지는 않았다. 향후 저널리즘을 성장 가능한 직종으로 만드는 데에도 관심이 있었다. 퓰리처는 일생 동안 뉴욕의 컬럼비아 대학과 인연을 맺었다. 퓰리처의 엄청난 재정 지원 덕에 그 대학은 세계 최초의 언론학교를 설립했다. 하지만 그것이 전부는 아니었다. 유언장을 통해 퓰리처는 대학에 퓰리처상을 위한 상금으로 50만 달러를 기부했다. 퓰리처상은 미국에서 가장 명망 있는 상 가운데 하나이다. 그것은 음악뿐만 아니라 언론과 문학 분야의 업적을 인정하는 상이다. 퓰리처상은 퓰리처가 사망한지 7년 후인 1917년에 최초로 수여되었다.

조셉 퓰리처의 삶과 업적은 아메리칸 드림의 성공적 실현을 효과적으로 보여준다. 사실상 아무것도 없이 시작한 사람이 일반 대중은 꿈도 못 꾸는 부와 명예를 누리는 위치까지 오를 수 있었다. 그러나 그는 또한 자신의 유산을 잘 깨닫고 있었다. 그는 언론인으로서 남긴 업적으로만 기억되는 것은 원치 않았다. 기록적인 판매부수와 은행 잔고는 충분히 만족스럽지 못했다. 하지만 최초의 언론학교 설립과 퓰리처상 제정을 통해 그는 영원히 이름을 남길 수 있었다.

> epitomize ~의 전형이다

Reading Comprehension
1 (B) 2 (D) 3 (A) 4 ① It was first awarded in 1917. ② It is awarded for achievements in literature, journalism, and music. 5 (C) 6 (B)

Organizing & Summarizing
A 1 Civil War   2 *New York World*
3 yellow journalism 4 Columbia University
5 Pulitzer Prizes   6 in 1917

B 1 the Civil War
2 failing newspapers
3 *New York World*
4 yellow journalism
5 Columbia University
6 journalism, literature, and music

조셉 퓰리처는 헝가리에서 태어나 나중에 미국으로 건너가 남북전쟁에 참여했다. 종전 후에는 기자가 되었다. 그는 젊고 야망이 있었으며 언론사업을 속속들이 배우고 싶어했다. 오래지 않아 그는 망해가는 신문사들에 투자하기 시작했다. 그것들을

성공적으로 회생시켜 상당한 이윤을 남기고 되팔았다. 그가 내린 최선의 선택 가운데 하나는 1883년에 〈뉴욕 월드〉지를 사들인 것이었다. 1895년경 그것은 미국에서 가장 판매부수가 많은 신문이 되었다. 대중매체 분야의 성공에 이어 곧 부와 권력이 뒤따랐다. 황색저널리즘의 발명이 성공에 크게 기여했다. 그의 신문은 선정주의와 추문을 이용해 판매부수를 늘렸다. 많은 사람들이 도덕성 또는 도덕성 결여를 문제 삼았지만 신문은 기록적인 수치로 팔려나갔다. 하지만 퓰리처는 이윤을 남기는 데만 관심이 있었던 것은 아니었다. 그는 컬럼비아 대학에 최초의 언론학교를 세웠다. 그가 사망한 후 대학은 퓰리처상을 제정했고, 이는 언론, 문학, 음악 분야에 수여되는 명망 있는 상이다. 궁극적으로, 퓰리처는 바닥에서 출발해 부를 획득한 아메리칸 드림의 상징이었다.

Unit 12 The History of Magazines

Thinking about the Topic
Answers can vary. It is best to elicit as many answers from students as possible.

Vocabulary Focus
B
1 refine 다듬다; 개량하다
2 distribution 분배
3 inaugural 시작의, 처음의
4 advent 출현, 도래
5 authoritative 권위 있는, 믿을 만한
6 devise 고안하다, 생각해내다
7 explode 급속히 증가하다
8 breathtaking 깜짝 놀랄 만한
9 cater 만족시키다, 영합하다
10 periodical 정기간행물

잡지의 역사
최초의 영어 잡지는 18세기 초 영국에서 시작되었다. 〈젠틀맨스 매거진〉이 1731년 런던에서 출판되어 그 분야의 문을 최초로 열었다. 그것은 흔히 영어로 된 최초의 일반잡지로 간주된다. 창설자인 에드워드 케이브는 "잡지"라는 단어를 최초로 사용했으며 정기 간행물을 독자에게 전달하는 성공적 배포 시스템을 만들었다. 같은 시기에 미국 잡지들의 대다수는 영국 잡지의 재발행판이었다. 19세기가 되어서야 비로소 잡지가 미국에 영향력을 미치기 시작했다.

1800년대 초 미국에는 잡지가 전국적으로 100종도 되지 않았다. 또한 대다수는 판매부수도 매우 적고 수명도 짧았다. 하지만 19세기 중반이 되자 잡지의 수는 거의 1천 종으로 늘어났다. 이러한 현상에는 두 가지 이유가 있었다. 첫째, 당시는 남북전쟁 시기였다. 미국은 나뉘어졌고 잡지는 전쟁에 관한 의견을 표출할 수 있는 손쉬운 방법이었다. 둘째, 기술 발전으로 인쇄가 더 빠르고 저렴해졌다. 이 덕분에 일반 대중은 더 쉽게 잡지를 구할 수 있었다. 20세기가 시작될 무렵에는 미국에서만 5천 종이 넘는 잡지가 있었다.

미국에서 잡지의 인기가 높았던 또 다른 중요한 이유는 〈내셔널 지오그래픽〉이라는 단 하나의 잡지 때문이었다. 그것은 1888년 처음 창간되었다. 지금은 〈내셔널 지오그래픽〉이 전 세계적으로 가장 유명한 잡지 가운데 하나가 되었다. 그 잡지의 초창기 편집자들은 전 세계에서 입수한 깜짝 놀랄만한 사진들과 문화 기사들을 이용해 독자들을 놀라게 했다. 그 잡지를 보면 미국 독자들과 이후에는 전 세계 독자들이 꿈에서나 볼 수 있던 곳들을 바로 집과 사무실에서 만날 수 있었다. 그 잡지는 19세기의 많은 미국 잡지 가운데 유일하게 살아남은 잡지이기도 하다. 20세기 초반에 1차 대전이 일어나면서 잡지의 역사에 변화가 생겼다.

1923년 〈타임〉지가 세계 최초의 "뉴스 전문지"로 창간되었다. 그것은 직설적이면서도 권위가 있었다. 〈타임〉지는 미래의 뉴스 잡지와 여타 대중매체의 논조를 결정지었다. 1900년대 중반 무렵 미국인들은 개인의 정체성에 관심을 갖기 시작했고 잡지도 마찬가지였다. 스포츠, 취미생활, 건강과 같은 관심사들을 전문으로 삼게 되었다. 일부 잡지들은 심지어 특정한 성(性)을 위해 출판되기도 했다. 경제와 금융도 인기 있는 주제가 되었다. 현대의 잡지들은 여전히 특정 독자층을 겨냥하는 전통을 고수하고 있다. 하지만 오늘날 많은 사람들은 종이로 된 매체에서 관심을 돌려 더 쉽게 접할 수 있는 온라인 매체로 돌아서고 있다.

> circulation (잡지, 신문 따위의) 배포, 발행부수

Reading Comprehension
1 (D)   2 (C)   3 (B)   4 ① *Time* was first established in 1923. ② It called itself a "news-only" magazine.   5 (A)
6 (B)

Organizing & Summarizing
A
1 *The Gentleman's Magazine*
2 100 magazines
3 Civil War
4 *National Geographic*
5 specialized magazines
6 news-only

B
1 in London in 1731
2 their British counterparts
3 Civil War discussions
4 *National Geographic*
5 global stories
6 *Time* magazine

1731년 런던에서는 최초의 영어 잡지인 〈젠틀맨스 매거진〉이 창간되었다. 이 시기는 또한 "잡지"라는 단어가 최초로 사용된 때이기도 했다. 미국에서 같은 기간에 나온 잡지들은 영국 잡지의 재발행판에 지나지 않았다. 그 후 1800년대 초에는 미국에 100개도 되지 않는 잡지만 있었다. 하지만 19세기 중반 경이 되자 남북전쟁 논의에 대한 관심 증가와 발전된 기술 덕분에 잡지의 수가 늘어났다. 더 좋은 장비 덕분에 잡지가 더 저렴해졌다. 잡지 수는 전국적으로 1천 개가 넘었다. 또한 1888년에는 〈내셔널 지오그래픽〉이 창간되었다. 사진과 전 세계의 문화 기사들이 독자를 끌어들였다. 20세기에는 잡지가 더욱 성장했다. 잡지는 스포츠, 뉴스, 심지어 성과 같은 주제를 더 전문적으로 다뤘다. 1923년에는 〈타임〉지가 최초의 뉴스 전문 잡지로 창간되었다. 논조는 직설적이고 권위가 있었다. 오늘날에는 대다수 잡지들이 온라인으로 진출했다.

Vocabulary Expansion

Part A

A JOURNALISM: circulation, interview, magazine, periodical, reporter, subscription
MUSIC: conductor, ensemble, instrument, note, recital, symphony

B
| 1 publisher | 2 corporation | 3 profession |
| 4 media | 5 New York | |

C
1 New York	2 reporters	3 corporation
4 circulation	5 Central Park	6 conductor
7 lawyer	8 media	
9 journalists / reporters		10 negotiator

Part B

A SPORTS: baseball, cricket, golf, lacrosse, soccer, volleyball
HOBBIES: cooking, gardening, painting, photography, quilting, woodworking

B
| 1 final | 2 economical | 3 pitch |
| 4 collapse | 5 frequency | |

C
1 golf	2 economical	3 frequency
4 final	5 collapse	6 pitch
7 first	8 crowd	9 quilting
10 lacrosse		

Psychology 심리학

Basic Knowledge Building

1. 감각기억, 단기기억, 장기기억

기억이란 정보를 저장하는 정신적 능력을 말한다. 종종 세 가지 기억으로 구분한다. 감각기억은 아주 단시간 감각 자극으로 받은 인상을 저장한다. 이 기억은 자동적으로 일어나며 겨우 1초 정도만 지속된다. 단기기억은 약 20초간 정보를 저장하며 분석과 해석 작업이 이루어진다. 일반적으로, 사람들은 단기기억 속에 7±2 개 정도의 정보를 기억할 수 있다. 흔한 예가 7자리 전화번호이다. 마지막으로, 장기기억이란 정보가 뇌에 영구 저장되는 것을 말한다. 하지만 정보가 지속되기 위해서는 자주 상기를 시켜야 한다.

Q. T ☑ F ☐

capacity 능력 distinguish 구별하다 retain 기억하다
interpret 해석하다 permanent 영구적인 recall 상기하다

2. 서술기억과 절차기억

장기기억에는 두 가지 방식으로 정보가 저장된다. 서술기억은 의식적으로 배운 사실이나 개념, 사상을 기억하는 것이다. 따라서 정보를 말로 쉽게 전달할 수 있다. 좋은 예가 역사 시간에 배운 중요한 날짜를 기억하는 것이다. 또 다른 예는 영어의 시제를 상기하는 것이다. 대조적으로, 절차기억은 기술 및 과정에 대한 지식과 관련이 있다. 이 범주에는 그것을 하는 법은 알고 있지만 어떻게 배웠는지는 의식적으로 알지 못하는 것들과 관련이 있다. 예를 들어, 사람들은 수영을 하거나 피아노를 칠 줄 알지만 어떻게 하는지 말로 설명하지는 못한다.

Q. T ☐ F ☑

declarative 서술의 procedural 절차의 concept 개념
convey 전달하다 tense 시제 consciously 의식적으로
verbally 말로

3. 초두 효과와 최신 효과

어떤 목록에서 어떤 항목을 얼마나 잘 기억하는지는 떠올릴 항목의 위치에 따라 달라진다. 일반적으로 사람들은 목록 처음에 나오는 단어를 쉽게 상기한다. 이런 현상을 초두 효과라고 한다. 예를 들어, 어떤 사람이 이름이 적힌 긴 명단을 듣는다. 나중에 가운데에 있는 이름보다는 처음에 있는 이름들을 더 잘 기억한다. 최신 효과는 정반대의 현상이다. 이름이 적힌 동일한 목록을 주었을 경우 목록의 가장 뒤쪽에 있는 이름들을 가장 잘 기억한다. 초두 효과와 최신 효과 둘 다 어떻게 기억이 처음과 마지막 인상에 초점을 맞추는가를 보여준다. 하지만 중간 부분은 그만큼 쉽게 기억되지 않는다.

Q. T ☑ F ☐

> primacy 수위, 최고 recency 최근 opposite 반대의
> phenomenon 현상 impression 인상 accessible 접근하기 쉬운

4. 원초아, 자아, 초자아

지그문트 프로이트에 따르면 원초아, 자아, 초자아는 성격을 이루는 세 가지 구성요소이다. 그는 인간은 원초아를 지닌 채 태어난다고 주장했다. 원초아는 허기와 갈증 같은 인간의 기본적 욕구이다. 그것은 즉각적인 욕구 충족 외에는 관심을 두지 않는다. 그 욕구가 이성적인지 혹은 유해한 것인지는 개의치 않는다. 대조적으로, 자아는 출생 후 성장과 함께 발달한다. 자아는 다른 사람들도 역시 욕구가 있다는 것을 깨닫는다. 그러므로 자아는 현실의 원칙과 밀접한 관련이 있다. 타인의 욕구를 배려함과 동시에 현실적인 방법으로 원초아의 본능적 욕구를 충족시키려 한다. 마지막으로 발달하는 것이 초자아이다. 초자아는 개인의 양심을 통제한다. 무엇이 옳고 그른지 구별하는 역할을 한다.

Q. T☐ F☑

> component 구성요소 contend 주장하다 rational 이성적인
> contrast 대조 instinctual 본능의 conscience 양심
> simultaneously 동시에

5. 칼 융

칼 융은 스위스의 유명한 심리학자이자 정신과 의사이다. 융은 처음에는 지그문트 프로이드와 함께 작업했다. 나중에 그는 많은 프로이드 이론에 반대하게 되었다. 융은 분석 심리학 분야를 열었다. 융 이론의 핵심은 무의식에 대한 사고이다. 융에게는 인간의 무의식이 두 가지 요소로 되어 있다. 한 가지는 개인 영역이다. 이것은 억압된 기억으로 이루어져 있다. 다른 것은 집단 영역이다. 융은 과거든 현재든 각 개인이 인류의 나머지와 어떤 행동과 경험을 공유한다고 믿었다. 그는 또한 꿈이 보편적인 원형의 저장소라고 주장했다.

Q. T☑ F☐

> psychologist 심리학자 psychiatrist 정신과의사
> analytic 분석적인 be comprised of ~로 구성되다
> repress 억압하다 maintain 주장하다 archetype 원형

6. 아브라함 매슬로의 욕구위계 이론

아브라함 매슬로는 20세기의 미국 심리학자이다. 그는 1940년대에 욕구위계 이론을 발표했다. 그의 위계 이론은 어떤 욕구가 다른 욕구에 비해 어떻게 더 중요한지를 설명해준다. 다섯 단계의 인간 욕구가 피라미드 형태로 조직되어 있다. 호흡과 식욕 같은 기본 욕구가 피라미드의 하부에 자리잡고 있다. 다음 단계에는 가령 개인의 건강이나 고용과 같은 안전에 대한 욕구가 자리잡고 있다. 안전 위에는 사랑, 애정, 소속감이 있다. 친구들이 있으면 이런 욕구를 충족시킬 수도 있다. 다음 단계는 자존심인데, 개인적인 성취와 존경으로 실현이 된다. 마지막으로, 매슬로는 피라미드의 가장 꼭대기에 자기 실현을 두었다. 이 영역에는 창조성과 도덕성이 해당된다. 하위 욕구가 충족되어야만 상위 욕구도 충족될 수 있다.

Q. T☑ F☐

> hierarchy 위계 ascend 올라가다 self-esteem 자존심
> achievement 성취감 creativity 독창성 morality 도덕성
> fulfill 채우다, 성취하다

7. 장 피아제의 인지 발달 이론

스위스의 심리학자인 장 피아제는 아이들의 사고가 어떻게 발달하는지 관찰한 후 1952년에 혁신적인 이론을 발표했다. 그는 아동의 지식은 스키마(도식) 또는 기초 지식 구조망으로 이루어져 있다고 설명했다. 스키마는 아동이 이전의 경험을 조직하고 새로운 경험을 이해하는 데 도움을 준다. 더욱이, 피아제는 아동의 인지 발달에 네 단계가 있다고 보았다. 최초의 단계는 감각운동기로, 출생 후부터 2세까지 지속된다. 다음은 전조작기로, 2세부터 7세까지에 해당된다. 7세부터 11세까지의 구체적 조작기가 다음에 온다. 그리고 마지막은 11세에서부터 성인기 동안 지속되는 형식적 조작기이다. 보다 복잡한 사고는 후반 단계에서 일어난다. 또한, 이 단계들은 항상 동일한 순서로 진행된다.

Q. T☐ F☑

> publish 발표하다 previous 이전 surmise 추측하다
> cognitive 인지의 concrete 구체적인

8. 관찰학습

관찰학습 이론은 인간이 타인을 관찰함으로써 배우게 된다는 사고에 기초를 두고 있다. 하지만, 이것은 단순한 모방이 아니다. 인간은 타인의 행동을 보고 무엇을 해야 하는지 뿐만 아니라 무엇을 하지 말아야 하는지를 배울 수 있다. 관찰학습은 캐나다 심리학자인 앨버트 반두라와 주로 관련이 있다. 그는 이러한 학습을 모델링이라고 불렀다. 그는 모델링에 필요한 네 가지 조건을 들었다. 주의집중, 세부사항에 대한 파지, 운동재생, 그리고 동기부여/기회이다. 관찰학습은 삶의 모든 단계에서 일어날 수 있다. 하지만, 반두라는 그것이 아동기에 가장 흔히 일어난다고 했다. 이 시기는 역할 모델이 가장 큰 영향을 미치는 시기이다.

Q. T☑ F☐

> observational 관찰의 imitation 모방 associate 관련 짓다
> retention 보유 reproduction 재생

9. 플라시보 효과

플라시보란 약효가 없는 일종의 위약이다. 유당정이 흔한 예이다. 환자가 유당정만 복용한 후 회복되기 시작하면 이것이 플라시보 효과 때문이라고 할 수 있다. 분명히, 유당정은 아무런 작용도 하지 않았다. 하지만 환자는 위약을 복용하면 자신의 상태가 나아질 것이라고 믿기 때문에 효과가 나타난다. 본질적으로, 플라시보 효과는 물질보다 정신이 우선하는 효과이다. 의약품이나 치료를 믿기만 해도 일부 환자는 충분히 치료

효과를 본다. 일부 전문가들은 심지어 플라시보가 30퍼센트 이상의 효과가 있다고 주장한다. 이 수치는 정신적인 요소가 환자의 신체적 건강과 많은 관련이 있다는 것을 의미한다.

Q. T ☑ F ☐

> fake 가짜의   medicinal 의학의   improve 향상되다
> therapy 치료법   effective 효과가 있는   imply 암시하다

10. 구매자의 후회

구매자의 후회는 구매자가 대단히 값비싼 물건을 산 뒤에 느끼는 불안감을 말한다. 구매를 한 후 곧 구매자는 자신의 행동에 의문을 갖거나 후회를 하기 시작한다. 이 후회는 여러 요소에 근거할 수 있다. 구매자는 잘못된 선택을 했다고 생각할 수도 있다. 또는 너무 비싸게 샀다고 생각할 수도 있다. 구매자의 후회는 심리적으로 설명 가능하다. 구매 전의 긍정적인 감정이 그러한 상황과 연관이 있다. 예를 들면, 더 기분이 좋아지거나 다른 사람의 부러움을 받을 수 있는 것이다. 하지만 나중에는 부정적인 감정이 앞선다. 예를 들어, 빚을 지거나 다른 것을 구매할 수 없는 상황에 처할 수도 있다.

Q. T ☑ F ☐

> remorse 후회   anxiety 불안감   excessive 과도한
> purchase 구매   fore 전면, 앞부분

11. 각인

각인은 많은 동물 종에게서 볼 수 있는 가장 흔한 학습 방법 가운데 하나다. 본질적으로, 짐승의 새끼는 어미의 특징을 익힌다. 일부 연구에 따르면 어떤 새들은 처음 보는 것이 누구이든지 또는 무엇이든지 간에 처음 본 것을 어미라고 여긴다. 각인을 최초로 발견한 것은 19세기 집에서 기르는 닭에게서였다. 나중에, 동물행동학자 콘라드 로렌츠는 오리 새끼와 거위 새끼의 습성을 연구했다. 로렌츠는 어린 새들이 태어난 지 13시간에서 16시간 안에 그들 앞에서 처음으로 움직인 물체에 각인된다는 것을 발견했다. 종종 그들은 로렌츠에게 각인이 되었다. 그는 이 시기를 "결정적 시기"라고 불렀다.

Q. T ☐ F ☑

> imprinting 각인   essentially 본질적으로   attach 애착을 느끼게 하다
> ethologist 동물행동학자   behavior 습성

12. 색채 심리학

색채 심리학은 색채가 인간의 기분, 감정, 행동에 미치는 영향을 연구하는 학문이다. 지지자들은 사람들이 어떤 색깔에 비슷한 반응을 보인다고 믿는다. 이 반응은 심리적인 동시에 생리적이다. 하지만 색채 심리학은 주요 과학 분야로 간주되지는 않는다. 비판가들은 문화마다 색채를 다르게 본다고 주장한다. 또한 다양한 색채가 갖는 의미는 시간이 흐르면서 바뀐다. 하지만 색채 치료는 계속해 영향을 미친다. 예를 들어, 의사들은 빨간색이 사람들에게 자극을 주며 분홍색은 진정 효과를 가진다고 믿는다. 파란색 역시 이완 효과가 있다고 여겨진다. 이런 이유 때문에 오늘날 색채 심리학은 광고와 스포츠에서 더 큰 역할을 한다.

Q. T ☑ F ☐

> proponent 지지자   reaction 반응   practitioner 의사
> calm 진정시키다   motivate 동기를 부여하다

Unit 13 Howard Gardner and Multiple Intelligences

Thinking about the Topic

Answers can vary. It is best to elicit as many answers from students as possible.

Vocabulary Focus

B
1 unitary 단일한, 통일된
2 evaluation 평가, 측정
3 enroll 등록하다, 입학하다
4 existential 존재의
5 embrace 포용하다, 받아들이다
6 potential 잠재력
7 controversial 논란을 일으키는
8 flawed 흠이 있는, 결함이 있는
9 constitute 구성하다
10 curiosity 호기심

하워드 가드너와 다중지능

하워드 가드너는 1943년 펜실베이니아에서 출생했다. 10대 때에는 재능 있는 음악가로 인정받았다. 그 후 1961년 하버드 대학교에 입학해서 역사를 전공했지만 학문적 호기심은 재빨리 사회과학과 심리학으로 옮겨갔다. 가드너는 1965년에 대학을 우등으로 졸업하고 하버드 대학원에 진학했다. 그는 곧 '프로젝트 제로'의 일원이 되었는데, 그것은 아동, 성인, 조직 등의 학습 과정 발달을 연구하는 연구팀이었다. 그 프로젝트에서 가드너는 인간의 인지에 대해 연구하고 인간 지능에 관한 자신만의 이론을 정립했다. 나중에 저서인 〈마음의 틀: 다중지능 이론〉(1983)을 통해 그의 이론을 발표했다.

가드너의 다중지능 이론(MI)은 인간 지능의 구성요소와 측정법을 다시 규정하려고 시도한다. 전통적으로, 지능은 지성을 나타내는 유일한 단위라고 여겨졌다. 지능지수(IQ)를 이용해 수리-논리와 언어 분야에서 점수를 매겼다. 하지만 가드너는 이런 식의 평가는 사람들이 실제로 가진 다양한 능력을 측정할 수 없기 때문에 부족하다고 믿었다. 예를 들어, 그는 수학 점수가 높은 학생이 반드시 다른 학생보다 지능지수가 높은 것은 아니라고 주장한다. 이에 대해, 다중지능 이론은 보다 다양한 인간의 재능과 지성을 포괄한다. 가드너가 제안한 핵심

지능 분야로는 대인관계, 개인 내적 요소, 음악, 공간, 언어, 논리-수리, 그리고 신체-운동 분야 등이 있다. 나중에 가드너는 지능을 측정할 수 있는 기준으로 자연, 정신, 실존, 도덕과 같은 몇 가지 요소도 제안했다.

가드너는 자신의 이론을 아동교육에도 적용해야 한다고 생각한다. 미국에서는 전통적으로 교육의 초점이 읽기, 쓰기, 수학에 집중되어 있었다. 가드너는 이 때문에 주요 과목은 못하지만 다른 과목은 잘 하는 학생들을 제한할 수 있다고 믿는다. 교사들은 다중지능 이론을 교육에 응용해 다양한 방법으로 각 학생의 요구에 부응할 수 있다. 그리고 다중지능은 각 아동의 서로 다른 지적 욕구를 평가하는 기초가 된다. 지능이 높건 낮건 교사는 학생을 도울 수 있다. 궁극적으로, 가드너는 이러한 형태의 평가와 교육을 통해 개인의 지적 능력을 최대화할 수 있다고 믿었다.

오늘날, 가드너의 다중지능 이론은 심리학과 교육 분야에서 매우 논란이 되고 있다. 일반적으로, 그의 이론은 학술적인 심리학자들한테는 인정을 받지 못하고 있지만 북미의 많은 교육자들은 이 이론을 수용한다. 많은 학교들에서는 조직화된 교과 과정을 시행하며 다중지능 이론에 따라 교실 활동을 설계한다. 논란이 있긴 하지만 하워드 가드너는 적어도 전통주의자들로 하여금 지능을 측정하는 방법과 학생을 가르치는 방법의 기초를 다시 살펴보게 했다.

cognition 인지

Reading Comprehension

1 (B) 2 (D) 3 (B) 4 ① It typically focuses on core abilities like reading, writing, and math. ② He wants the individual needs of each student evaluated and addressed in the classroom. 5 (A) 6 (C)

Organizing & Summarizing

Ⓐ 1 Project Zero 2 IQ test
   3 math & science 4 bodily-kinesthetic
   5 core subjects
   6 strengths and weaknesses

Ⓑ 1 Project Zero
   2 cognition and intelligence
   3 multiple intelligences
   4 math and science
   5 strengths and weaknesses
   6 remain controversial

하워드 가드너는 하버드 출신의 심리학자이자 사회과학자였다. 그는 '프로젝트 제로'에서 일했는데, 이 팀은 인간의 학습과정을 연구했다. 가드너는 인지와 지능에 매료되어 다중지능 이론(MI)을 만들었다. 다중지능 이론은 인간의 다양한 능력을 고려한다. 이것은 전통적인 지능지수 검사와는 반대인데, 전통적인 방법은 수학과 과학 분야의 능력에만 초점을 둔다. 가드너는 또한 다중지능 이론을 학교 교육에도 적용해야 한다고 믿는다. 그는 학생들이 전통적인 시스템에 의해 제한을 받는다고 느낀다. 하지만 다중지능 이론을 이용해 교사들은 학생의 장점과 단점 모두에 초점을 맞출 수 있다. 일부 학교에서는 학생 평가와 교육에 다중지능 이론을 활용한다. 하지만 가드너의 이론은 전통주의자들에게는 논란거리로 남아 있다.

Unit 14 Behaviorism, Cognitivism, and Constructionism

Thinking about the Topic

Answers can vary. It is best to elicit as many answers from students as possible.

Vocabulary Focus

Ⓑ 1 mechanical 기계적인
   2 substantially 충분히, 넉넉히; 실제로
   3 overshadow ~을 못해 보이게 하다
   4 rigid 완고한, 엄격한
   5 plausible 그럴싸한, 그럴듯한
   6 alter 바꾸다, 변경하다
   7 theory 이론
   8 acknowledge 인정하다
   9 framework 틀, 기반
   10 external 외부의, 외적인

행동주의, 인지주의, 구성주의

인간의 학습 과정은 19세기경부터 과학적인 연구가 이루어졌다. 현대 학습 이론은 학습 과정 동안 머리 속에서 어떤 작용이 일어나는지를 설명하고자 한다. 이 설명들은 대개 행동주의, 인지주의, 구성주의의 세 가지 범주 가운데 하나에 해당된다. 이 이론들이 모든 사람의 학습 과정에 대한 명확한 해결책을 제시해 주지는 않는다. 하지만 인간이 지식을 습득하고 쌓아나가는 일반적인 패턴을 설명해 준다.

행동주의는 미국의 심리학자인 B. F. 스키너와 밀접한 관련이 있다. 스키너는 학습이 이른바 조작적 조건화에 기초한다고 주장했다. 간단히 말해, 개인의 행동은 보상이나 처벌에 의해 강화된다. 따라서 학습 행동은 개인의 행동에 대한 긍정적 또는 부정적 반응에 의해 바뀔 수 있다. 표면적으로는, 스키너의 설명이 그럴 듯해 보인다. 하지만 그 '표면'은 기본적 오류를 가지고 있다. 행동주의는 행동에 영향을 미치는 가시적이거나 외부적인 자극에 기초를 둔다. 개인의 내적 사고나 감정은 고려하지 않는다. 20세기 후반에는 인지주의 이론이 행동주의의 제한성을 극복하기 시작했다.

인지주의는 정신적인 면에 초점을 맞춘다는 점에서 행동주의와 차이가 있다. 그래서 사고가 인지주의 진영의 핵심이다. 행동주의에 반기를 든 중요한 반대자 가운데 한 사람이 노엄 촘스키이다. 그는 언어학자로서 언어는 내부적 기전이 없이는 존재할 수 없다고 주장했다. 이러한 견해는 행동주의적 접근 방식이 지닌 중요한 결점을 드러냈다. 하지만 인지주의는 행동주의보다 완전할지는 모르지만 구조에 융통성이 없다. 많은 이론가들은 뇌를 추적 가능한 입출력 과정을 지닌 일종의 컴퓨터로 본다. 이러한 접근 방법은 학습과 인간 행동의 내부 작용을 다루는 데 있어 너무 기계적이다. 따라서 경험이 인간에게 미치는 영향과 인간이 그것을 어떻게 처리하는지를 상당 부분 다루지 못한다. 이는 구성주의와 다른 점이다.

구성주의는 인간은 각자의 경험에서 의미와 지식을 쌓아간다고 주장한다. 대표적 제안자 가운데 한 사람인 장 피아제에 따르면, 사람들은 그런 다음 경험을 동화시키거나 경험에 순응한다. 동화는 새로운 경험을 기존의 사고방식의 틀 안에 넣는다. 이 틀은 변하지 않는다. 동화는 새로운 경험이 개인이 실재를 인식하는 기존의 틀을 변화시킬 때 일어난다. 비판가들은 구성주의의 중요한 문제 중 하나가 사람들이 저마다 독특한 틀을 가지고 서로 다르게 동화 또는 순응하는 것이라고 주장한다. 그러므로, 구성주의는 폭넓게 적용될 수 있는 단일한 이론이 될 수 없다. 그렇지만, 이것이 장점이 될 수도 있다. 인지주의나 행동주의와 달리 구성주의는 어떻게 인간이 사회적, 학문적으로 자기만의 독특한 경험을 살려 자신의 세상을 형성하는지를 가장 잘 설명해 준다.

> divergence 차이, 불일치

Reading Comprehension

1 (C)   2 (D)   3 (C)   4 ① Noam Chomsky revealed the limitations of behaviorism. ② He used language to claim that internal processes are important.   5 (A)   6 (B)

Organizing & Summarizing

Ⓐ 1 B.F. Skinner 2 operant conditioning
   3 reinforcement 4 human language
   5 prior knowledge 6 Jean Piaget
   7 assimilation 8 individuality

Ⓑ 1 B.F. Skinner
   2 operant conditioning
   3 like a computer
   4 Jean Piaget
   5 assimilate and accommodate
   6 the individuality of each person

행동주의, 인지주의, 구성주의는 세 가지 주요 학습 이론이다. 행동주의는 B. F. 스키너에 의해 대중화 되었다. 그것은 보상과 처벌에 기초를 두고 있다. 스키너는 이것을 조작적 조건화라고 불렀다. 하지만 이 개념은 내부적 자극이 아닌, 외부적 자극에 주로 의존한다. 대조적으로, 인지주의는 정신 상태에 의존한다. 언어학자 노엄 촘스키가 중요한 제안자이다. 인지주의는 인간의 뇌를 컴퓨터처럼 정보를 처리하는 장치로 본다. 이 과정에서 이전의 경험이 중요한 역할을 한다. 하지만 이 학습 이론은 어떻게 학습이 새로운 경험과 연관되는지를 충분히 설명하지 못한다. 구성주의는 이러한 설명을 해 준다. 장 피아제가 중요한 지지자였다. 그는 인간이 새로운 경험을 동화하고 순응한다고 믿었다. 동화는 사고 방식의 틀 속에 새로운 경험을 저장한다. 순응도 마찬가지지만 새로운 경험이 전체적 정신적 실재에 변화를 일으킨다. 결국, 구성주의는 이전의 개념들과 달리 각 사람의 개별성을 고려한다.

Vocabulary Expansion

Part A

Ⓐ **SENSE:** auditory, gustatory, kinesthetic, olfactory, tactile, visual
   PERSONALITY: agreeable, confident, enthusiastic, generous, obedient, trustworthy

Ⓑ 1 scholar   2 practitioner   3 human
   4 guess   5 judge

Ⓒ 1 dentist   2 generous   3 geologists
   4 enthusiastic 5 surgeon   6 tactile
   7 psychiatrist / psychologist   8 olfactory
   9 spiritual   10 estimated

Part B

Ⓐ **REWRAD:** bounty, compliment, prize, respect, satisfaction, trophy
   PUNISHMENT: community service, detention, fine, hard labor, prison, suspension

Ⓑ 1 recur   2 agitate   3 president
   4 critic   5 debut

Ⓒ 1 reminisces 2 recurring   3 compliments
   4 bounty   5 agitated   6 pyramids
   7 critics   8 prison   9 detention
   10 fine

Economics 경제학

Basic Knowledge Building

1. 애덤 스미스

애덤 스미스는 스코틀랜드의 정치 경제학자이면서 사회학자였다. 1776년에 그는 걸작인 〈국부론〉을 발표했다. 이 책은 현대 자본주의 사회의 기초를 마련했다. 그것은 전반적 현대 경제에 관한 최초의 서적으로 간주된다. 스미스는 경쟁과 자유시장이 소비자, 기업, 정부를 비롯해 모든 이들에게 도움이 된다고 믿었다. 그는 자유시장이 가격을 낮출 뿐 아니라 서비스와 재화의 다양성도 보장한다고 주장했다. 정부 규제가 거의 없는 자유시장이라는 개념은 혁신적이었다. 그것은 나중에 19세기에 가서 자유방임주의로 알려지게 되었다.

Q. T☐ F☑

> masterpiece 걸작 capitalist 자본주의 competition 경쟁
> benefit 이익이 되다 diversity 다양성 groundbreaking 혁신적인

2. 토머스 맬서스

토머스 맬서스는 18세기와 19세기에 살았던 영국의 정치경제학자였다. 그는 저서인 〈인구론〉(1798)에서 인간 사회는 인구 증가와 식량 부족 때문에 궁극적으로 생계경제로 돌아갈 것이라고 말했다. 이 이론은 맬서스의 격변설이라고 알려져 있다. 이 이론에 따르면, 인구는 기하급수적으로는 증가하지만 농작물은 산술적으로 증가한다. 결국, 식량이 인구 증가를 따라잡을 수 없게 된다. 그래서 제대로 된 긴급 대책을 세우지 않으면 사회는 위축되어 결국에는 대단히 황량한 결과를 맞이할 것이다.

Q. T☑ F☐

> ultimately 궁극에는, 결국 subsistence 생계 catastrophe 대재앙
> exponentially 기하급수적으로 arithmetically 산술적으로
> bleak 황량한 eventually 결국

3. GDP와 GNP

GDP와 GNP는 둘 다 한 국가의 경제를 측정하는 중요한 기준이다. 하지만 많은 사람들이 이 두 가지를 자주 혼동한다. GDP는 국내 총생산이다. 한 국가에서 1년 동안 생산되는 모든 재화와 용역을 말한다. 하지만 GNP는 국민 총생산을 말한다. 그것은 해외에 거주하는 국민이 벌어들인 수입을 GDP와 합한 액수와 동일하다. 또한 GNP는 해당 국가에서 외국인이 벌어들인 수입을 뺀다. 더 간단히 말해, GDP는 한 해 동안 해당 지역에서 생산된 모든 양을 말하고, GNP는 거주지에 상관없이 해당 국가의 국민이 생산한 총 생산량을 말한다.

Q. T☑ F☐

> critical 중요한 stand for ~을 나타내다, 상징하다 domestic 국내의
> gross 총계의 earning 수입 subtract 빼다

4. 수요와 공급

수요와 공급의 법칙은 모든 시장경제의 기초다. 공급은 공급자가 일정 기간 동안 재화나 용역을 시장에 공급하고자 하는 의지나 능력을 말한다. 수요는 소비자가 일정 기간 동안 재화나 용역을 구매하고자 하는 의지나 능력을 말한다. 경쟁 시장에서는 수요가 공급보다 클 경우 가격이 오른다. 반대로, 공급이 수요를 초과하면 가격은 내려간다. 따라서 시장의 역할은 가격이 안정되도록 수요와 공급의 균형을 맞추는 것이다.

Q. T☐ F☑

> supply 공급 demand 수요 willingness 의지
> on the contrary 반면에, 반대로 stable 안정된

5. 칼 마르크스

칼 마르크스는 독일의 혁명적 사상가였다. 그의 뛰어난 업적 가운데 마르크스 경제학이 있다. 이 이론은 계급 투쟁이라는 개념에 기초하고 있다. 마르크스는 두 주요 계층을 부르주아와 프롤레타리아라고 명명했다. 첫 번째는 지배 또는 우세 계층이고 두 번째는 노동 계층이다. 마르크스에게 프롤레타리아가 생산자들이기 때문에 사회에 대단히 중요하다. 제품은 그들의 노동력에서 나온다. 부르주아나 자본가들은 노동자를 이용할 뿐이다. 마르크스 경제학에 따르면, 자본주의 사회에서는 기술 때문에 결국 많은 노동자들이 일자리를 잃게 된다. 이로 인해 프롤레타리아 폭동이 일어난다. 노동자들은 투쟁에서 승리할 것이고 생산력을 장악할 것이다. 결국, 경제적 구분을 사라지게 될 것이다.

Q. T☑ F☐

> revolutionary 혁신적인 notable 유명한 dominant 지배적인
> revolt 폭동 emerge 나타나다 dissolve 사라지다

6. 알프레드 마샬

알프레드 마샬은 1842년부터 1924년까지 살았다. 그는 영국의 유명한 경제학자로, 20년 이상 케임브리지 대학에서 교편을 잡았다. 마샬은 재화나 용역의 가격이 어떻게 결정되는지 새로운 방식으로 설명하여 경제학에 기여했다. 마샬 이전에는 일부 경제학자들이 가격 결정에서 생산 비용이 주된 요소라고 생각했다. 다른 이들은 한계 효용이 가장 중요하다고 생각해서 누군가 어떤 것을 더 많이 가질수록 더 많은 양에 대해 더 적게 지불하려고 한다고 주장했다. 하지만 마샬은 이런 생각을 융합시켜 어떻게 수요와 공급의 상호작용을 통해 가격이 변하는지를 설명했다. 이러한 융합 덕분에 현대의 경제적 사고가 뚜렷해졌다.

Q. T☐ F☑

> contribute to ~에 공헌하다 factor 요인, 요소 utility 효용
> fuse 융합시키다 clarify 명백히 하다

7. 케인즈 이론

영국의 경제학자 존 메이너드 케인즈는 20세기 초반에 자신의 이론을 개발했다. 그 이론은 대공황 기간에 만들어졌다. 케인즈는 고전경제학 이론을 거슬렀다. 예를 들어, 그는 아담 스미스의 원칙들에 동의하지 않았다. 스미스는 시장을 그냥 내버려 두어야 한다고 믿었다. 정부는 꼭 필요한 때가 아니면 개입하지 말아야 했다. 반면에, 케인즈는 경제 성장을 자극하는 것이 정부가 할 일이라고 믿었다. 정부는 이자율, 세금, 지출을 조절함으로써 경기 침체를 막고 민간 부문을 안정시킬 수 있었다. 케인즈 이론은 대공황을 대처해 나가는 데 효과적이었으며 그 이후로 여러 세계 경제체제의 중추 역할을 했다.

Q. T ☑ F ☐

> depression 불황 intervene 개입하다
> absolutely 절대적으로 stimulate 자극하다 adjustment 조절
> thwart 방해하다 economic downturn 경기 하락

8. 프리드리히 하이에크

프리드리히 하이에크는 20세기에 활동했던 중요한 경제학자였다. 그는 오스트리아에서 출생했다. 고국에서 공식 교육을 받은 후 나중에 영국과 미국에서 대학 교수로 재직했다. 그는 사회주의를 강하게 비판했다. 경제에 대한 시각도 케인즈 이론과는 반대였다. 하이에크는 모든 종류의 정부 간섭은 무익하다고 믿었다. 국가의 조치로 높은 실업률과 경기침체를 막을 수는 없었다. 더욱이, 하이에크는 정부 간섭이 개인에게도 위험하다고 믿었다. 국민들이 자유를 잃을 수 있었다. 1974년 하이에크는 노벨 경제학상을 받았다.

Q. T ☐ F ☑

> professorship 대학교수직 critic 비평가 oppose 반대하다
> meddling 간섭 futile 무익한 unemployment 실업
> intervention 개입

9. 밀턴 프리드먼과 통화주의

밀턴 프리드먼은 미국의 경제학자이다. 그는 20세기에 통화주의를 창시했다. 이 이론은 국가의 통화 공급이 인플레이션과 성장에 영향을 미치기 때문에 중요하다고 주장한다. 그러므로, 중앙은행과 같은 금융감독기관은 통화 공급을 조절해 물가를 안정시켜야 한다. 일반적으로, 통화주의자들은 매년 통화 공급량을 늘릴 필요가 있다고 본다. 프리드먼과 그의 지지자들에 따르면, 약 3~4퍼센트를 투입하면 물가가 안정된다. '통화 속도' 역시 중요하다. 속도는 달러 하나가 매년 몇 번이나 사용되는지를 측정한다. 따라서, 그 속도를 가지고 매년 얼마나 많은 통화를 추가해야 하는지를 결정한다.

Q. T ☑ F ☐

> founder 창시자 monetarism 통화주의
> critical 매우 중요한, 결정적인 adjust 조절하다 proponent 지지자
> injection 투입 velocity 속도 dictate 결정하다

10. 은행권의 역사

은행권 즉 지폐는 아마도 6세기에서 9세기 사이에 고대 중국에서 최초로 사용되었을 것이다. 금속으로 된 동전이 부족해서 만들어졌다. 진정한 의미에서 최초의 은행권이 등장한 것은 16세기나 17세기 유럽에서였다. 민간기관이 만들었고 유통량도 많지 않았다. 유럽에서는 18세기가 되어서야 비로소 은행권이 정부의 지원을 받았다. 하지만 미국에서는 1700년대에 국가가 발행한 인쇄된 은행권이 처음으로 도입되었다. 오늘날 많은 나라에서는 은행권 지폐가 동전을 완전히 대체했다.

Q. T ☐ F ☑

> banknote 은행권 institution 기관 circulation 유통
> replace 대체하다 currency 통화

11. 매몰 비용

경제학에서 매몰 비용이란 쉽게 말해 회복 불가능한 비용을 말한다. 흔히 매몰 비용은 경제적 손실과 동일하지만 둘 사이에는 분명한 차이가 있다. 매몰 비용은 과거에 지불한 비용을 말한다. 매몰 비용은 초기 가격과는 더 이상 관련이 없다. 한편, 경제적 손실은 최초 가격과 나중 가격 사이의 차이를 말한다. 예를 들어, 차를 한 대 살 때 지불한 비용은 매몰 비용이다. 그 가격은 절대 변하지 않고 차는 시간이 흐르면서 가치가 하락하게 된다. 아마도 2년 후면 차주는 자동차를 살 때 치렀던 비용보다 낮은 가격에 차를 팔기로 할 수도 있다. 이 가격 차이가 정확하게 차주의 경제적 손실을 나타낸다.

Q. T ☐ F ☑

> equate 동일시하다 distinction 차이 relevant 관련이 있는
> depreciate 가치가 하락하다 accurately 정확하게

12. 세계무역기구

세계무역기구(WTO)는 1995년 설립되었다. 그것은 스위스 제네바에 본부를 두고 있다. 오늘날 활동하고 있는 회원국은 140개국이 넘는다. WTO는 여러 가지 국제적인 기능을 한다. 가장 중요한 것은 물론 무역이다. WTO는 국가 간의 무역과 상업을 더욱 원활하게 하려고 한다. 게다가, 더 국제화된 사회에서 자유무역을 확대하고자 한다. 또한 사법적인 역할도 한다. 국가 간 분쟁이 발생할 경우 WTO는 분쟁을 해결한다. 여러 면에서 WTO가 부유한 국가만을 위해서 존재하는 것처럼 보일 수도 있다. 하지만 개발 도상국에게도 기술과 선진 경제 전략으로 도움을 주고 있다.

Q. T ☑ F ☐

> establish 설립하다 commerce 통상, 상업 judicial 사법적인
> dispute 분쟁 strategy 전략

Unit 15 John Ruskin

Thinking about the Topic
Answers can vary. It is best to elicit as many answers from students as possible.

Vocabulary Focus

B
1. rational 합리적인
2. enormous 어마어마한, 엄청난
3. accumulate 쌓다; 쌓이다
4. reformer 개혁가
5. advocate 옹호하다, 지지하다
6. decline 감소, 하락
7. intervene 개입하다
8. realm 영역
9. ultimately 결국, 궁극에는
10. subsist 살아가다, 생활해 나가다

존 러스킨

19세기 영국은 빅토리아 여왕의 통치 하에 엄청난 번영을 누리며 변화를 겪었다. 영국은 해외 식민지를 통해 막대한 부를 축적했다. 산업혁명 덕분에 도시 거주자의 수는 급격히 증가했다. 또한 많은 사상가, 예술가, 과학자들이 다양한 문화 운동과 사회 개혁을 옹호했다. 존 러스킨도 이러한 지식인 가운데 한 사람이었다.

러스킨은 빅토리아 시대의 영향력 있는 미술비평가이자 사회사상가였다. 그는 1819년 런던에서 출생해 1900년까지 살았다. 그는 여러 분야에 관심이 있었으며 문학, 미술, 건축 등을 포함해 다양한 영역에서 영향력을 행사했다. 그는 미술이 사회적 가치관과 도덕성의 표현이라고 믿었다. 그것이 사회적 정의와도 밀접한 관련이 있다고 생각했다. 그러므로 미술의 몰락은 전반적인 사회 위기뿐만 아니라 문화적 위기의 징후이다. 미술에 대한 이러한 견해 때문에 러스킨은 자연스럽게 사회적 상황에도 관심을 갖게 되었다.

그 당시 영국은 사회 계층의 구성에 커다란 변화를 겪고 있었다. 교육을 받은 대규모 중산층이 서서히 성장했고 신흥 상인들이 상류층에 합류했다. 하지만 노동 계층은 여전히 빈곤한 생활을 벗어나지 못했다. 많은 노동자들은 아주 낮은 임금으로 생활해야 했다. 많은 아동들이 공장과 광산에서 노동을 강요당했다. 그들은 또한 주거 공간도 없었다. 이러한 비극적 상황은 산업혁명 후에 있었던 자유방임 자본주의의 급속한 발달 때문이었다.

이러한 사회적 상황에 반대하여 존 러스킨은 1860년에 자유방임 자본주의를 비판하는 일련의 글을 발표했다. 이 글들은 나중에 〈나중에 온 이 사람에게도〉(1862)라는 책으로 묶여졌다. 이 글에서 러스킨은 산업혁명에 따른 규격화된 노동을 맹렬히 비판했다. 그는 또한 숙련공이거나 비숙련공이거나 모든 노동자들은 고정된 임금을 받아야 한다고 주장했다. 차별 임금은 노동자들로 하여금 일자리를 얻기 위해 임금 삭감을 감수해야 하는 결과만 낳을 뿐이다. 이러한 경쟁은 모든 노동자와 사회 전반에 해롭다.

러스킨의 견해는 자유방임 경제학의 창시자로 알려진 애덤 스미스와는 정반대를 이룬다. 애덤 스미스는 그의 저서 〈국부론〉(1776)에서 자유 시장에서 개인과 기업 들의 경쟁은 궁극적으로 사회 전체에 이익이 된다고 주장했다. 그렇기 때문에 정부는 시장에 개입해서는 안 된다. 시장은 소비자와 생산자의 합리적인 선택과 결정에 의해 움직일 것이다.

하지만 러스킨은 자유 경쟁으로 인해 가난한 자들은 부자들을 더욱 부자로 만드는 도구로 전락할 뿐이라고 믿었다. 그는 사회에서 모든 생산은 인류 전체의 더 큰 이익을 위해 이루어져야 한다고 생각했다. 그래서 주거 환경 개선, 보편적인 무료 교육, 노령연금과 같은 사회 개혁을 주장했다. 그는 또한 소득세에 누진세율을 매겨야 한다고 주장했다. 여러 면에서 러스킨은 선구적인 사회 개혁가였다.

> laissez-faire 자유방임의

Reading Comprehension

1 (D)　2 (A)　3 (B)　4 ① Individual competition which benefits society ② Government with a "hands-off" approach to the market　5 (B)　6 (C)

Organizing & Summarizing

A
1. art critic
2. laissez-fair capitalism
3. child labor practices
4. Adam Smith
5. *Unto This Last*
6. universal education

B
1. an art critic
2. the Industrial Revolution
3. laissez-fair capitalism
4. overcrowded
5. the free market
6. fixed wages

존 러스킨은 19세기 영국의 미술비평가이자 사회개혁가였다. 그는 미술이 사회의 중요한 기둥이라고 믿었다. 그가 살았던 당시의 영국 사회는 격동기를 맞고 있었다. 산업혁명으로 사회 계층과 근로 환경에 큰 변화가 일었다. 교육을 받은 중산층이 더 많아졌다. 자유방임 자본주의도 점점 더 보편화되었다. 러스킨은 노동자 계층이 잊혀져 가고 있다고 생각했다. 임금은 낮았고, 주거지는 좁았으며, 아이들은 노동을 강요당했다. 러스킨은 이러한 끔찍한 상황을 바꿀 사회 개혁을 이루고자 했다. 그는 자유시장과 애덤 스미스의 견해에 반대했다. 러스킨은 그러한 시스템이 가난한 자는 억압하고 부자들을 더욱 부유하게 만들 뿐이라고 믿었다. 그는 또한 생산은 선택된 계층이 아니라 인류 전체에게 도움이 되어야 한다고 믿었다. 궁극적으로, 그는 고정 임금과 주거의 개선, 보편적인 무상 교육, 퇴직 연금제도를 주장했다.

Unit 16 The Theory of Marginal Utility

Thinking about the Topic
Answers can vary. It is best to elicit as many answers from students as possible.

Vocabulary Focus
B
1. alternative 대안적인
2. benefit 유익, 혜택
3. consumption 소비
4. assume 가정하다
5. bundle 묶음, 다발, 꾸러미
6. attain 달성하다, 도달하다
7. quantify 정량화하다, 양을 나타내다
8. inversely 역으로, 반비례로
9. affect 영향을 주다
10. subsequent 다음의, 뒤의, 그 이후의

한계 효용 이론

배가 고픈 사람이 뷔페 식사를 할 경우 첫 번째, 두 번째, 세 번째 접시 중 어떤 접시에서 가장 큰 만족감을 느낄까? 말할 필요도 없이, 첫 번째 접시의 만족감이 가장 크고 세 번째 접시의 만족감이 가장 적을 것이다. 경제학에서는 재화나 용역에서 소비자가 느끼는 이러한 만족감을 효용이라고 부른다. 또한 소비자가 재화나 용역을 한 단위 사용함으로써 얻게 되는 추가적 만족감을 한계 효용이라고 한다.

한계 효용은 가격 결정을 설명하기 위해 만든 경제학적 개념이다. 그 용어는 오스트리아 경제학자인 프리드리히 폰 비저가 처음 사용했고, 나중에 영국의 경제학자인 알프레드 마샬에 의해 널리 알려졌다. 마샬은 한계 효용이 유익에 기초하고 있다고 설명했다. 그것은 소비자가 재화나 용역을 한 단위 더 소비했을 때 느끼는 유익을 말한다. 이 유익은 한 사람이 소비하는 단위에 반비례한다. 한 사람이 구매한 제품의 단위 수가 많을수록 얻는 만족감은 적어진다. 따라서 소비자는 한계 효용과 가격이 같아질 때까지 소비량을 변화시킨다.

예를 들어, 롤러코스터를 아주 좋아하는 어떤 십대 소년이 있다고 하자. 어느 날 놀이공원에 가서 가장 좋아하는 놀이기구를 다섯 번 탄다. 첫 번째가 가장 신나고 만족감도 클 것이다. 매번 탈 때마다 조금씩 덜 신나고 만족감도 줄 것이다. 그래서 한계 효용은 첫 번째 놀이기구를 탄 뒤로 줄어들게 된다. 이 예에서 보듯이 그 십대의 수요 가격은 가장 처음에 가장 높고 놀이기구를 자꾸 탈수록 감소하게 된다. 다시 말해, 소년은 처음 놀이기구를 탄 뒤로는 매번 놀이기구를 탈 때마다 더 적은 금액을 지불하려고 할 것이다. 따라서 수요 가격은 구입하는 수량이 늘수록 감소하게 된다.

마샬이 살았던 시대에는 가장 기본적인 의미에서 효용이라는 것이 유용성을 의미했다. 또한 어떤 재화나 용역이 지닌 효용의 양을 측정할 수 있다고 생각했다. 하지만 실제로 개별적인 재화나 용역의 한계 효용을 수량화하기란 대단히 어렵다. 그렇기 때문에 오늘날 경제학에서는 정량화라는 개념을 도입했다. 이러한 취지에서 정량화는 소비묶음이라 불리는 다양한 재화와 용역의 조합에 대한 선호도를 보여주는 것이다. 현재, 한계 효용은 효용의 수량화된 변화를 의미한다. 다시 말해, 재화나 용역의 양과 종류가 더 많으면 한계 효용에 미치는 영향이 달라진다.

> demand price 수요 가격

Reading Comprehension
1 (A) 2 (D) 3 (B) 4 ① They thought it could be measured. ② They use qualification in combination with quantity. 5 (C) 6 (B)

Organizing & Summarizing
A
1. pricing
2. Alfred Marshall
3. demand price
4. marginal utility and price
5. consumer satisfaction
6. consumption bundles

B
1. Alfred Marshall
2. customer satisfaction
3. inversely related
4. marginal utility and price
5. the quantity of utility
6. consumption bundles

한계 효용 이론은 오스트리아의 경제학자인 프리드리히 폰 비저가 처음 생각해냈다. 나중에는 영국의 경제학자인 알프레드 마샬에 의해 널리 알려졌다. 효용이라는 개념은 소비자 만족과 밀접한 관련이 있다. 이 이론에 따르면 소비자가 얻는 유익은 소비자가 구매하는 재화나 용역의 단위 수에 반비례한다. 소비하는 단위 수가 많을수록 유익은 줄어든다. 게다가, 소비자가 어떤 재화나 용역을 더 원할수록 수요 가격은 높아지고 그렇지 않을 경우 반대가 된다. 또한 시간이 흐르면 소비자는 한계 효용과 가격이 같아질 때까지 소비량을 바꾼다. 예전에는 경제학자들이 양을 쉽게 측정할 수 있다고 믿었다. 하지만 오늘날에는 양이 더 복잡하다고 알려졌다. 그래서 경제학자들은 소비묶

음이라는 개념을 도입했다. 이것은 재화와 용역을 조합해서 정량화한다. 이들 조합의 다양성과 양이 가격 결정에 영향을 미칠 수 있다.

Vocabulary Expansion

Part A

Ⓐ **MONEY:** banknote, currency, check, dime, penny, quarter
ECONOMICS: consumer, demand, product, supply, utility, vendor

Ⓑ 1 government 2 architecture 3 stop
4 authority 5 economy

Ⓒ 1 monarchies 2 economy 3 floor plan
4 supply 5 principal 6 currency
7 Depression 8 utility 9 judge
10 consumers

Part B

Ⓐ **GOODS:** beverages, cosmetics, duplex, laptop, sneakers, vehicle
SERVICES: banking, catering, counseling, education, entertainment, tourism

Ⓑ 1 conform 2 recess 3 cost
4 rally 5 defend

Ⓒ 1 tourism 2 formula 3 vehicles
4 defend 5 shrank 6 beverages
7 rallied 8 challenged 9 catering
10 conform

Law 법학

Basic Knowledge Building

1. 함무라비 법전

많은 학자들은 함무라비 법전을 성문화된 최초의 법전으로 본다. 그것은 기원전 1700년대 중반에 바빌로니아의 함무라비 왕이 제정했다. 법전은 돌판에 새겨졌다. 그것은 1901년 이란에서 발견되어 현재 파리 루브르 박물관에 있다. 그 안에는 절도, 노상강도, 간통과 같은 범죄에 대한 처벌 조항이 들어 있다. 이제까지 알려진 가장 초기 형태의 금전적 가치들도 법전에 나와 있다. 그 예로는 벌금, 차용액에 붙는 이자, 조세, 심지어 상속에 관한 조항도 있다.

Q. T ☑ F ☐

penalty 처벌 inscribe 새기다 robbery 강도 adultery 간음, 간통
taxation 조세 inheritance 상속

2. 12표법

12표법은 기원전 450년 경의 초기 로마법이다. 일부 학자들은 평민에 대한 차별을 줄이기 위해 이 법전이 만들어졌다고 본다. 평민들은 구술되는 로마법을 이해하지 못했다. 하지만 12표법을 통해 법을 더 정확히 알고 남에게 속지 않을 수 있었다. 12표법은 결혼, 재산, 민사소송, 부채, 상속 같은 주제에 관한 다양한 법을 개괄했다. 원래, 그 법은 모든 로마인들이 볼 수 있도록 상아 명판에 새겨서 로마 광장에 비치되어 있었다.

Q. T ☑ F ☐

reduce 줄이다 corruption 부패 discrimination 차별
oral 구두의 outline 개요를 나타내다 property 재산

3. 전통 중국법

전통적인 중국법은 아마도 기원전 11세기경에 생겼을 것이다. 그 후 기원전 4세기 초에 이회가 6권의 법전으로 편찬했다. 전통 중국법은 두 가지 중국 철학인 유가와 법가에 기초를 두고 있었다. 유가는 윤리적 규범과 효를 강조한 반면 법가는 성문화된 법전을 통해 지배자를 지지하면서 개별적 자치에 반대했다. 전통적인 중국법은 일반 평민과 귀족들 사이에서 질서를 확립하는 데 도움이 되었다. 전통 법률 가운데 많은 부분이 19세기 후반까지도 시행되었다. 하지만 중국에서 1911년에 일어난 혁명으로 전통 법률에 변화가 일어났다. 그 시점 이후로, 더 시민적이고 서양의 영향을 받은 법이 등장했다.

Q. T ☐ F ☑

compile 편찬하다, 하나로 모으다 legalism 법가 filial piety 효
autonomy 자치 populace 서민

4. 법의 지배와 마그나카르타

법의 지배는 적용되는 문맥에 따라 뜻이 달라지기 때문에 융통성이 있는 용어이다. 어떤 경우에는 정부가 정해진 법을 따라야 한다는 것을 의미한다. 다른 경우 법의 지배는 아무도 법 위에 올 수 없다는 것을 의미한다. 1215년에 나온 마그나카르타는 법의 지배를 보여주는 중요한 역사적 사례이다. 그것은 영국의 존왕이 마지못해 승인한 것으로, 결국 영국 헌법의 기초가 되었다. 하지만 애초의 목적은 거듭되는 존왕의 보통법 침해를 막고 백성들을 보호하는 것이었다. 마그나카르타는 군주에 의한 잠재적인 전제 권력을 제한하고 억제하기 위해 마련된 최초의 법률 가운데 하나였다.

Q. T ☐ F ☑

flexible 융통성 있는, 유연한   context 문맥   reluctantly 마지못해
constrain 억제하다   tyrannical 전제적인

5. 동물 재판

동물 재판은 13세기부터 18세기까지 주로 유럽에서 시행되었다. 때때로 인간에게 해를 끼친 동물이 기소되었다. 피소된 동물은 말 그대로 법정에 세워져서 범죄 혐의를 추궁 받았다. 기록으로 남아 있는 동물 범죄는 살인에서부터 재물 손상에 이르기까지 다양했다. 유죄로 입증되면 해당 동물은 똑같은 상황에서 인간에게 가해지는 처벌과 똑같은 처벌을 받았다. 그래서 유죄가 입증된 동물은 때때로 추방되거나 심지어 처형을 당하기도 했다. 동물 재판에서는 돼지나 말, 소와 같은 가축들이 가장 흔한 피고였다. 하지만 집에 사는 쥐가 범죄 행위로 기소된 기록도 있다.

Q. T ☐ F ☑

criminal 범죄의   accuse 기소하다, 고발하다   exile 추방하다
execute 처형하다   domesticate 가축으로 기르다

6. 원형교도소

원형교도소는 영국 철학자 제레미 벤덤이 18세기 후반에 고안한 혁신적인 교도소이다. 그는 교도소 당국이 언제고 수감자들을 관찰할 수 있기를 바랐다. 그래서 간수들이 수감자들을 볼 수 있는 교도소를 설계했다. 하지만 수감자들은 그들이 감시를 받고 있는지 아닌지를 몰랐다. 원형 건물 한가운데 중앙탑을 세웠다. 특수한 조명 기술을 사용해 탑에 있는 감시자가 잘 보이지 않도록 했다. 관리자들은 수감자들에 대해 심리적으로 대단히 유리한 위치에 있었다. 오늘날 많은 현대식 교도소가 벤덤의 원래 설계에 기초해 만들어진다.

Q. T ☑ F ☐

revolutionary 혁명적인   circular 원형의   administration 행정
psychological 심리적인   population 인구

7. 성문헌법과 불문헌법

오늘날, 대다수의 국가에는 사람들이 준수해야 하는 성문법이 있다. 더 구체적으로 말하자면, 성문헌법은 한 국가의 기본법과 원칙들을 글로 적어 설명한 문서이다. 그것에는 또한 정부의 구체적인 의무가 명시되기도 한다. 그런가 하면, 일부 국가의 경우에는 불문헌법이 대단히 영향력을 가지기도 한다. 불문헌법에는 어떠한 공식 문서도 존재하지 않는다. 하지만 법과 절차들은 한 국가의 역사에서 오랜 세월에 걸쳐 시행되었기 때문에 인정받는다. 그리하여 그것들은 마치 글로 된 것처럼 국가에 없어서는 안 될 존재가 된다.

Q. T ☐ F ☑

constitution 헌법   principle 원칙   specific 구체적인
influential 영향력이 있는   essential 필수적인

8. 미국의 권리장전

미국의 권리장전은 미국 헌법에 생긴 최초 10개의 수정조항이다. 그것은 1791년 의회의 승인을 받았다. 권리장전은 개인의 자유와 권리를 보장하고 더 나아가 개인을 보호하기 위해 정부의 권한을 제한한다. 권리장전에 수록된 기본권의 예로는 언론, 종교의 자유와 무기 소유권 등이 있다. 또한 범죄로 피소된 국민들이 "잔인하고 비범한 처벌"을 받지 않도록 보호한다. 또한 범죄 소송 절차에서 시민들은 "신속하고 공정한 재판"을 보장받는다. 권리장전은 항상 미국 법률이 기초가 되어서 미국의 가치를 구현했다.

Q. T ☑ F ☐

amendment 수정조항   ratify 승인하다   guarantee 보장하다
embody 수록하다   foundation 기초

9. 미국의 연방대법원

연방대법원은 연방사법제도의 최고 기관이자 미국에서 항소할 수 있는 마지막 법원이다. 그것은 미 헌법 제3조에 근거해 만들어졌다. 대법원은 한 명의 대법원장과 8명의 판사로 이루어져 있다. 각 법관은 대통령이 임명하며 상원의 승인 또는 인준을 받아야 한다. 해마다 대법원은 국가와 연방 차원에서 올라온 수천 건의 소송을 검토하고, 법 해석이 가장 필요한 소송을 골라 소송 내용을 듣는다. 대법원에서 재판이 진행되는 경우는 거의 없다. 아주 흔히, 대법원까지 올라가는 소송은 초미의 관심사가 된다. 그 결정이 대중에게 흔히 중요한 영향을 미칠 수 있기 때문에 논쟁의 여지가 있다.

Q. T ☑ F ☐

appeal 항소   confirm 인준하다   interpretation 해석
controversial 논쟁의 여지가 있는   impact 영향

10. 일사부재리의 원칙

법률에서 일사부재리라는 개념은 한 사람이 같은 상황에서 동일 범죄에 대해 재판을 두 번 받지 않는다는 개념이다. 미국에서는 수정헌법 제5조에 명시되어 있다. 일사부재리는 법원에서 한 사건에 대해 판결을 한 상태에서 개인에게 정부가 계속해서 권력을 남용하는 것을 막는다. 미국에서는 무죄 평결이든 유죄 평결이든 간에 피고를 다시 재판할 수 없으며 동일 범죄에 대해 두 번 이상 처벌할 수 없다.

Q. T ☐ F ☑

jeopardy 위험   embed 새기다   amendment 수정조항
acquittal 무죄 평결   conviction 유죄 평결

11. 민법과 형법

형법은 범죄와 처벌을 규정한다. 그것은 정부가 개인 또는 집단을 범죄 혐의로 기소하는 것을 포함한다. 재판에서 검사는 합리적으로 의심할 여지 없이 피고가 유죄라는 것을 입증해야 한다. 만약 유죄로 입증되면 피고는 집행유예나 징역, 가장 극단적으로는 사형까지 선고 받게 된다. 반면에, 민법은 대개 두

개인 또는 집단 간에 흔히 법률 소송의 형태로 법적인 절차가 이루어지는 것을 포함한다. 패소자는 징역을 사는 대신 보통 배상금을 물어야 한다. 일반적으로, 민사소송에서 승소하기 위해서는 증거만 충분하면 된다.

Q. T ☑ F ☐

> prosecution 기소 probation 집행유예 extreme 극단적인
> monetary 재정적인 sufficient 충분한

12. 소환장과 구속영장

소환장은 법원이 발부하여 어떤 사람에게 법정에 출두하여 증언을 하도록 요구하는 것이다. 출두를 거부하면 처벌을 받게 된다. 소환장은 출두해야 하는 사람에게 필요한 사항, 출두 시간과 장소를 자세히 적은 공문서이다. 소환장에 불응하면 법정 모독죄가 적용될 수 있다. 이러한 위반으로 당사자는 범법자로 기소될 수도 있다. 한편, 구속영장은 개인을 바로 체포하기 위해 판사나 다른 사법기관에서 발부한다. 일반적으로, 구속영장을 발부하기 위해서는 범죄 구성에 대한 정당한 근거가 있어야 한다.

Q. T ☐ F ☑

> testify 증언하다 comply 순응하다 contempt 모독 violation 침해 judicial 사법의

Unit 17 Major Legal Systems

Thinking about the Topic
Answers can vary. It is best to elicit as many answers from students as possible.

Vocabulary Focus
B 1 precedent 선례, 전례
2 rigid 엄격한
3 render ~가 되게 하다, 주다, 하다,
4 jury 배심원단
5 enforce 집행하다
6 chaos 혼돈, 혼란
7 valid 유효한
8 reconcile 화해하다
9 prevalent 널리 퍼진, 횡행하는
10 neutral 중립적인

주요 법률 제도

법률 제도란 한 국가를 통치하는 일련의 법률과 그것을 해석하고 시행하는 방식을 말한다. 이러한 법률은 한 국가의 사회, 정치, 경제적 기초가 된다. 전형적으로, 법률 제도는 국민의 권리와 국민이 따라야 할 규칙과 원칙을 규정한다. 물론, 어떤 법의 해석은 국가마다 다를 수 있다. 하지만 정해진 법률 제도가 없으면 국가가 제 기능을 할 수 없다. 쉽게 혼란에 빠지게 된다. 한 국가의 법률 제도는 일반적으로 역사적 요소와 다른 나라들과의 관계에 근거하여 결정된다. 현대 사회에서는 대륙법, 영미법, 종교법의 세 가지가 가장 일반적이다.

대륙법은 세계적으로 가장 흔한 법률 제도이며 다른 두 가지보다 더 일찍 사용되었다. 그것은 로마법에서부터 시작되었다. 그래서 대륙법은 성문법과 규칙을 중심으로 이루어진다. 재판 과정에서 재판관은 이미 정해진 법을 시행할 뿐이다. 대륙법의 기초가 되는 것은 각 법률 문제에 한 가지 유효한 해결책이 있다는 생각이다. 대륙법에서는 공개재판이 흔하지 않다. 재판관들은 비공개 법정에서 증거를 검토하고 증언을 듣는다. 그런 다음 정보와 법에 근거해 판결을 내린다. 이런 식의 법률 절차는 영미법 제도와는 정반대이다.

영미법은 18세기 영국에서 시작된, 더 현대적인 법률 제도이다. 또한 그것은 미국법의 기초가 되었다. 대륙법과 달리 영미법은 법령이나 엄격한 법전보다는 판례에 기초를 둔다. 판례란 법 해석에 기초를 둔 법원의 이전 판결을 말한다. 영미법에서는 중립적인 재판관이나 배심원단 앞에서 논쟁을 통해 분쟁을 조정한다. 궁극적으로는, 재판관이나 배심원이 사건의 증거나 사실에 기초해 판결을 내린다. 그러면 최종 판결은 기본적으로 새로운 판례 즉 법이 되어 미래의 법률 문제에서 무게가 실리게 된다.

오늘날 세계에서 주요한 마지막 법률 제도로 종교법이 있다. 기본적으로, 그 법률은 인간의 삶을 관장하기 위해 신에게서 나왔다고 여겨진다. 흔히 성스러운 문서에 기록되어 있다. 일반적으로, 종교법에는 신에게서 물려받은 것으로 여겨지는 도덕률이 포함된다. 예로는 이슬람법, 기독교법, 힌두법이 있다. 때로는 종교적인 신념이 단순한 길잡이로만 쓰인다. 다른 경우에는 한 국가의 전체 법률 제도의 기초가 되기도 한다. 하지만 일부 국가에서 종교법은 종종 대륙법과 같은 또 다른 형태의 법률 제도와 결합된다.

> weigh in on ~에 영향을 미치다

Reading Comprehension
1 (B)   2 (C)   3 (B)   4 A precedent is a previous decision by a court based on its own interpretation of a law.   5 (A)   6 (D)

Organizing & Summarizing
A 1 Roman law codes 2 hear testimony
3 U.S. legal system 4 new precedent
5 moral codes 6 another legal system

B 1 early Roman codes
2 open trials or juries
3 the U.S. legal system

41

4 on precedent
5 moral guidance
6 another legal system

오늘날 세계에는 세 가지 주요한 법률 제도가 있다. 대륙법은 가장 널리 사용되는 법률 제도로, 초기 로마법에서 유래했다. 그것은 명확하게 규정된 성문법에 기초한다. 재판관들은 일반적으로 이 법을 적용해 판결을 한다. 판결은 확실하며 공개 재판이나 배심원이 별로 필요하지 않다. 영미법은 18세기 영국에서 시작되어 나중에 미국 법률 제도의 기초가 되었다. 이 법률 제도는 판례에 기초한다. 법은 지속적으로 진화하며 법원에서 현행법을 해석하기 때문에 미래의 법에 영향을 준다. 배심원에 의한 재판도 일반적이다. 종교법 제도에서는 법이 특정 신에 의해 인간과 연결되어 있다. 때로는 이러한 법이 도덕적 안내자의 역할만 한다. 다른 경우에는 한 국가의 전체 법률 제도의 기초가 된다. 하지만 종교법은 일반적으로 또 다른 법률 제도와 결합되어 국민에게 도움을 준다.

Unit 18 The Code of Hammurabi

Thinking about the Topic
Answers can vary. It is best to elicit as many answers from students as possible.

Vocabulary Focus
B 1 engrave 새겨 넣다
2 righteousness 의로움
3 optimistic 낙관적인
4 malpractice 과실, 과오
5 encompass 에워싸다; 포함하다
6 primitive 원시적인, 초기의
7 inheritance 상속
8 civil 시민의, 문민의
9 epilogue 끝맺음, 결말
10 carve 새기다, 조각하다

함무라비 법전

1901년 프랑스의 고고학팀은 이란 서부의 수사라는 메소포타미아의 폐허 도시에서 현무암으로 된 돌기둥을 발견했다. 검은 석판은 높이가 약 7피트 정도로 고대법이 새겨져 있었다. 법전은 그것을 만든 왕의 이름을 따 함무라비 법전이라 명명되었다 오늘날에는 파리의 루브르 박물관에 소장되어 있다. 그것은 현재까지 발견된 가장 잘 보존된 법전의 원본 가운데 하나다.

함무라비 법전은 쐐기 모양의 초기 문자인 설형문자로 돌기둥의 앞뒤에 새겨져 있다. 법 조항들이 석판의 앞뒤에 모두 적혀 있다. 함무라비는 자신을 "약하고 억압받은 자의 보호자"로 소개한다. 그런 다음 신들이 어떻게 "그 땅의 정의"를 보존하도록 그에게 법전을 하사했는지 설명한다. 법전의 법률부에는 바빌로니아의 일상 생활과 관련된 282가지 법이 나와 있다. 법률은 모든 사람들이 이해할 수 있도록 쉬운 말로 적혀 있다. 법전은 함무라비가 그의 법을 자자손손 물려주도록 명하는 서정적인 결말로 끝맺는다.

학자들은 함무라비 법전을 원시적인 헌법으로 본다. 그것은 국가를 다스리는 기본법과 국민의 기본적 자유를 보장한다. 심지어 왕도 어떤 기본법은 바꿀 수 없었기 때문에 폭정으로부터 백성을 보호해 준다. 또한 법전에는 가족의 권리뿐만 아니라 공정한 재판과 금전적인 문제도 언급되어 있다. 심지어 의사의 과실과 같은 여러 가지 불의에 대한 벌칙도 포함되어 있다. 게다가, 법전은 이자율과 상속 및 조세에 관한 지침의 형태로 명확한 경제적 기준도 정하고 있다. 이러한 방식들은 인류 역사에서 가장 오래된 경제 제도에 관한 기록으로 여겨진다. 형법이라는 맥락에서 볼 때, 함무라비 법전은 "눈에는 눈"의 정신을 따른다. 다시 말해, 처벌의 강도가 범죄의 강도와 동일하다. 이 원칙은 부분적으로 범죄에 비해 상대적으로 과도한 처벌을 막으려는 의도도 있다.

함무라비 법전의 가장 매력적인 부분은 인도적 정신이다. 법전은 왕을 옹호하지도 않고 왕에게 전권을 허락하지도 않는다. 부유한 자나 가진 자를 보호하지도 않는다. 대신에, 가난한 자와 약한 자, 여성과 어린이에게 힘을 주고 보호한다. 더욱이, 어조는 낙관적이다. 미래의 더 나은 삶과 전반적인 평화에 대한 희망을 내세운다. 분명히 함무라비 법전은 오래된 형태로 법의 지배를 보여주는 훌륭한 법률의 예이다.

> cuneiform 쐐기 형태의   omnipotent 전능한

Reading Comprehension
1 (B)   2 (A)   3 (C)   4 ① Scholars say it is an early expression of a constitution. ② It protected the civil liberties of Babylonian citizens.   5 (B)   6 (C)

Organizing & Summarizing
A 1 282 laws   2 Louvre Museum
3 civil liberties   4 eye for an eye
5 excessive punishment
6 no special privilege

B 1 282 codes in cuneiform
2 maintain righteousness
3 the power of the king
4 taxation and inheritance
5 eye-for-an-eye measures
6 excessive punishment

함무라비 법전은 현재까지 발견된 가장 초기의 법률이다. 그것은 7피트 높이의 석판으로, 282개의 법률이 설형문자로 새겨져 있다. 오늘날까지도 남아 있어서 파리의 루브르 박물관에서 볼 수 있다. 함무라비왕은 법전을 통해 그 땅의 정의를 유지하고 약한 자를 보호하고자 했다. 여러 면에서 그것은 왕의 권력을 제한하고 모든 백성을 위해 기본적인 법과 자유를 확립했기 때문에 원시적인 헌법이다. 조세와 상속에 관한 법률은 현재까지 알려진 가장 이른 경제법이다. 함무라비 법전은 법에 있어 "눈에는 눈" 원칙을 적용했다. 과도한 처벌을 금지했다는 점에서 그것은 더 현대적인 법률의 모범이라 할 수 있다. 또한 폭정에 대해 백성을 보호하고 전반적인 평화를 불어넣는다. 부유한 자에게 특권을 허락하지 않는다. 오히려 가난한 자, 여성, 아동을 보호한다.

Vocabulary Expansion

Part A

Ⓐ **LEGAL:** defendant, jury, judge, prosecution, testimony, witness
RELIGIOUS: cathedral, imam, monk, nun, priest, temple

Ⓑ 1 ruler 2 crime 3 prison
4 constitution 5 familial

Ⓒ 1 filial 2 signature 3 arson
4 guards / jailers 5 testimony
6 maternal 7 amendments 8 witness
9 monks 10 constitution

Part A

Ⓐ **PRIMITIVE:** arrowhead, cave, flint, hunter-gatherer, nomad, spear
MODERN: aircraft, automobile, biotechnology, nuclear, patent, satellite

Ⓑ 1 violation 2 amend 3 deceive
4 liable 5 vacate

Ⓒ 1 exempt 2 hunter-gatherers / nomads
3 nuclear 4 deceive 5 amend
6 satellites 7 guarantee 8 liable
9 vacate 10 violations

Ecology 생태학

Basic Knowledge Building

1. 생물권

1875년 지질학자인 에두아르트 쥐스는 모든 생물들이 사는 지역을 설명하기 위해 생물권이라는 용어를 사용했다. 그가 처음 사용한 뒤로 그 용어는 더 발전해서 지금은 지구의 모든 생태계를 가리키는 말이 되었다. 여기에는 지구상의 모든 생명체와 그것이 흙, 물, 공기와 상호 작용하는 것까지 포함된다. 생물권은 최초의 생명체가 등장하기 시작했던 약 35억년 전에 발달했던 것으로 생각된다. 오늘날 일부 과학자들은 생물권 자체가 일종의 거대 생물체라고 주장한다. 모든 식물, 동물, 다른 생명체들은 전체를 구성하는 일부일 뿐이다.

Q. T☐ F☑

biosphere 생물권 geologist 지질학자 initial 처음의
ecosystem 생태계 organism 유기체, 생물체
interaction 상호작용

2. 생태계

한 지역 내에 서식하는 동물과 식물의 종류가 중요하긴 하지만 이 생물체들에게 물이나 기온 같은 무생물적 요소가 미치는 영향도 크다. 생태계라는 말은 한 지역 내의 동식물과 무생물 환경 사이의 관계를 설명하기 위해 만들어졌다. 예를 들어, 비와 일조량은 특정 지역에 서식하는 동식물의 종류와 수에 큰 영향을 끼칠 수 있다. 대부분의 생태계는 정적이지 않다. 그들은 시간을 두고 바뀐다. 그 결과, 한 지역에서 서로 다른 시기에 여러 종의 동식물을 볼 수 있다.

Q. T☐ F☑

impact 영향 temperature 온도 significant 중요한 coin 만들다
population 개체군 static 정적인

3. 먹이사슬

모든 생명체는 태양으로부터 에너지를 얻는다. 식물은 태양을 직접 이용해 당분의 형태로 에너지를 만든다. 동물은 식물이나 다른 동물을 먹어서 에너지를 얻는다. 이러한 에너지 경로를 먹이사슬이라고 한다. 모든 먹이사슬의 기반은 식물에서 비롯된다. 1차 소비자는 식물을 먹는 동물이다. 2차 소비자는 1차 소비자를 잡아먹는 동물이고 그런 식으로 계속된다. 각 먹이사슬의 끝에는 분해자가 있다. 이들은 박테리아나 균류로서, 유기물을 분해해 양분을 토양으로 되돌려서 식물이 사용하게 해준다.

Q. T☑ F☐

base 기부, 기반 primary 1차의 consumer 소비자
secondary 2차의 decomposer 분해자

4. 생태 천이

판 구조 운동으로 새로운 땅이 형성되면 거기에는 많은 생물이 살지 못한다. 대개는 지의류나 다른 내한성 식물만 자랄 수 있다. 여러 세대에 걸쳐 식물의 뿌리와 침식작용으로 암석이 서서히 잘게 부서진다. 이렇게 섞이고 나면 더 많은 식물이 자라게 된다. 잡초가 가장 처음 등장하며 잔디가 그 뒤를 잇는다. 식물이 죽으면 유기물이 부패하면서 토양이 두터워진다. 식물이 점점 더 많아지면서 작은 동물들이 등장한다. 비가 충분히 내리면 마침내 나무가 뿌리를 내리게 된다. 그렇지 않은 경우는 그 지역이 초원지역으로 남는다. 시간을 두고 일어나는 이 모든 환경적 변화를 생태 천이라고 한다.

Q. T☐ F☑

> lichen 지의류 hardy 내한성의 erosion 침식작용 decay 부패하다
> sufficient 충분한

5. 생물다양성

생물다양성이란 특정 지역 내에 서식하는 종의 다양성을 말한다. 생물다양성은 흔히 그 지역의 건강도를 측정하는 데 사용된다. 만약 한 지역의 생물다양성이 감소하면 그 지역의 건강도도 떨어진 것이다. 일반적으로, 지구에서 종이 가장 다양한 지역은 적도 부근이며 생물다양성은 극지방 쪽으로 갈수록 떨어진다. 생물다양성이 가장 큰 곳으로 두 군데의 생태 핵심 분포지역이 있다. 첫 번째는 브라질의 열대우림이다. 그곳에는 백만 종이 넘는 곤충이 있는데, 절반이 브라질에만 서식한다. 두 번째는 마다가스카르이다. 그 섬은 6천5백만 년 전에 아프리카에서 떨어져 나온 후 고립되어 수많은 자생종들의 보금자리가 되었다.

Q. T☑ F☐

> variety 다양성 gauge 측정하다 decline 감소하다
> hotspot 핵심분포지역 separate 분리하다

6. 우림

우림이란 간단히 말해서 비가 많이 내리는 산림지역이다. 우림은 열대 지역에도 있고 온대 지역에도 있다. 일반적으로, 우림은 여러 층으로 이루어져 있다. 최상층은 신생층이라고 한다. 이것은 가장 키가 큰 나무의 최상부로 이루어져 있다. 여기에는 동물이 거의 살지 않는다. 천개층이 두 번째 층이다. 나무 꼭대기로 이루어진 거의 연속적인 군엽이다. 이 층은 생물학적 다양성이 가장 높은 지역이다. 천개층 아래에는 하층이 있고, 다음은 임상이다. 대다수의 사람들이 생각하는 것과 달리 임상은 햇빛이 이곳까지 비치지 않기 때문에 사실상 거의 공지이다.

Q. T☑ F☐

> tropical 열대의 temperate 온대의 emergent 신생의
> foliage 군엽 understory 하층 canopy 천개

7. 생물량

생물량이란 일정한 시점에 주어진 지역 안에 살고 있는 생물과 다른 생물학적 물질의 전체 무게이다. 생물량은 특정한 종이나 자연 집단을 설명하는 데 쓰일 수도 있지만, 가장 흔하게는 먹이사슬에서 어떤 생물의 위치 즉 영양 단계를 설명하는 데 쓰인다. 다시 말해, 생물량은 먹이사슬의 어떤 단계에서 모든 생물의 무게를 나타낸다. 예를 들어, 소는 풀보다 무게가 훨씬 더 나간다. 하지만 소가 평생 동안 먹는 풀의 무게를 더하면 소의 생물량보다 훨씬 많다. 이런 식으로 어떤 들판에서 살 수 있는 소의 수를 그 들판의 생물량을 계산하여 추정해 낼 수 있다.

Q. T☐ F☑

> particular 특별한 species 종 trophic 영양의
> estimate 추정하다 calculate 계산하다

8. 바이오스피어 2

바이오스피어 2는 1991년 애리조나에 지어진 대형 인공 생태계 돔이다. 거기에는 열대우림, 해양, 사바나, 사막, 심지어 사람도 있었다. 바이오스피어 2는 자급자족하는 생태계가 되었으면 하는 바람으로 지어졌다. 하지만 맨 처음에는 내부의 산소 농도가 너무 낮아 추가적으로 공기를 주입해야 했다. 더욱이, 돔 안에 사는 사람들은 먹고 살 만한 식물을 경작할 수가 없었다. 지금은 많은 사람들이 바이오스피어 2를 실패작이라고 생각한다. 하지만 기술적으로는 바이오스피어 2가 성공작이었다고 보는 사람들도 있다. 그 구조물은 현재까지 만들어진 최대의 폐쇄 생태계이다.

Q. T☑ F☐

> artificial 인공적인 ecological 생태학적
> self-sustaining 자급자족의 additional 추가적인
> consider 간주하다, 생각하다

9. 물의 순환

지구상에서 물은 총량이 한정되어 있어서 끊임없이 재사용된다. 공기 중에 있는 물은 거의 대부분 호수, 강, 바다와 같은 수원에서 증발되어 생기거나 식물의 증산작용으로 생긴다. 일단 물이 공기 중에 있으면 강수가 되어 내린다. 강수는 호수와 강으로 내리거나 땅속으로 흘러 들어간다. 지하의 물은 식물이 흡수하거나 강과 바다로 흘러간다. 그러면 소비되고 처리된 물이 전부 다시 사용되면서 새로운 물의 순환이 시작된다.

Q. T☐ F☑

> hydrologic 물의 recycle 재활용하다 evaporation 증발
> transpiration 증산작용 precipitation 강수
> consume 쓰다, 소비하다

10. 탄소 순환

모든 생물의 주된 성분은 탄소이다. 그것은 당, 단백질, 지방을 구성한다. 탄소는 모든 생물에게 대단히 중요하기 때문에 다음 세대에 영양분이 충분하도록 재활용해야 한다. 이렇게 탄소가 재활용되는 과정을 탄소 순환이라고 한다. 예를 들면, 식물은 공기 중에서 다량의 이산화탄소를 흡수해 당과 전분으로 전환한다. 동물은 식물을 먹고 나서 신진대사에 일부 탄소를 사용하고 나머지는 이산화탄소 가스의 형태로 배출한다. 하지만 많은 이산화탄소는 연소에 의해서도 대기 속으로 배출된다. 나무나 석유를 태우면 안에 있던 탄소가 나와서 공기 중 이산화탄소의 양이 늘게 된다.

Q. T ☑ F ☐

> ensure 보장하다 illustrate 실례를 들다 convert 전환하다
> metabolic 신진대사의 excrete 배출하다, 배설하다

11. 생물 증폭

생물 증폭은 독성 화학물질이 먹이사슬의 위쪽으로 올라가면서 더욱 농축되는 경향을 말한다. 작동원리는 아주 단순하다. 물에 소량의 독소가 있으면 그 물을 섭취하는 식물도 그 독소를 섭취하게 된다. 식물은 끊임없이 물이 필요하므로 시간이 지나면서 독성 수준이 높아진다. 그 다음에 그 식물을 먹는 동물은 더 많은 독소를 섭취한다. 평생 동안 다량의 식물을 먹기 때문이다. 이러한 독소 농축은 그 화학물질이 먹이사슬로 올라갈수록 계속 증가한다. 그래서 먹이사슬의 가장 위쪽에 있는 동물은 아래쪽에 있는 동물보다 더 많은 독소가 몸에 쌓인다.

Q. T ☑ F ☐

> magnification 증폭 concentrate 농축되다 toxin 독소
> constantly 끊임없이 progress 나아가다 ultimately 결국, 궁극에는

12. 부영양화

부영양화는 수원에서 조류가 급격히 증가하는 것을 말한다. 이러한 현상은 예를 들어 농지에서 흘러나온 비료와 같은 영양분이 더해져서 아주 흔하게 일어난다. 부영양화는 심각한 영향을 끼칠 수 있다. 처음에는, 양분 때문에 수면을 따라 조류의 양이 급격히 증가한다. 이것은 햇빛을 차단해 바닥에 사는 식물을 죽게 만든다. 하지만 환경에 가해지는 피해는 여기에서 끝나지 않는다. 일단 넘치는 양분을 다 쓰고 나면 조류가 죽기 시작한다. 조류가 분해되면서 물속의 산소가 전부 소모된다. 단기간에 수중의 모든 어류가 죽고 그 지역에는 생물이 거의 자취를 감추게 된다.

Q. T ☐ F ☑

> alga (pl. algae) 조류, 바닷말 shield 가리다 excess 과도한
> decomposition 분해 devoid of ~이 전혀 없는

Unit 19 Keystone Species

Thinking about the Topic
Answers can vary. It is best to elicit as many answers from students as possible.

Vocabulary Focus

B
1 subjective 주관적인
2 dub 이름 붙이다
3 allocate 할당하다, 책정하다
4 predator 포식자
5 abundance 풍부, 풍요
6 consensus 합의, 의견 일치
7 graze 목초[풀]을 먹다
8 unchecked 통제되지 않은
9 reluctance 내키지 않음, 마지못함
10 collapse 무너지다, 붕괴하다

핵심종

1960년대 초반에 생태학자인 로버트 페인은 미국 서해안에 서식하고 있는 생물 종을 연구하고 있었다. 그는 한 종류의 불가사리가 생태계에서 중요한 역할을 하는 것을 발견했다. 그것은 포식자였음에도 불구하고 초식동물의 수를 조절해서 그 지역의 다른 종들에게 도움을 주었다. 그 불가사리를 제거하자 두 종류의 홍합이 손쓸 수 없게 늘어났다. 그것들은 수가 증가하면서 다른 종을 몰아냈다. 본질적으로, 그 불가사리는 해안 지역의 다양성을 책임지고 있었던 것이다. 페인은 곧 자신의 연구성과를 발표하고 생태계에서 가장 중요한 역할을 하는 생물을 핵심종이라고 명명했다.

그의 획기적인 발표 이후로 핵심종은 보다 명확하게 규정되었다. 대다수의 생물학자들은 그것을 한 지역 내에서 주요한 역할을 하는 종으로 규정한다. 그들은 또한 상대적으로 그 수를 감안할 때 예상보다 훨씬 더 큰 영향을 미친다. 하지만 이러한 정의는 여전히 매우 주관적이다. 그 결과, 어떤 무리가 핵심종인지 아닌지를 놓고 과학자들 사이에 의견 차이가 생길 수 있다.

의견 일치를 보지 못해 약간의 마찰이 생겼다. 주된 이유는 핵심종이 환경보존 노력의 중요한 대상이 되기 때문이다. 핵심종은 해당 지역에 직접적으로 영향을 미치기 때문에 그것이 없으면 생태계가 파괴될 수 있다. 그래서 핵심종이 번성하도록 하기 위해 상당한 자원을 배분한다. 핵심종을 제대로 가려내지 못하면 환경보존 노력이 헛수고가 될 수 있다.

또 다른 쟁점은 핵심종의 정의를 확대하는 것이다. 페인의 원래 연구는 포식자만 중요하다고 언급했다. 더 최근에 와서는 생물학자들이 먹이가 되는 일부 종과 식물을 핵심종으로 명명했다. 그들은 해당 생태계에 미치는 영향이 핵심종 선정에서 가장 중요한 고려 대상이 되어야 한다고 주장한다. 문제의 핵

심종의 역할은 본질적인 게 아니다. 하지만 원래의 범위를 넘어 그 이론을 받아들이는 데는 여전히 거리낌이 존재한다.

핵심종 이론은 아직 시작 단계에 불과하다. 이론이 완성될 때까지는 환경보호론자들이 사용에 제한을 둘 것이다. 하지만 그것은 성공을 거두기도 했다. 아주 최근에는 미국의 옐로우스톤 국립공원에 늑대를 다시 들여 놓았다. 처음에는 지역 주민들이 그 포식동물이 사슴과 다른 작은 포유동물에게 미칠 부정적인 영향을 우려했다. 하지만 과학자들은 그것이 핵심종이라서 그 지역 야생생물의 건강도와 다양성을 향상시킬 것이라고 주장했다. 그 이후 늑대는 수가 증가했다. 늑대와 함께 사슴의 수도 증가했다. 더 진전된 연구를 통해 핵심종 이론은 환경보존 노력에서 훨씬 더 큰 역할을 하게 될 것이다.

> mussel 홍합

Reading Comprehension

1 (D)　2 (B)　3 (A)　4 The role of the species within an ecosystem is not as important as its impact upon it.
5 (C)　6 (D)

Organizing & Summarizing

Ⓐ　1　Robert Paine　　2　a type of starfish
　　3　their numbers　　4　subjective
　　5　plants & prey animals
　　6　reintroduction of wolves

Ⓑ　1　Robert Paine
　　2　a keystone species
　　3　conservation efforts
　　4　being targeted for aid
　　5　non-predators
　　6　the reintroduction of wolves

1960년대 초반 로버트 페인은 불가사리가 미국 서부 해안의 생태계에 중요한 역할을 한다는 것을 알았다. 그것은 포식자로서 그 지역 초식동물의 수를 조절했다. 그는 그 불가사리를 핵심종이라고 불렀다. 핵심종은 해당 지역에서 중요한 역할을 하는 생물이다. 하지만 핵심종의 정의를 둘러싸고 의견 차이가 있었다. 한 가지 이유는 핵심종이 환경보존 노력에 중요하기 때문이다. 그러므로, 오인할 경우 잘못된 종을 목표로 삼아 지원하는 결과를 낳을 수 있다. 두 번째 이유는 과학자들이 포식자가 아닌 동물을 핵심종으로 간주하고 싶어하기 때문이다. 핵심종 이론이 완성된 이론은 아니지만 효과는 입증되었다. 미국 옐로우스톤 국립공원에 늑대를 다시 들여온 결과 핵심종이 다른 동물들에게 이익을 가져온다는 것이 밝혀졌다.

Unit 20 Mutualism vs. Commensalism

Thinking about the Topic

Answers can vary. It is best to elicit as many answers from students as possible.

Vocabulary Focus

Ⓑ　1　inhabit 살다, 거주하다
　　2　leftover 먹다 남은 것, 음식 찌꺼기
　　3　scavenger 청소 동물, 청소부
　　4　sweep 샅샅이 찾다
　　5　capable 능력이 있는, 할 수 있는
　　6　immune 면역이 된
　　7　benefit 도움이 되다, 이롭다
　　8　arrangement 화합, 타협
　　9　symbiosis 공생
　　10　unaffected 영향을 받지 않는

상리공생 대 편리공생

산호초는 가장 다양한 생태계 가운데 하나이다. 이 지역에 사는 종은 서로에게 대단히 의존도가 높다. 산호초는 조류와 산호 동물의 공생 관계의 결과로 형성된다. 두 종은 상호 이익이 되는 관계에 있다. 산호초는 먹이를 얻고 조류는 보호를 받는다. 이러한 관계는 주요한 공생 관계 가운데 한 가지인 상리공생으로 알려져 있다.

일반적으로, 공생은 한 지역 내의 다른 종 사이의 다양한 관계를 설명하기 위해 사용하는 광의의 용어이다. 상리공생은 종 간의 가장 긍정적인 관계이다. 산호초 내에는 수많은 상리공생 관계가 존재한다. 가장 잘 알려진 것이 말미잘과 흰동가리의 관계이다. 말미잘의 독침은 물고기를 마비시킬 수 있다. 흰동가리는 그 가시에 면역이 있기 때문에 말미잘의 촉수 사이를 헤엄치며 포식자들로부터 보호를 받는다. 그 대가로 흰동가리는 종종 숙주인 말미잘에게 작은 물고기 조각을 준다. 게다가, 미끼 역할을 해서 덩치가 큰 먹이를 말미잘 쪽으로 유혹한다.

산호초에는 편리공생이라는 또 다른 종류의 공생 관계가 있다. 이 관계에서는 한 종이 이익을 보지만 다른 종은 이익을 보지도 해를 입지도 않는다. 편리공생을 뜻하는 영어 단어 'commensalism'은 글자 그대로 '한 식탁을 공유하는'이라는 뜻이다. 이것은 최초로 관찰된 동물들이 남은 먹이를 같이 나눠 먹고 있었기 때문이다. 이러한 공생 관계에서 포식자들은 먹이의 사체를 전부 다 먹는 일이 별로 없다. 나머지는 공짜 먹이를 차지하는 청소동물들이 재빨리 먹어 치운다. 청소동물은 혜택을 받는 반면 포식자는 영향을 받지 않는 것이다.

하지만 편리공생은 먹이를 넘어선 관계까지 포함한다. 예를 들어, 말미잘게 역시 말미잘 속에서 흰동가리와 함께 산다. 말미잘게는 여과섭식 동물이기 때문에 먹이를 얻기 위해 물을 쓸어 담을 수 있는 장소가 필요하다. 감히 말미잘에게 접근하는 포식자는 거의 없기 때문에 말미잘은 말미잘게에게 보호처를 제공한다. 하지만 말미잘은 서비스의 대가로 말미잘게에게서 아무것도 얻는 게 없다.

사실, 공생 관계의 유형을 정의하는 것은 쉽지 않다. 예를 들어, 말미잘게처럼 말미잘 사이에서 사는 청소새우 역시 편리공생 동물이다. 하지만 때로는 말미잘 가운데 사는 흰동가리와 상리공생 관계를 이루기도 한다. 이러한 이유로 일부 과학자들은 청소새우가 편리공생 동물이 아닐 수도 있다고 생각한다. 청소새우는 흰동가리를 청소하며 생태계를 정화하는 데 도움을 준다. 이것은 말미잘에게 간접적인 도움을 주기 때문에 이 관계는 사실상 상리공생 관계일 수도 있다.

mutualistic 상리공생의　commensal 편리공생의

Reading Comprehension

1 (A)　2 (B)　3 (D)　4 They are protected from predators since few will come close to an anemone.
5 (C)　6 (C)

Organizing & Summarizing

Ⓐ　1 interdependent relationship
　　2 clearly distinguished
　　3 both species benefit
　　4 algae & coral
　　5 unaffected
　　6 sea anemones & porcelain crabs

Ⓑ　1 highly dependent on each other
　　2 the coral animals and algae
　　3 sea anemones and clownfish
　　4 at the table together
　　5 the other is unaffected
　　6 the porcelain crab

산호초에 사는 동물들은 상호 의존도가 대단히 높다. 산호초 자체가 산호 동물과 조류의 공생 관계의 결과물이다. 이것을 상리공생이라고 한다. 산호초에서 발견되는 다른 종류의 상리공생은 말미잘과 흰동가리의 관계이다. 흰동가리는 말미잘의 보호를 받고 말미잘에게 먹이를 공급해 주고 더 큰 먹이를 위한 미끼 역할을 한다. 편리공생은 또 다른 종류의 공생 관계이다. 이 용어는 "한 식탁을 공유하는"이라 뜻인데, 최초로 관찰된 편리공생 동물이 포식자가 남긴 먹이를 먹고 있었기 때문이다. 현재는 이 용어가 한 종은 이익을 얻는 반면 다른 종은 영향을 받지 않는 경우에 사용된다. 한 가지 예가 말미잘과 말미잘게의 관계이다. 하지만 공생 관계는 대단히 복잡하기 때문에 관계의 정확한 종류를 분명히 정의하기는 힘들다.

Vocabulary Expansion

Part A

Ⓐ　**PREDATOR:** cobra, crocodile, lion, shark, starfish, wolf
　　PREY: cow, deer, horse, mouse, mussel, zebra

Ⓑ　1 species　　2 ecosystem　　3 resource
　　4 disaster　　5 food chain

Ⓒ　1 deserts　　2 crocodiles　　3 species
　　4 eutrophication　5 amphibians　6 famine
　　7 decomposers　8 rainforest　　9 prey
　　10 funds

Part A

Ⓐ　**HELPFUL:** advantageous, beneficial, gainful, useful, profitable, valuable
　　HARMFUL: damaging, dangerous, destructive, detrimental, hazardous, injurious

Ⓑ　1 similar　　2 divergent　　3 consumerism
　　4 endanger　　5 magnification

Ⓒ　1 endangering　2 hazardous　　3 divergent
　　4 precipitation　5 valuable　　　6 secure
　　7 beneficial　　8 destructive
　　9 commensalism　　　　　　　10 evaporation